MAYBE IT'S ME

ALSO BY EILEEN POLLACK

Fiction

The Professor of Immortality
The Bible of Dirty Jokes
A Perfect Life
Breaking and Entering
In the Mouth
Paradise, New York
The Rabbi in the Attic
Whisper Whisper Jesse, Whisper Whisper Josh:
A Story About AIDS

Nonfiction

The Only Woman in the Room: Why Science Is Still a Boys' Club
Woman Walking Ahead: In Search of
Catherine Weldon and Sitting Bull
Creative Nonfiction: A Guide to Form, Content, and Style

MAYBE IT'S ME

ON BEING THE WRONG KIND
OF WOMAN

EILEEN POLLACK

DELPHINIUM BOOKS

MAYBE IT'S ME

For information, address DELPHINIUM BOOKS, INC.,
16350 Ventura Boulevard, Suite D
PO Box 803
Encino, CA 91436

Library of Congress Cataloguing-in-Publication Data is
available on request.
ISBN 978-1-953002-07-5
22 23 24 25   LSC 10 9 8 7 6 5 4 3 2 1

First Edition

Jacket and interior design by Colin Dockrill

To Barbara Kane, for helping me see
that being wrong can be very right

CONTENTS

PIGEONS

NOT LONG AGO, I went back to my elementary school, a Gothic brick-and-mortar fortress whose Escher-like stairs dead-end on floors that lie halfway between other floors and whose halls branch off into mysterious tunnels that suddenly disgorge a student into the cafeteria, or the girls' locker room, or the balcony of benches overlooking the auditorium that doubles as the gym. I wasn't surprised to find my younger self crying at the back of this or that classroom, or staring up at some adult whose behavior baffled me, or wandering the gloomy stairwells, wondering if I would ever find my way to a sunnier, less confusing, less confining life outside.

What startled me was how often I glimpsed the ghosts of classmates whose existence I had forgotten. The ones whose lives, even then, must have been far more troubled than my own, and who—even though there were fewer than one hundred students in my class—disappeared from my consciousness long before the rest of us had moved on to high school, let alone college. Seeing those ghostly classmates, I wanted to bend down and comfort them, as I had comforted my own younger self. I wanted to assure them everything would be all right. But I felt the way a doctor must feel approaching a patient who is waiting for a pathology report the doctor knows contains nothing but devastating news.

My own malady wasn't fatal, although it felt so at the time. The symptoms started in third grade, the day a stranger appeared at our classroom door and summoned me to the hall. My classmates and I were making cardboard headbands on which to glue the feathers we had won for good behavior.

A good Indian was defined by her ability to walk to the bathroom without speaking to her partner or digging a finger in his spine. (That was the year we discovered how vulnerable the human body is. Twist a thumb between two vertebrae and watch your victim writhe. Place the tip of your shoe at the back of his rigid knee and effect collapse.) The edges of my headband kept sticking to my fingers. Not that I had any feathers to paste on the cardboard anyway.

"This is Mr. Spiro, the school psychologist," my teacher said. "He wants to talk to you in his office." Then she went back in and shut the door.

I had been causing a lot of trouble. The year before, my teacher had joked she was going to bring in her dirty laundry to keep me occupied. In reality, Mrs. Hoos had the sense to let me do whatever I wanted, as long as I didn't disturb my neighbors. At the start of each day, I stowed a dozen books beneath my seat and read them one by one, looking up to see if she was teaching us something new, which she rarely was.

I still love Gertrude Hoos, who was as lumpy and soft as the bag of dirty laundry I gladly would have washed if only she had brought it in. But my third-grade teacher, Mrs. Neff, was made of starchier, sterner stuff. By God, if we were reading aloud, paragraph by painful paragraph, I was going to sit there with my book open to the appropriate page and not read a word ahead. If we were learning to add, I would sit there and learn to add, even if I already had learned that skill by keeping score when my grandmother and I played gin.

Mrs. Neff gave me a workbook in which I could teach myself to multiply, but working in that workbook was a privilege and not a right. The more bored I grew, the more I misbehaved, for which I lost the privilege of working in my workbook. Multiplication began to seem like a meal I would never get to eat because I was too exhausted by my hunger to reach the plate. This continued until Mrs. Neff and I each wished the other gone. And since she was the teacher, she had the power to make her wish come true.

Warily, I followed Mr. Spiro to the third floor of our building and then down the main hall, where we entered a narrow door, traversed a short, dark passage, and climbed a few more steps. The room was oddly shaped, with low, slanted ceilings that met at a peak on top. We were in the belfry! You could see it from the playground, where the older kids frightened us with stories about the vampires who lived inside. There was an open window along one wall, but the office was so hot I could barely breathe.

Mr. Spiro settled behind his desk and motioned me to sit in the chair beside it. Bushy black curls exploded from his head like the lines a cartoonist draws to indicate a character is confused or drunk. *Mr. Spiral*, I remember thinking, which is how, four decades later, I can still recall his name. His heavy brows, gigantic nose, and thickly thatched mustache seemed connected to his glasses, like the disguises you could buy at Woolworth's. His suit was white, with thin red stripes, like the boxes movie popcorn came in, and he wore a bright red bow-tie. This was 1964. I had never seen a man in a shirt that wasn't white or a suit that wasn't dark or a tie that called attention to itself, and I felt the thrill and dread any child would feel at being selected from the audience by a clown.

He must have sensed I distrusted him. "Would you like some Oreos?" he asked, then slid a packet across the desk. I can still see those cookies, so chocolaty rich and round, the red thread around their cellophane cocoon just waiting to be unzipped. But a voice in my head warned me to be careful. It was as if that clown had motioned me to sniff the bright pink carnation fastened to his lapel.

"How do I know these cookies aren't poisoned?" I asked.

The bushy black brows shot up. "Do you really think I would poison you?"

"Well," I said, "you're a stranger. How do I know you wouldn't?"

I don't remember what happened next. He probably reassured me the Oreos were fit to eat. I don't remember if I ate them. All I know is he changed the subject. In a falsely jolly tone, he said: "So! I hear you want to be an authoress!"

If he had asked if I wanted to be an author, I would have told him yes. But I had never heard that word, *authoress*, and it seemed dangerous as a snake. *Authoress*, it hissed, like *otherness*, or *adulteress*, a word I had encountered in a novel and didn't quite understand, except to know I didn't want to be one. "Who told you that?" I demanded.

"Why, your teacher, Mrs. Neff."

"That's because she doesn't like me. She probably told you a lot of other lies, but those aren't true either."

He began scribbling on a pad, and even a child of eight knows anything a school psychologist writes about you on a pad can't be any good. Outside, on the ledge, a pair of plump gray pigeons bobbled back and forth like seedy vaudeville comics (this was the Catskills, after all), pigeon variations of Don Rickles and Buddy Hackett, who sidestepped toward each other, traded a dirty joke, bumped shoulders in raunchy glee, and shuckled back across the stage.

"Well then." He finished writing. "I hear you are a very bright little girl, and I would like you to take some tests that are designed to show if you are smart enough to skip a grade."

Tests? I thought. *What kind of tests? Who suggested I skip a grade?*

Then it came to me: Mrs. Neff. If she couldn't get rid of me any other way, she would skip me a year ahead. I would miss Harry and Eric, the boys I couldn't resist jabbing in the spine as we walked down the hall. But fourth grade had to be less boring than third. *Bring on the tests!* I thought, expecting a mimeographed sheet of addition and subtraction problems or some paragraphs to read aloud.

Mr. Spiro brought out a flipbook. He showed me drawing after drawing, asking me to describe what was missing from each. But how could a person know what was missing from a picture if there was nothing to compare it to? Did *every* house have a chimney? Was the daisy missing a petal, or had someone merely plucked it?

After we finished with the flipbook, Mr. Spiro brought out a board fitted with colored shapes. He would flash a pattern on a card and ask me to reproduce it. As I recall, he timed me. But as vivid as my memory is for people and events, I have a terrible time remembering patterns and facts. Had the purple triangle been positioned above or below the line? Had the rectangle been blue or green? And who decreed that playing with colored shapes should determine if a child was ready to skip a grade? It wasn't enough to be smart; you needed to be smart in the ways grownups wanted you to be smart.

Finally, Mr. Spiro presented me with a test like the ones I was used to taking. "If you want to buy three pencils," he began, "and one pencil costs four cents, how much would it cost you to buy all three?"

I was about to add three and four when I realized this required a different kind of math. I could have figured out the answer by adding four three times, but something about being so bored that I had misbehaved, which had denied me the chance to work in my workbook, which had denied me the chance to learn to multiply, which seemed to be preventing me from going on to fourth grade, where I might be less bored and less tempted to misbehave, made me cry out: "That isn't fair!"

But when Mr. Spiro asked me what wasn't fair, I couldn't put my grievance into words. We sat in silent stalemate until a pigeon flew in the room. It flapped around our heads and beat its wings against the walls. But this struck me as no stranger than anything else that had happened in that room; for all I knew, Mr. Spiro had trained the pigeon to fly in on cue and test some aspect of my psychology I would need to skip to the fourth grade. The safest response, I decided, was no response at all.

Mr. Spiro, on the other hand, leapt up on his desk and started waving his arms and shouting. Imagine sitting in a chair looking up at a full-grown man in a red-and-white-striped suit who is standing on his desk flailing at a pigeon. I might have understood if he had been flailing at a bee, but what harm could a pigeon do? At last, the pigeon found a crevice at the very top of the belfry and disappeared inside. My final glimpse of its bobbing rear is the image I still see whenever I hear the word *pigeonholed*.

Mr. Spiro smoothed his suit, climbed down from his desk, and asked why I hadn't been more upset. Hadn't I noticed a pigeon was in the room?

All these years later, I still remember what I said. "Why should I be upset? This isn't my office. I'm not the one who has to clean up after it."

Then I remember nothing more until a disheveled Mr. Spiro led me back to class. Later, he told my mother I wasn't emotionally ready to skip a grade. The experience left me more resentful than ever. I misbehaved more and more. The following year, my teacher grew so impatient with my incessant talking that in front of everyone else she said: "Eileen, has anyone ever told you how obnoxious you are?"

Obnoxious, I repeated, delighted and appalled by the toxicity of the word. Obnoxious, was I? Fine. I shunned the company of the other girls and hung around with the roughest boys, who were even more obnoxious than I was. I still did well on tests—what was I supposed to do, pretend I didn't know how to add (or multiply)? But I refused to act the part of the well-mannered little lady the grownups wanted me to play.

I looked for Mr. Spiro, but I never saw the man again. I searched in vain for his secret office. From outside, on the playground, I could look up and see the belfry. But the windows were boarded up, and the pigeons, like me, couldn't find a way to get inside.

That is, until the first day of sixth grade. Climbing to the third floor of our building, I followed the directions I had been given to the dead-end passage to my class, where I saw a small alcove that led to what once must have been Mr. Spiro's office. My teacher that year—let's call him Mr. F—had persuaded the administration to allow him to board up the windows and use the belfry as a darkroom. Or he hadn't bothered to ask permission and simply went ahead and did it.

Mr. F seemed even more bored by school than I was. At least once a day, he would put his feet up on his desk, tell us how desperate he was to quit teaching and work full-time as a photographer, then lovingly describe the Hasselblad camera he was saving to buy. Unfortunately, my parents and Mr. F's parents were friends, which meant they couldn't complain or ask that I be transferred to another class. If anyone else misbehaved, Mr. F pushed him into the darkroom and we heard terrible bangs and crashes. But nothing I did, no matter how unruly, earned me a timid reprimand. My status as the smartest girl, coupled with my complete disregard for other people's feelings and my lack of social grace, would have made me a pariah anyway. But Mr. F brought that fate upon me sooner by handing back a test on which I had scored an A, asking me to stand, and demanding of my classmates that they try to be more like me.

Complaining about being praised is like complaining about being pretty. Even then I knew it was better to be me than Pablo Rodriguez, whose parents were migrant farmers and who, in sixth grade, could barely read or write, or the Buck brothers, Phil and Gregory, who seemed to get punished for no reason other than being large and male and Black. But if I was so unhappy, it defies me to imagine how much angrier and unhappier kids like Pablo or Phil or Gregory must have been.

A few weeks into term, I developed a crush on the boy across the aisle. He was handsome, thin, and lithe, with curly red hair and freckles. His name was Walter Rustic, which is why, whenever I read that ballad about the passionate shepherd wooing his lass ("Come live with me, and be my love,/ and we will some new pleasures prove"), I imagine Walter Rustic saying those lines to me.

All of us were at the stage where we chased each other around the playground and tried to throw each other down in that hysteria-tinged way of not-quite-adolescents who don't know any other means to touch or be touched. I was wearing a new coat, which Walter grabbed to slow me. As ecstatic as I was that he found me worthy of pursuit, I was upset that he ripped the lining. My mother was always scolding me for ruining my clothes, and I was sure I would get in trouble.

I hate to think that I squealed on Walter. I prefer to believe Mr. F saw the ripped coat and asked me who had torn it. Either way, I watched in horror as he tugged Walter by the ear into that dreadful belfry—*the darkroom*, I suddenly thought—and we listened to the thwacks and grunts of a grown man throwing a boy half his size against a wall. I covered my ears and wondered what had happened to that pigeon. Had it made a nest inside that wall? What could it find to eat? Maybe it subsisted on the crumbs of Oreos left by children who accepted Mr. Spiro's gift.

Then Walter disappeared. Not that day. Or the next. But he didn't graduate from high school with the rest of us. My lack of popularity had reached such spectacular heights by then I couldn't be bothered to consider that anyone else might be miserable for better reasons.

But miserable they must have been. Kids killed themselves and killed each other. One of my classmates hiked out into the woods, put his rifle in his mouth, and pulled the trigger. Another set fire to her house with her family asleep inside. A carload of kids died or were maimed in a drunk-driving accident. But no matter who disappeared or how, no one saw fit to discuss the matter with us. The job of a school psychologist isn't, as people think, to offer counseling for troubled kids; it's to administer IQ tests.

I have no memory of Walter Rustic after we left sixth grade. If I hadn't gone back to my elementary school, I might have lived another forty years without wondering where he went. As it is, I called a friend who had been in that sixth-grade class. Walter? she said. Hadn't I heard? He'd had a problem with drugs. Maybe mental illness had been involved. She didn't know all the facts— she had gotten the information secondhand from her brother, who had been friends with Walter's older brother, Frank, before Frank left town for Vegas. But Walter had been living on the streets in Corpus Christi, Texas, and he had fallen asleep in a dumpster. A

9

garbage truck came along and turned the dumpster upside down, and Walter's skull got crushed.

Walter? Homeless? Crushed?

I called his brother and left a message, but Frank didn't return my call. I googled Walter and found a record of his arrest for attempted robbery in Queens, New York, in 1980, when we would have been twenty-four. But that created more mysteries than it solved. The records indicated that Walter served two years of his sentence before being released "to another agency." Had anyone helped him kick his habit? Treated him for mental illness? How and why had he moved to Texas?

I called the paper in Corpus Christi (I realized as I dialed that the name means *body of Christ*), and the editor sent me Walter's obit. I hoped there would be a photo so I could see what the handsome, redheaded boy on whom I'd had a crush looked like as a man, but the only photo showed a body in a bag being handed down from a trash compactor.

According to the story, on December 22, 1986, Walter had crawled inside the dumpster behind Incarnate Word Junior High, trying to keep warm and sleep. The next morning, the sanitation workers hooked the dumpster to their truck and tipped it back. A groundskeeper at Incarnate Word saw a man trying to scramble out of the dumpster and screamed for the workers to stop, but the roar of the engine prevented his warning from being heard. The lid came down on Walter's neck.

The fire department needed an hour to remove his body. When they did, they saw that he was barefoot and wearing rags. They were able to figure out who the man was only because he was wearing a hospital ID around his wrist. Apparently, Walter had visited the ER the night before to have a swollen ankle x-rayed. There was a bottle of antibiotics in his pocket. He hadn't been in town very long. A few days earlier, he had been arrested for refusing to give his name, but he listed his address as the Search for Truth Mission. Not that anyone there remembered him.

An article published on Christmas Day ("Officials close the book on man's grisly death") added only that Walter Rustic had been a "native of Liberty, N.Y., a town of 4,293 near the Catskill Mountains" and neither his mother nor his brother could be reached for comment. And so, the reporter wrote, "The sad case of the man who died in a dumpster is closed."

Except the sad case had a happier coda. In 1988, a shelter for homeless men was opened in Walter's honor not far from where he died. The Rustic House for Men offers a hot meal and a place to sleep for vagrants, although most people probably assume the name is intended to connote a rural retreat rather than to honor the ragged, barefoot man who died in a dumpster a few blocks away.

I figured I had the facts. But I still seemed to be missing something. I dialed Walter's brother one last time. An elderly woman answered and told me that she was Walter's brother's mother. Which meant she was Walter's mother, too.

"You knew Walter in sixth grade?" she said. "He's been in your mind all these years?"

I wanted to lie and say I had been thinking about her son for forty years and was very, very sorry he had been beaten up on my account. Instead, I asked if Walter ever talked about Mr. F. But his mother said Walter never talked about school at all. He made it to junior year before dropping out. I wanted to ask her why, but it's hard to press a dead friend's mother as to whether he had been mentally ill or addicted to drugs. All she would say was Walter had loved to travel. He traveled from state to state to state, calling her now and then to say hello and ask her to send him money so he could get something to eat. His favorite place had been Tupelo, Mississippi, where he visited Elvis Presley's birthplace. Another time, he called her on New Year's Eve and told her that he had been picked up as a vagrant, and the police liked him so much they invited him to join their party and share their pizza.

Then, on Christmas Eve 1986, she was sitting in her house in North Carolina—she had moved there a few years earlier—wrapping a present for Walter when she got "the horrible phone call" telling her that he had died. She hadn't even known he was in Texas, but she flew to Corpus Christi and spoke to the sisters at Incarnate Word, who told her that her son had died in the arms of two nuns, and she got some comfort in hearing that, as she still derives comfort from knowing the Rustic House for Men takes in vagrants like her son "and gives them a hot meal and a warm clean place to sleep and keeps them there awhile until they're ready to get a job or go out on the road again."

I have no doubt Walter would have ended up homeless or dead even if he had been blessed with a more caring sixth-grade teacher. I was only twelve years old. I don't hold myself responsible for the beating Walter received that day. But being thrown against a wall doesn't do anyone any good. It isn't much fun to occupy any of the circles of hell to which all but the most popular and well-adjusted students find themselves consigned. But schools fail different children in different ways. Kids like Pablo grow up unable to read and write, with no way to earn a living. Kids like Walter Rustic grow up to be dead.

And kids like me? We make it through. We end up who we were meant to be. Sometimes, we end up someone better. Despite Mrs. Neff's refusal to allow me to work in my workbook, despite Mr. Spiro's decision that I wasn't ready to skip a grade, despite a similar decision the following year to advance the two smartest boys while leaving me behind because—as the principal claimed—girls don't finish courses in science or math, I studied those courses on my own and got accepted to Yale, where, despite being very far behind my mostly male classmates, I graduated Phi Beta Kappa, *summa cum laude*, with a degree in physics.

I was too angry and confused and lacking in confidence to go on to physics grad school. But I'm not sure how much I care. What gadget might I have invented, what small theorem might I have proved, that could have mattered half as much as my being forced to learn compassion? I gave up the chance to spend my life multiplying and dividing so I could become an authoress and tell the stories of all those poor pigeons who didn't make it out of school alive, who survived childhood but not adulthood, who are missing from our community. Although how can we measure what we have lost? To what can we compare their absence?

THIN AIR

ONE AFTERNOON, I WAS riding my bike when I saw a bright turquoise-and-yellow bird on the hill behind the high school. I hopped off and crept closer, but the bird didn't startle or fly away. I pedaled furiously to my house, where I announced, "I found a parrot!" and asked my father to help me catch it.

My family already had me pegged as a drama queen with an overripe imagination, so my dad figured this was a fictitious bird, and he said in a tone I was too young to interpret, "I don't have time now, pussycat. Why don't you take the cage in the basement [my sister previously had owned a canary that I coveted], put some Saltines in the bottom, open the door, and say 'Polly want a cracker?'"

I should have guessed this was a trap not for the parrot but for me. A few years earlier, my father had explained I could catch a bird by sprinkling salt on its tail, at which everyone in my family sat on the porch and watched as I toddled around the yard with our big red wooden shaker. This is one of my earliest memories—the birds standing on the lawn until I was just within reach, then hopping a few yards farther. I was certain the next time I tried, the salt would immobilize the bird by making its tail too heavy for it to fly.

But the next robin, and then the next, flew up in the willow. I stood there licking the top of my magic shaker as laughter swelled behind my back, until I realized everyone I loved was laughing at me for falling for the prank they'd played. (Even today, I can feel the lacquered surface of that shaker against my tongue, taste the tang of my humiliation.)

But the last laugh was on my family. The shock on my father's face when I pedaled up with a tropical bird in the cage simultaneously hurt my feelings—I understood he hadn't actually believed I'd found a parrot—and provided me with my first experience of turning a figment of my story-telling imagination into a vivid three-dimensional presence my audience could see, right there in its cage, hopping about and preening. The bird turned out to be a parakeet, but I felt as if I had been talking about an invisible friend for months, to my family's winks and nods, only to produce my invisible friend at dinner.

Like any self-pitying youngest child, I had been longing for a small, malleable companion to whom I could confide my woes. Despite what my family thought, I was too literal to make one up. A few years earlier, my first-grade teacher had grown so frustrated with my incessant chattering she suggested I sit quietly at my desk and "write a story." I was so hazy about the notion of what a story was that I copied out a song ("I'm looking over a four-leaf clover that I overlooked before . . ."). When she pointed out my error, I returned to my seat and copied out "Cinderella."

This time, Mrs. Prettyman explained I was supposed to *make up a story*, a statement that baffled me, given that *making up a story* was exactly the sort of lie I got scolded for at home. When she managed to convey what *making up a story* meant, I nearly levitated from my chair. That was where stories came from? People just made them up? Intoxicated by the power of *making something up*, I wrote another story, and then another.

But that didn't mean I felt free to invent a friend who didn't exist. Other than the Poppin' Fresh Doughboy, who I convinced myself resided in a shoebox beneath my bed, the parakeet I found behind the school was as close as I would ever come to a small, pliable companion who understood me.

Of course, I needed to name that companion first. And to name him—or her—I needed to determine his—or her—sex. Considering I was ignorant of how to do this with a human being, determining the gender of a parakeet was beyond my expertise. My parents weren't about to flip the parakeet upside down and spread its legs. Instead, my mother suggested we drive to Woolworth's and find a book about how to care for birds.

If you grew up in a rural town in the early 1960s, a visit to the pet department at your local Woolworth's was no small adventure. The instinct to care for a creature smaller than oneself runs very deep in our species. As does the instinct to engage in interior decoration. Not only could you buy a turtle, you could spoil your pet by providing it with a kidney-shaped plastic habitat, complete with an island in the middle, which demanded to be furnished with a nifty green umbrella whose purpose seemed to be to prevent your turtle from getting fried in the unrelenting sun on top of your bookcase. I refused to leave the store until my mother agreed to buy one of those beautiful orange boxes of Hartz Mountain bird food; a contraption I could clip to my parakeet's cage so he/she could take a bath; a packet of sanded covers for its perch and similarly sanded sheets for the bottom of the cage; a bell made of seeds; and the ever-important cuttlebone, so the bird could whittle down its beak and thereby prevent it from growing too big to fit its face.

We also brought home a book called *Caring For Your Budgie*, "budgie" being the Australian word for parakeet. This was how I learned you could determine a budgie's sex by looking at its cere, the part of the beak where it had its nostrils. In adult males, the cere was bright blue, and in females pinkish gray. (I was mature enough to know you couldn't determine a person's gender by the color of his/her nose, but I couldn't help thinking how much less frightening it would be if boys had blue noses and girls had pink noses and the sex act consisted of the interested parties giving each other Eskimo kisses of the sort my father and I exchanged.)

Knowing my budgie's gender allowed me to select its name. No one replied to our ad in the local paper, but deep down I knew my budgie had escaped from someone's house, which meant he already had a name, given to him by a child who mourned him. Like a kidnapper who wants a victim to forget his former life, I decided to come up with a name so distinctive it would blot out its owner's memories of what he was called before.

The name I came up with was Ish Kabibble. This is an unusual name, I know. But I had grown up in the Borscht Belt, and I knew Ish Kabibble had been a famous vaudeville comic who used the nonsense-phrase *ish kabibble* to mean "What, I should care?," and even though I wasn't yet aware of this performer's contribution to American culture, the phrase having entered the vernacular as the Alfred E. New-manesque "What, me worry?," I'd heard it often enough that it bubbled up from my unconscious to provide the moniker for a clownishly colored bird that hopped maniacally around its cage, chirping onomatopoeic gibberish.

Although, after I read the book, I realized my parakeet was capable of producing not only gibberish, but human speech.

Talk? This bird could talk? The next time my mother needed to go to Woolworth's, I hurried to the pet department, where I was astonished to discover a 45-rpm recording whose sole purpose was to teach a parakeet to talk. I couldn't wait to set up Ish Kabibble's cage next to my family's record player and provide my new pet with the power of human speech.

I wish I could say I wanted my bird to talk so he could share his innermost thoughts. Since then, I have become fascinated by animal behaviorists who carry on conversations with parrots and apes, and I often find myself thinking about a chimp who used sign language to describe the terrible day, many years earlier, when he had watched hunters kill his mother. As a child, though, all I wanted was a companion who could say: *I love you. I understand you.*

The voice on the recording did nothing but repeat the sentence "HELL-o, BAY-bee, want a KISS?" until everyone in our house walked around sing-songing that phrase aloud ("HELL-o, BAY-bee, want a KISS?"), as if we were propositioning a houseful of imaginary lovers. Even the cat took to listening to the recording, head cocked, like the dog you see listening to its master's voice on albums by RCA. The cat seemed more likely to speak than the bird; she would leap onto the counter and paw thoughtfully at the cage, as if, should she manage to unlatch the door, she might be able to sweet-talk poor Ish into hopping out voluntarily (*HELL-o, BAY-bee, want a KISS?*).

At that point, my mother suggested—strongly—I move my parakeet to our attic. She claimed to be concerned for Ish's safety. But I suspect if she had heard that recording one more time ("HELL-o, BAY-bee, want a KISS?"), she was going to make a parakeet fricassee and serve it to the cat. Also, I think she disdained the parakeet for its lack of cleanliness; while the cat was civilized enough to go down to the basement to use her litter box, Ish had no choice but to spatter the counter with stray droppings, the husks of the seeds he ate, and the feathers he shed whenever the cat stuck a paw in his cage and scared him.

We had a cleaning lady, Helen, who showed up once a week to clean our house, but my mother was the sort of housekeeper who cleaned the house *before* the cleaning lady arrived, and to spare Helen the need to clean the droppings, seeds, and feathers, I moved my parakeet to the attic. For a while, I replaced the goal of teaching my pet to talk with training him to perform the tricks *Caring For Your Budgie* promised he could learn. I no longer held much faith in anything *Caring For Your Budgie* promised, but the steps outlined in the book did result in Ish hopping on my finger, running up and down my arm, and consenting to ride a small stuffed horse.

All of this—the failed attempt to teach my parakeet to talk, the successful attempt to teach him to perch on my finger—lasted six months, at which I understood that any creature who can demonstrate his affection only by trying to tear off your fingernail is never going to be the soulmate you hoped you'd found. By then, I needed to be reminded to change the sandpaper at the bottom of my soulmate's cage so he wouldn't be forced to stand knee deep in his own droppings, if a bird can be said to have knees.

The person who took to reminding me of my parakeet's existence was Helen. One day, I went upstairs and surprised her making kissy noises at the cage. She grew flustered, then summoned the courage to ask the bird's name. When I told her, she tried to repeat it, then gave up and asked where I had gotten him. I told her about finding Ish behind the school, then said most people got their birds at Woolworth's.

"Really? You can just go in and buy a bird at Woolworth's?" She confided she always had wanted a bird but hadn't been allowed to keep pets as a girl, and I had the sense that even as a grownup she didn't think she had the right to just walk into Woolworth's and buy one.

I didn't know much about Helen, except that she was an orphan whose foster parents had mistreated her and, the minute she turned sixteen, forced her to go to work. She was overweight and poorly dressed, with heavy, pale legs made dumpier by the white ankle-socks and saddle shoes she wore, a grating, nasal voice, and a reading level that caused my mother to leave her notes printed in block capitals with a vocabulary as simple as one would use with a child.

Still, she was what my mother and the other ladies in the neighborhood called "a sweet soul," and they took pride in making her nice lunches and setting them on real china instead of paper plates. They presented her with outdated clothes and castoffs. And they paid her a higher wage than they otherwise might have paid.

Occasionally, my mother hired Helen to babysit for me. Helen was very kind and never found the heart to reprimand me, no matter how badly I misbehaved. But I was uneasy in her presence, the way children tend to be around the people who clean their family's toilets and scrub their floors. When I was young, I tried to avoid her, but as I grew older, I came to understand it was rude to leave the room when Helen came in, and we sometimes engaged in awkward, brief conversations.

Once, while I was hammering out a particularly soppy version of "Over the Rainbow" on the piano, I realized Helen had tiptoed in to listen. "Would you play that again?" she asked. No one ever requested I play anything on the piano once, let alone provide an encore. Happy to oblige, I played an even schmaltzier rendition, which caused Helen to swab her eyes with the sleeve of her shapeless housedress. "That's always been my favorite song," she said, at which the image of Helen as an orphan, lonely and abused, listening to Judy Garland sing "Over the Rainbow," brought a sensation to my chest for which I had no name, although I imagine now it would be *compassion*.

Sadly, this made me more uncomfortable in Helen's presence. I even felt queasy around my parakeet, sensing that here was the very bluebird that might, if it escaped its cage, fly over the rainbow, way up high, to a place where the dreams you dared to dream really did come true and you didn't have to clean people's houses all day.

Maybe it was in the hope of reaching her own private Oz that Helen shocked my mother by dating a man my mother described as a *real no-goodnik*. It was like a Catskills version of a Eudora Welty story (although the fiancé's surname, Friend, reminds me of the seductive villain in Joyce Carol Oates's chilling "Where Are You Going, Where Have You Been?"). This fiancé was a rough character—a lumberjack, my mother thought. He had been in and out of jail, and surely he was marrying poor, naïve Helen to take advantage of her good nature and live off her earnings.

But in a rare show of independence, Helen ignored my mother's advice and married her jailbird. She retired from cleaning houses and gave birth to a daughter, Helen Lynne. Helen tried to give Helen Lynne the childhood she never had, doting on her, buying her everything she asked for, and Helen Lynne grew up to be a beautiful, blonde little girl, who, by third or fourth grade, could read and write and do arithmetic better than her mother.

By then, Helen had gone back to cleaning houses. As my mother predicted, the jailbird refused to work. And Helen wanted to give her daughter the advantages she never had. Every afternoon, after school let out, Helen Lynne would find her mother at whatever house she was cleaning. At first, my mother and her friends petted and fussed over Helen Lynne. Then they decided her mother was *spoiling her rotten*. Helen Lynne didn't speak to her mother with respect, and the older she grew, the more disrespectful she became.

Eventually, Helen Lynne got a job as a bank teller, but she still lived at home, sponging off her mother. Somehow, my mother and her friends came to suspect that Helen Lynne and her father beat Helen, that Helen Lynne and her father shared a single bed and made Helen sleep on the floor. This wasn't taking place in another part of town. Helen and her family lived in an apartment down the street from my house. But she might as well have lived on Mars for all anyone seemed able to protect her.

My parents retired and moved away, but my mother remained in touch with our former neighbors, who kept her apprised of the scandals concerning Helen. Finally, my mother called me at college to say that Helen had been discovered lying dead in the doorway to her apartment. She showed no signs of violence, but my mother and her friends felt certain Helen's husband and daughter were responsible. *They scared her to death,* my mother said. *No one will ever be prosecuted for that crime, but they murdered that poor woman as surely as if they had put a gun to her head.*

My mother's account of the funeral, which Helen Lynne *hadn't even had the good graces to attend*, made me think of an afternoon a few years earlier when I had been home on break from college and was using my Smith Corona to type the first draft of a story for a fiction-writing seminar. Helen came in to clean and asked if I minded if she asked a question.

Of course not, I said.

"Well," she said, "when most people type, they look at something on the table next to them. But when you type, you're looking into thin air."

Um, I said. I'm writing a story. I'm making it up as I go along.

"Really? That's how stories get written? Someone just

makes them up? Gee, that seems spooky. It's as if you're writing something only you can see."

I got a chill when Helen said that. Could she honestly not know what I had figured out in first grade—that writers make up their stories?

"So, does that mean you could write a story about *anything*?" She laughed a laugh that sounded like curdled milk. "Maybe you could write a story about me."

But I never did write that story. As much as I blamed my mother for treating Helen as a servant—a job for which she and the other ladies paid Helen a generous wage, providing her with the only independence and kindness she ever knew—the only request Helen ever made of any of us, she made of me. And I never fulfilled that wish.

Although it wasn't for lack of trying. At first, I made up a story about a cleaning lady who is mistreated by her foster parents and seeks to escape her lonely, hardworking life by marrying a no-good lumberjack and bearing him a child, only to suffer far worse degradation at the hands of the daughter whose love she craves. But I couldn't get inside Helen's head. And I couldn't figure out the point of writing an account of Helen's life, except to say she had been a sweet, uncomplicated soul who lived in misery and died in pain at her husband's and daughter's hands.

Years went by. Then, a few months ago, a neighbor of mine bought two parakeets for her kids. "Eileen," she said, "you wouldn't happen to know how a person can tell if a parakeet is male or female, do you?" As I stunned her with the information that a male parakeet's nose is blue and a female's nose is pink, all my memories came flying back—how I had found Ish behind the school, how I tried to teach him to talk, how my mother banished him to the attic, how she complained about having to clean the cage, how she called me at Yale to ask if she could give my bird to Helen, who, *out of the clear blue sky*, had asked if she could have him. Sure, I told my mother, and oh, by the way, if Helen wants to change the bird's name, she can.

Yet even as this flock of memories came home to roost, I realized I had no idea what happened to my pet after Helen died. Had the parakeet been there in the apartment when Helen's husband and daughter heaped her with abuse? Had she poured out her heart to poor Ish? By what name had she addressed him? Surely she hadn't kept a name she couldn't pronounce, a name that meant—not that Helen knew this—she didn't have any cause to worry. Had she serenaded her poor caged bird with some nasal but heartfelt version of "Over the Rainbow"? Had she inherited the recording I bought at Woolworth's and played it for her pet until he finally learned to greet her and ask did she want a kiss? Had Ish been there when she died? Had he cried out in an attempt to bring her help? If only he had been able to convey to the authorities what Helen's no-goodnik of a husband had done to kill her!

All this made me think of Gustave Flaubert's famous story "A Simple Heart," in which a servant named Felicity pours out her woes to her parrot, Loulou, and then, after Loulou dies, asks to have him stuffed. "A Simple Heart" is a beautiful and touching tale. But even if Monty Python hadn't made famous the ultimate dead-parrot sketch, I would find it difficult to believe a woman would be so ignorant as to turn a wormy stuffed parrot into a sort of god, imagining as she dies the bird is carrying her up to heaven.

No, the story that seems more relevant is "Death in the Woods" by Sherwood Anderson, in which the narrator struggles to understand an incident that happened to him years earlier, when he and the men in his hometown discovered the strangely youthful corpse of a local farmwife. At the time, the narrator was too young to understand what to make of the woman's death. But in the decades that followed, he pieced together the facts of her life, and he uses his imagination to fill in the rest.

The woman, he says, grew up as an orphan and was bound at an early age to a German farmer, who brutalized and harassed her. Later, she was brutalized and harassed by her husband, and then by their son. At the time of her death, she was carrying groceries home from town. Overcome by weariness, she sat in the snow to rest, then fell asleep. A pack of dogs, trying to get the meat from her knapsack, dragged her here and there, uncovering her nakedness.

The story of the woman's death, the narrator says, was "like music heard from far off," and the notes "needed to be picked up slowly one at a time. Something had to be understood." What needed to be understood is that the woman who died "was one destined to feed animal life. . . . She was feeding animal life before she was born, as a child, as a young woman working on the farm of the German, after she married, when she grew old and when she died. . . . On the night when she died she was hurrying homeward, bearing on her body food for animal life."

A story so complete has its own beauty, the narrator goes on. But the beauty of the woman's life isn't the reason he tells her story. He tells it because *it deserves to be told*—and no one else can tell it.

Like Anderson's narrator, I needed years to understand the simple rightness of the events that led me to discover a parakeet behind the school, then give him to our cleaning lady in the hope he might provide her with some solace and companionship. And even if that parakeet never did learn to speak, he bore witness to the tragedy of her life and death and allowed her story to be recorded among the few recorded stories of the billions of human (and nonhuman) creatures who have lived and died.

And yet, like Anderson and his narrator, I find that I am still dissatisfied. I can't help but wonder what happened to my parakeet after his owner died. I can't imagine poor Ish surviving in the care of Helen's no-goodnik husband. But what of Helen Lynne? What became of her? How could I have allowed my mother and her friends to judge the girl so harshly? What child can be corrupted to such a horrifying extent merely by her mother *spoiling* her? How could everyone have failed to see such an obvious and unsettling truth? A dumpy, long-suffering mother . . . a beautiful little girl . . . a no-goodnik of a jailbird father . . .

I am certain Helen's daughter has a story of her own to tell, and all I can do is hope the sight of her mother's pet cowering in his cage brought to life some flutter of compassion, some fledgling comprehension of what harm had been done to *her*, and maybe, just maybe, Helen Lynne kept that parakeet for herself.

THE JEWISH SHAH

"THE SHAH OF IRAN is Jewish," my father would remind us whenever the newspaper ran a story about Iran, which was often those days, the sixties and early seventies. One issue of *Life* showed a magnificent red silk tent supporting a chandelier over a resplendent array of emperors and ambassadors dining in the desert at the shah's celebration of twenty-five-hundred years of Persian history and thirty years of his own Pahlavi regime. My father knew the shah was Jewish because he had been told the secret by his best friend from dental school, with whom he also had served in World War II.

"Just don't tell anyone," my father warned. "If the shah knew that we knew his secret, he would send his police to bump us off."

I loved to hear this story. As far as I could tell, it was the only romantic part of my father's life. I had little respect for his profession, or the role he had served in the war, fixing the teeth of British soldiers in Calcutta, India. His best friend, Sidney Polivy, another Jewish dentist from New York, used to joke that he and my father should slip over the border to Iran and visit the shah, who happened to be his cousin. As Sidney told the tale, four of his uncle's sons had fled Russia in their teens to avoid conscription by the czar. The fifth cousin went east instead of west, making his way over the Caucasus Mountains to Persia. He tried to earn a living as a peddler but eventually joined or was inducted into a troop of Cossacks. He hid his origins, became a Muslim, and rose quickly through the ranks. There was a coup. He changed his name and declared himself the shah. At the start of World War II, he threw in with Hitler, and his brothers in America washed their hands of their black-sheep relative. But seeing as how Sidney and my father were in the neighborhood, they might as well stop by.

My father and his friend never made it to Iran. Victory was declared, and the men were sent home. My father opened a dental practice in the Catskills, and Sidney in the Bronx. "We drifted apart," my father said. "We would correspond, but not as often." Sidney and his wife drove up to Liberty to see my parents. "Then we had a falling out," my mother said. "They never came back." She wasn't sure why.

It bothered my father that he and his friend lost contact. "We were like two brothers." He shook his head. "But what can you do?" The years slipped by. My father was looking forward to seeing Sidney at their thirtieth dental-school reunion. "Your mother and I had just walked in when someone ran up to me and said, 'Your friend Sidney just died.' I nearly fainted. It hit me like a ton of bricks."

Telling the story about the shah must have been a way for my father to keep his friend's memory alive. Besides, he believed the story. I wanted to believe it, too. And in the fall of 2000, when I had a year off from teaching and a grant to do some research, I decided to find out if it could be true.

The first thing I learned was there had, in fact, been a squad of Cossacks operating in Iran when Sidney's cousin would have lived there. The friendship between the brutal Qajar shahs and the Russian czars had been cozy for many years, and the Russians established a crack "Cossack Brigade" of Persian soldiers commanded by Russian officers. In 1911, when the last Qajar shah tried to stage a return to his homeland, the British landed troops across the south while the Russians deployed several thousand men across the north. With its central location and staggering reserves of oil, Persia had long been a focus of interest by Western powers. The Qajar shahs tried to stay neutral, but the British, Russians, and Turks used World War I as an excuse to grab pieces of the country. Parliament was dissolved. Pestilence and famine flared. By the time the smoke cleared, Turkey was defeated, Russia had been weakened by a revolution, and the British were in charge. They demanded the Qajar shah dismiss the Russian officers who commanded his Cossacks. Under General Sir Edmund Ironside, the British decided to withdraw from northern Persia and consolidate their forces in the south. But they couldn't leave the north undefended. Searching for a Persian officer to lead the de-Russified Cossack Brigade, Ironside was stopped by an imposing colonel named Reza Khan. As Ironside confided to his journal, Reza Khan stood over six feet tall, with broad shoulders "and a most distinguished face. His hooked nose and sparkling eyes gave him a look of animation." Reza Khan was shivering from malaria, but he "handled himself well and never went on sick leave." After extracting promises that Reza Khan wouldn't attack the British as they were leaving nor use force to depose the Qajar shah, Ironside withdrew. No doubt he guessed Reza Khan eventually would oust the shah—Reza Khan made no attempt to hide his contempt for the ruling class—but Ironside harbored no love for the shah himself.

Still, it was quite a feat for Reza Khan to rouse the demoralized Cossack Brigade to march on the shah's headquarters in Tehran. Calling on his men to remember the years they spent "fighting neck-deep in mud and filth," denied decent food and pay, Reza Khan stood on a stool and announced he had been "inspired by God to rectify this intolerable situation." Though he later seemed embarrassed to have invoked

God on his own behalf, the oration proved effective. At midnight on February 20, 1921, a small force of Cossacks conquered Tehran with only a few shots fired. Reza Khan allowed the shah to remain on the throne for four more years, but Reza Khan ran the country, gaining his countrymen's respect by refusing to sell their wealth to foreign kings. As minister of war, Reza Khan acted less from a desire to take the throne than to root out corruption and bolster Persia's defense. With his towering height and fiery eyes, Reza Khan intimidated most opponents. He raged at anyone who disobeyed. An inelegant speaker, he at least had the sense to keep his speeches brief.

In 1925, eager to enforce a series of Western reforms, Reza Khan took steps to seize power. The constitution prohibited a man of humble birth from becoming shah, so he tried to push through a measure that would turn Persia into a republic; if he couldn't be king, he might be president. Although the clergy defeated this resolution, the parliament abolished the ruling class and required every citizen to take a family name. Choosing as his own name "Pahlavi," a term for the pre-Arabic language of Persia, Reza Khan pressed parliament to dismantle the Qajar dynasty. In December 1925, the assembly named Reza Khan the new *Shahanshah*, the King of Kings. As such, Reza Shah catapulted his subjects into the most energetic program of Westernization any monarch ever unleashed. Trains ran on time. Streets were paved for cars, camels targeted for slaughter. Women were forbidden to wear the veil. Reza Shah's men stopped mullahs on the street, tore off their turbans, and shaved their beards. Everyone wore Western clothes. Girls were sent to school. The shah laid the cornerstone for the country's first university. Hospitals sprang up, with newly trained physicians.

Strongly nationalistic, Reza Shah tried to replace his people's allegiance to Islam with a higher love for Persia.

Continually harking back to the glories of the Aryan tribes that settled the region centuries before the Arabs flooded in, Reza Shah went so far as to rename the country "Iran" in their honor. To quell the mullahs' fury, he made a few token pilgrimages to Islam's holy sites. But no one could mistake Reza Shah for a religious man. When his son, Mohammed-Reza, dared relate a vision in which a holy figure of Islam saved him from a fall, Reza Shah erupted in fury. "Rubbish, sir! If those saints could make miracles they would have saved themselves from being killed like chickens."

Hated as much as loved, Reza Shah certainly would have stayed in power if not for World War II. Bitter toward the British and Russians for their high-handed imperialism, he was in no rush to join the Allies. He admired Hitler's efficiency in bringing Germany back from ruin. The Germans and Iranians shared a glorious Aryan past (Hitler generously decreed that Iranians could marry Germans). Although Reza Shah never signed a pact with Hitler, the Allies feared he might. The strategic location of Iran provided an excuse for the Allies to invade. Reza Shah died in exile, and his son needed decades to win back his country, but Reza Khan threw his long shadow over Iran for many years.

Could he possibly have been a Jew? The official genealogy (for much of my information I have relied on Cyrus Ghani's excellent account *Iran and the Rise of Reza Shah: From Qajar Collapse to Pahlavi Rule*) gives Reza Khan's year of birth as 1878, in the village of Alasht, a tiny mountain town on the Iranian-Russian border. According to this story, Reza Khan's father died when the boy was forty days old. His mother, a persecuted second wife, took her infant son and fled across the snowy mountains to Tehran, nearly losing the child to cold and hunger.

At fifteen, Reza Khan supposedly followed an uncle's footsteps into the Cossack Brigade. By 1912, the young soldier's proficiency with machine guns had earned him a captaincy, with a promotion to colonel three years later. Around 1903, Reza Khan married a girl named Tajmah, who bore him a girl before he divorced her and married the eldest daughter of a brigadier general in the regular army. This second wife, Taj al Molouk, provided Reza Khan with twins, one of whom became his heir, Mohammed-Reza, as well as with two younger children. In 1922, Reza Khan married a third wife, whom he divorced the next year to marry the beautiful sixteen-year-old daughter of a Qajar prince.

If the official biography is true, then Sidney Polivy's story cannot be. But the collapse of the Pahlavi dynasty in 1979 led Iranian journalists to delve more deeply into Reza Shah's background. Especially revealing is *The Unknown Life of the Shah* by Amir Taheri, who served as editor of Iran's largest daily paper, *Kayhan*, between 1973 and 1979, and later wrote for *The Washington Post* and the *Sunday Times* of London. Reza Khan's origins were obscure, Taheri notes. The elaborate pedigree in which his ancestry was traced back to the earliest Aryan tribes was manufactured after Reza Khan was on the throne. Even then, the story remained riddled with inconsistencies. Taheri thinks the stories of Reza Khan's Aryan roots were concocted to serve the needs of a new regime that wanted to distinguish itself from the alien rule of the Turcoman Qajars. Once Reza Khan ran the army, no one was going to challenge what he said.

Certainly, once his son built up the terrifying SAVAK, no one was going to point out the discrepancies in the Pahlavi genealogy. Reza Khan's birth date was established early in his rule. "But it was not until 1972 that the house in which he was supposed to have been born was identified, renovated and turned into a museum," Taheri writes. Journalists invited to visit Alasht for the dedication "found almost no one who could claim to have even the remotest memory of Reza Khan's family. In a society of extended families and close clan relations this could mean only one thing: Reza Khan's family had no roots in Alasht. . . . Reza Khan himself almost never spoke of his ancestors. Did he bear them a grudge for having left him destitute and at the mercy of fate?"

Taheri might be right that Reza Khan was lying to conceal his humble origins. But everyone knew Reza Khan came from a humble family. The mere fact he wasn't a Qajar prince would have kept him from being shah. At the start, Reza Khan's only ambition was to rule the army. Little would have disqualified him from that post except an enemy's proof that he wasn't a Muslim.

The Pahlavi genealogy is so thin anyone could invent a background for Reza Khan that doesn't contradict the few verifiable facts. But the fit between the Polivy story and the holes in Reza Khan's genealogy seems too eerie to ignore. The official Pahlavi history implies Reza Khan's father was killed in combat. But Taheri points out there were no major conflicts in Alasht—or anywhere in Iran—in 1878. Beyond that, Taheri finds it odd that Reza Khan's mother, no matter how disfavored, would immediately flee on foot over a snowy mountain. Many people died on such a trek. Why risk her infant son? And I couldn't help but wonder what happened to that mother. Why did none of the biographies mention the woman's name, let alone discuss what became of her? Why, of all the details Reza Khan could have given about his life, did he choose to recall that wintry climb? A teenage Russian boy crossing the Caucasus Mountains in winter might have almost died before he reached Tehran. Could that journey have been the kernel of truth at the heart of Reza Khan's lie?

The official version of Reza Khan's youth was that he joined the Cossack Brigade in 1892, but Taheri could find no evidence of Reza Khan's early years in Tehran or his service in the Brigade until he was twenty-two. "Thus Reza's military career did not begin with the Cossacks. Recent research shows that Reza joined the *Savadkuh fowj* in 1892. His uncle must have been able to secure him a place there thanks to contacts he still had in the region." But what became of that uncle? Why doesn't he appear in any later accounts of Reza Khan's life? Isn't it possible a teenage Jewish boy who worked his way across the mountains found himself starving and homeless and joined a Persian troop? Later, as Taheri says, when Reza Khan was more experienced, he might have been allowed to enter the more prestigious Cossack Brigade. Equally revealing are the insults heaped on Reza Khan by his second wife. Highly born and well-schooled, Taj al Moluk was fully literate while Reza Khan couldn't read or write Persian, spoke only a few thousand words, and, Taheri notes, rarely ventured beyond "the beaten track of stark expression." A boy can grow up unschooled, but by the time he is in his twenties, he knows more of his native language than a few thousand words. According to Donald Wilber's biography, Reza Khan didn't speak Persian with any regional accent, which made him seem to come from nowhere. He strikes me more as a man speaking and writing a second language than a poor but brilliant boy who grew up illiterate and never learned to properly read and write his own tongue.

The same argument could apply to Taj al Moluk's mockery of her husband "because he could not even remember the names of all the twelve Imams of Iranian shi'ism." Reza Khan's abstention from daily prayer or fasting on Ramadan can be explained by the religious indifference exhibited by many military men. But his wife accused him of ignorance, not indifference. It could be an accident that Reza Shah rarely referred to the deity as "Allah," preferring to use the Persian words for "Providence" or "God." His orders that he be served nothing but chicken, rice, and bread likely sprang from a soldier's Spartan tastes rather than a Jew's revulsion for unkosher food. Nationalism could account for Reza Shah's efforts to efface his country's Muslim past. But the sheer number of such idiosyncrasies makes it difficult to dismiss the Polivy claim out of hand. Could Reza Khan have been drawn to choose "Pahlavi" because it echoed the name he'd been given at birth?

Kathryn Babayan, my neighbor in Ann Arbor and a scholar of Iranian history and culture at the University of Michigan, gets politely doubtful when I go off on another tangent about Reza Khan being Jewish. While she acknowledges the diverse ancestry of many people in northern Iran—Babayan herself had a Russian-born grandmother who hid her Jewish birth from her family—she considers it a coincidence that my father's friend's story so neatly provides the missing pieces in the puzzle of Reza Khan's background. She finds it more likely Reza Khan was hiding his lower-class origins. Maybe he was a bastard, a shameful circumstance even now in Iran. She attributes his lack of facility with the Persian language and his ignorance of Islam to the poverty and isolation common in a rural province like Alasht. Reza Khan never went to school and learned most of what he knew in an army barracks. As a military leader, his hostility to Islam would have been in keeping with the widely held belief that fundamentalism was preventing Middle Eastern cultures from advancing.

Babayan also points out that Sidney Polivy's cousin would have had to change his name not once but twice—first to Reza Khan, then to Reza Pahlavi. And the choice of

"Pahlavi" doesn't strike her as odd. "People at that time had the word in their mouths. They knew it from an epic poem. They might not have known exactly what it meant, but the word was widely associated with the country's pre-Islamic past." What Babayan finds fascinating is that an effort by one person to camouflage his background can create a large enough gap in the historical record that other people are allowed "to color their cocoons any way they want." She marvels that a bunch of Jewish immigrants in the Bronx would have wanted to identify themselves with a Muslim shah. Perhaps the Polivy myth was an imaginative response to a feeling of uprootedness, an example of a family of exiles weaving an entire story around a similarity in a name and creating genealogical links with a figure then touted by the Western press as a forward-looking monarch who might bring democracy to a "backward" land. The interesting phenomenon, Babayan says, is how family stories and oral traditions get started, "how they create these webs of inter-connectedness. One doesn't have to ever have lived in a particular country to feel attached to it."

While I listen to my neighbor, her skepticism rubs off on me. But as soon as I get back home, I find myself returning to my belief that the Polivys and Pahlavis are related. Look at all those African Americans who maintained they were descended from Thomas Jefferson—and turned out to be right. How could a family of poorly educated Jews in the early 1900s make up the unlikely fact that their relative ended up in a troop of Iranian Cossacks? Who would even suspect there might be Cossacks in Iran? People whose names are similar to the names of famous people might be tempted to forge a link. But Sidney Polivy didn't tell his story to claim distinction; according to my father, he seemed more ashamed than proud.

I also find it hard to explain why Reza Khan would have been so tolerant toward the Jews if he wasn't one himself. In his *Comprehensive History of the Jews of Iran*, Habib Levy describes the reign of Cyrus the Great, who defeated the Babylonians, freed their Jewish captives, and allowed the Jews to return to Jerusalem and rebuild their Temple. So revered was Cyrus among the Jews that many former captives—Daniel, for one—followed him back to Persia. After Cyrus died, the Jews retained a strong presence in Persia, as the story of the secret Jewish queen, Esther, reminds Jews every year at Purim. But once the Arab invasion began in 642 C.E., Islam became the official state religion, with Jews, Christians, and Zoroastrians relegated to second-class minorities. Persian Jews were ordered to sew yellow patches on their clothes and to wear ridiculous hats. They weren't permitted to marry Muslims and were barred from many jobs. During the Crusades, Christians as well as Muslims made it their goal to convert the Jews. Although several Qajar shahs kept Jewish concubines and doctors, the majority of Persian Jews were considered unclean. For a Jew to appear in public in anything but rags was a provocation to a beating. Many Persian Jews relinquished their faith in public but practiced it at home. Especially in the north, where Reza Khan lived, many non-Muslims tried to pass as Muslims, the way many Russian Jews who lived outside the Pale tried to pass as Christians.

Reza Khan's assault on the Muslim clergy undoubtedly derived from his resolve to Westernize Iran. But that doesn't preclude the pride he might have taken in liberating the people from whom he'd sprung. Consider his actions to protect the Jews of Tehran from a riot that broke out in 1922, when the custodian of a Jewish school stood in front of a Muslim's burro to prevent it trampling a group of Jewish children. In retaliation, the city's Muslims met at their mosques and decided to attack the Jews. (Of the quarter of a million people then living in Tehran, five thousand were Jews, with fifty thousand Jews in a country of ten million.) To ward off a pogrom, the American ambassador to Iran, a rabbi named Joseph Saul Kornfeld, sought an audience with Reza Khan, then minister of war. No record of that meeting survives, but as soon as Kornfeld left, Reza Khan dispatched his cavalry to protect the Jews. Perhaps he acted out of humanitarian concern, but few military commanders had shown much concern for Jewish lives. Reza Shah's reforms in opening new occupations to Jews and allowing them to leave the ghetto led them to hail him as their savior. Not only did he permit non-Muslims to join the army, he granted Jewish soldiers leaves for Rosh Hashanah, Yom Kippur, the first two days of Succoth, and all eight days of Passover.

In 1943, a Jewish envoy investigating the status of Polish refugees in Tehran met a Jewish physician serving in the Iranian army. This doctor told the envoy that many years before, Reza Shah had asked him why he didn't change his religion, given that being Jewish prevented him from rising. According to the historian Amnon Netzer, the doctor told Reza Shah, "There is no value to you if I change the Lord of heaven for a fast promotion." To which Reza Shah replied, "You are right, and changing religion in the army is not necessary." After which the man received a promotion to colonel.

If Reza Shah's relatives in America washed their hands of him for being too chummy with the Nazis, the more provocative question is why he never signed a pact with Hitler. Reza Shah and the führer shared a hatred of Russia and Great Britain and an admiration for modernization and efficiency, no matter how achieved. Germany was Iran's most prominent trading partner. German announcers on Radio Tehran had been flooding the country for years with Nazi propaganda. And the shah's plans for improvement depended on several thousand German technicians, merchants, teachers, researchers, and military advisors living in Iran. That Reza Shah refused to sign a pact with Hitler seems more mysterious than his refusal to expel the Germans from Iran, as the Allies demanded.

According to Taheri, Reza Shah might have admired Germany's industrial might, but he held "no warm feelings for Hitler. He never took up an invitation to visit Germany and refused to reorganize the Iranian armed forces on the German model. He found Hitler's anti-Semitism odious and instructed the Iranian ambassador to Berlin to invite the German Jewish professors who had lost their positions to come and work in Iran." Taheri claims Hitler was so frustrated by his repeated failures to establish a pact with Iran that by the summer of 1941, he was planning to overthrow Reza Shah, seize the oil fields, and stage an invasion of British India by barreling through Iran, just as the Allies feared. Reza Shah's unwillingness to shake Hitler's hand might have stemmed from a wily soldier's instinct that Hitler would knife him in the back. But it might also have been influenced by hatred for a man whose persecution of the Jews was even worse than the czar's.

A Jewish peddler turned shah being cajoled by Hitler to join the Aryan cause might seem as fantastic as the little Jewish tailor in Charlie Chaplin's *Great Dictator* masquerading as the führer. But Reza Khan was no timid tailor. Even the few people who loved him described him as a solitary man who revealed nothing of his inner life. If he were a secret Jew, he wouldn't have told a soul. His son apparently believed his father was a Muslim, if not a very observant one; guileless assertions to that effect appear on page after page of Mohammed-Reza's memoirs. But many children have been shocked to find out a parent was a Jew. Look at Madeleine Albright.

Besides, Reza Khan wasn't the most confiding of dads. "He could be one of the pleasantest men in the world," Mohammed-Reza told a reporter, "yet he could be one of the most frightening." Once, Reza Shah pulled an imam from a mosque and beat him with an iron cane for criticizing his wife for going without a veil. If Reza Shah maintained he was a Moslem from Alasht, who would disagree? And really, what does any child know about his parents? Sometimes other families know our secrets better than we do.

Given my suspicions, it seemed only fair to ask Reza Khan's grandson, Reza Pahlavi, what he could confirm about his grandfather's birth. In November 2001, after decades of living quietly in the United States, Pahlavi had emerged as a prominent player in Iranian politics. According to *The Wall Street Journal*, Pahlavi's broadcasts from Los Angeles were stirring young Iranians who knew nothing of his father and liked Pahlavi's call for a secular, democratic state. When I phoned his headquarters in Virginia, Pahlavi's press secretary, Kamran Beigi, said with a giddy laugh that given the present circumstances, "You might need to come for the interview to Tehran!"

There seemed a good chance if I did get through to the youngest Pahlavi, he would treat me as a crackpot, especially if I asked him to donate DNA to test the Polivys' claims. And my father's fears resurfaced. "Do you really have to call the shah's grandson?" he asked. I assured him the SAVAK was long out of business and the ayatollahs would be more likely to make me a hero than kill me. My fear was that even if I weren't able to prove Reza Khan was a Jew, the mere whiff of suspicion might discredit his grandson. Imagine the propaganda. Not only was the first Pahlavi shah a Zionist tool,

he himself was a Jew! I told myself that with all the linger-
ing animosity toward his father's regime, Reza Pahlavi stood
little chance of taking back the throne. But who can predict
the future in Iran?

Unfortunately, before Beigi would set up an appointment with the deposed shah's grandson, he needed to know
the reason for my interest. I swallowed hard and told him,
and Beigi expressed dismay. He didn't consider my story
dangerous so much as irrelevant. With the number of calls
coming from Iran, Reza Pahlavi had little attention for anything else. The calls were so heartbreaking, describing the
deprivation of people so poor they were trying to sell their
kidneys, Beigi cried several times a day. Reza Pahlavi didn't
want to divert the world's attention to himself. His sole mission was to gain the right for Iranians to go to the polls and
vote. If they asked him to be their king, he would do so, but
that wasn't his objective. He had no ambition to restore the
monarchy, so his grandfather's origins didn't matter. "Reza
Pahlavi says over and over, the story isn't about him or his
wife and children. There are seventy million Iranians. The
story is about them."

As to the possibility some family of American Jews might
claim to be related to Reza Khan, Beigi considered that a
matter for historians. And even the historians wouldn't have
an easy job. "It is a very Western notion that any Iranian from
that time would have a written history of his birth," Beigi
said. "There is a gap in my own grandfather's origins. People
in those days had no last names or birth certificates. Usually, there was just their age recorded in the back of a Koran,
which was the only book in any house." The Polivys' claim
seemed no different from the "ten calls a day" Beigi receives
from people who want to claim a connection to Reza Pahlavi.
"I am myself just a poor Ph.D. student, yet they speak to me

and brag they have been in touch with the headquarters of Reza Pahlavi." Just a few days before, Reza Pahlavi had given a speech in California, and a woman called Beigi to say she had taken home the glass he drank from and would treasure it all her life.

But didn't Beigi want to give Reza Pahlavi the chance to deny the rumor that his grandfather was a Jew?

No, Beigi said, such stories didn't matter. He would give Reza Pahlavi my message, and if Reza Pahlavi had the time, he might answer (he never did). But Reza Pahlavi already had declined many requests for interviews. "We don't worry about how well presented he is in the United States. All that matters is how he is seen in Iran."

Like the existence of goblins that materialize only when the lights are turned off, the Polivy family story is impossible to prove. As Kathryn Babayan says, its value lies more in what it shows about the ways in which people fill in the gaps in history with stories that diminish their own sense of uprootedness and disconnection. What no one can deny is the story of the Jewish shah has forged a sixty-year bond between the Polivy family and my own, not to mention it has strengthened the connection between my father and me. Until I started this story, I knew only the roughest outlines of his friendship with Sidney Polivy or his experiences in the war.

"Sid and I met our first day of dent school at NYU in 1939," my father told me. "The professors divided us up according to the alphabet. Pollack and Polivy, it was always Pollack and Polivy, every little assignment, we did it together." Unlike my father, who had grown up in the Borscht Belt and loved telling raunchy jokes, Sidney was reserved. "He didn't have that good a sense of humor," my father said. "He didn't date that much, he wasn't very social." But Sidney demonstrated other qualities my father prized. "He was a square shooter. A hard worker. And he was handy with his hands, like I was."

By alphabet or fate, my father and his friend went through basic training together, then found themselves assigned to the same Liberty ship steaming out of Newport News, five hundred "fellas" stacked in hammocks five high in one clumsy troop-ship among thirty others like it, guarded from German subs by an escort of destroyers. The crossing took a month. My father was twenty-five. He had never been far from home or eaten unkosher food. (The men were supposed to get by on C-rations, but my father wouldn't touch a thing. Finally, the Jewish chaplain sat him down and said, "Listen, Abe, you have to eat. It doesn't matter what kind of meat it is—beef, pork, whatever—from here on, I say it's chicken.") As my father and Sidney steamed through the Straits of Gibraltar, across the Mediterranean and on through the Suez, they tried to figure out where they might end up. That's when Sidney told my father about the shah. "I kept pumping him for information. You know, the first time I heard it, I had my doubts. But he refrained from going into it. I said, 'We're going over to that part of the world, who knows where we'll end up, maybe we'll be stationed in Iran.' But Sidney refused to talk about it much."

Finally, the ship dumped the men in Bombay. They were herded on a train for an eight-day trek across the country. Both men suffered severe bouts of food poisoning, and by the time they reached Calcutta, they were desperate for a decent meal. Their first night, they were sitting in the court-yard of the magnificent Grand Hotel, worrying where they might get assigned. "We were plenty scared," my father said. "We could have been sent into the jungle with Stilwell, or over the hump to China with Merrill's Marauders." A full colonel walked in. My dad and Sidney jumped up, and my father, being the more gregarious, offered the man a drink.

"You two fellas just come in?" the colonel asked.

"Yessir!"

"Like it here?"

"Sure do!"

Well, this colonel was in charge of handing out dental assignments for the entire China-Burma-India theater of operations. "What would you fellas think of staying here in Calcutta with me?"

My father and Sidney spent the rest of the war a few miles apart, my father as the dentist for the 497th Port Battalion, and Sidney, the 508th. They couldn't believe their luck. One of the other dentists got sent into the jungle. He and a doctor took shelter in a trench; the other guy peeked out and got his head blown off, and the dentist had to spend an entire day and night with the headless corpse. Not that there weren't dangers in the city. Cholera struck, and my father woke each morning to find fresh corpses along the road. The soldiers were inoculated against that disease, but my father came down with dengue fever.

And the men he worked with didn't like Jews. The port battalions were composed mainly of stevedores charged with unloading supplies from ships and sending these by plane over the Himalayas to Stilwell's troop in China or the infantrymen cutting the Ledo and Burma Roads. My father was the first Jewish officer in his camp, and his first night in the officers' club "two rough characters from Montana" started railing against the kikes. "Oh, you sons of a gun," my father thought, "if you guys need dental work, just wait until I get you in my chair." Of course, the Jew haters from Montana liked my father so much, they ended up his friends. "They tried to make it up to me," my father said. "They channeled supplies I needed from the ships. For years after the war, we all exchanged Christmas cards."

Still, my father and Sidney knew how cushy they had it. The food was good. They got to travel. Sidney kept to himself, but my father found plenty of girls to date—English girls, Red Cross girls, American nurses. "There was a lot of shacking up. The guys would take a girl to the Vale of Kashmir for a weekend. I didn't do it, but I could have." My father's base, Camp Tollygunge, lay on the outskirts of an English country club. Every few weeks, my father and Sidney would get together for a round of golf. "Every hole had a kid waiting to get your ball in case you hit it in the water. They'd have guys on their hands and knees picking weeds from the fairway." The tennis courts were just as plush. "There was a little table with cold drinks beside the court. We had two kids, you know, like in the pros, to fetch our balls, and a waiter in a turban standing by." My father shrugged. "Tough war."

As was true for many soldiers, World War II provided my father with the most frightening yet exciting adventure of his life. After he got home, he never took another risk. He never traveled anywhere. The war forced the timid guys to be adventurous for a few years before they slipped back to being timid, and it drained a lifetime's supply of bravery from the rest. "I wouldn't want to do it again," he said. "But I wouldn't have wanted to miss it."

As was true for so many members of my own generation, I came to love adventure as much as my parents hated it. They lived in the same neighborhood for forty years; after leaving for college, I moved every few months. But wherever I went, I took an interest in Iran. Once, as I was leaving a library in Georgetown, a sweet Iranian man offered to shelter me with his umbrella. "Will you marry me?" he asked. "My father is very rich. He owns many goats. Tehran is a modern city. And women in my country no longer need to wear the veil." I tactfully declined—a wise decision, given that less than three years later Ayatollah Khomeini overthrew the son of the man the Polivys claimed as kin.

When Khomeini took over, I was working as a reporter in New Hampshire. "I have a secret I could sell to the Ayatollah," I confided to a friend. "The Shah of Iran—"

"—is Jewish," she said.

We stared at each other. "How did you know?" I asked. Oh, she said, a dorm-mate of hers at Wesleyan had told her years before. This woman's father had served as a dentist in India during World War II and considered sneaking off to visit the shah.

I lost contact with that friend. But somewhere, I knew, Sidney Polivy had a daughter.

Finally, I sat at my computer and ran a search for "Polivy." A Janet turned up, a professor in Toronto. I sent her an email. Was her father named Sidney, by any chance?

"No, my father was Calvin Polivy (son of David Polivy of the Bronx) and was a lawyer on Long Island. He was an artillery captain in Europe in W.W.II." Though she wasn't Sidney's daughter, Janet consulted her family tree. Her great-grandparents, Calman and Zlata Polivy, had given birth to five sons—Eugene, Harry, Paul, David, and Joe—as well as three daughters—Ella, Frieda, and Anna. The story Janet heard was that the eldest son, Eugene, ran away to the Caucasus Mountains to escape the czar's army, joined a rebel group in Persia, rose through the ranks, took over during a coup, and became the first Pahlavi shah. The family joke, she told me in an email, was that:

> we weren't speaking to him because he didn't send a wedding
> present when my father and uncles got married. The spooky

thing is that my father and the late Shah could have been twins! Same eyes, same hooked nose, same mustache, same shaped face! . . . Eugene is the brother who disappeared to the south and was never heard from again— though, again, I heard once that a letter did come saying he was fine—maybe even that he was a peddler—but not that he was becoming leader of Persia. Only my uncle Charlie can help with this, as my dad died a year and a half ago, and his younger brother died 3 months later.

As it turned out, Janet's uncle Charles had gotten his medical degree from NYU the year before my father and Sidney got their dental degrees from the same college. Odder still, Charles served in the China-Burma-India theater of operations, unaware that his cousin Sidney was in India. He and Sidney weren't all that close (Charles's grandfather, Calman, had a brother, Benjamin, who was Sidney's father), but Charles knew the family story. Charles's father, David, was born in 1884 in a village outside Kiev, so Eugene, the eldest brother, could well have been born in 1878, the year Reza Khan claimed as his birth date.

According to Charles, after Eugene went east, the Polivys never heard from him again. They sent him loads of mail but never got an answer. Much later, Charles's brother contacted the shah's widow and asked if the story was true, but she denied it. Although Charles doesn't believe the story, he promised to donate DNA if any of the shah's descendants could be persuaded to do the same ("I have plenty of blood to spare," he said wryly). He also gave me Sidney's daughter's name. She lived not far from him, in Hartford.

The next day, I sent Denise Polivy an email. When her reply came, I sensed her shock vibrating from the screen. She had gone to great lengths to track down people who knew her father, then finally gave up. She was "stunned and thrilled" to learn I was out there looking for her. She was forty-seven years old, a lawyer. She remembered my friend from college but had cut all her ties to Wesleyan except for her marriage to a classmate. "My father died when I was halfway through Wesleyan, which means that I spent a couple of the worst years of my life there."

Denise adored her dad. He was "a remote, revered figure" who spent a lot of time at work. Denise and her younger brother, Brian, felt trapped at home with their mother, who was "very, very depressed." Their father worshipped his wife and couldn't accept that this woman he loved was so unhappy. Maybe, if her father had spent more time at home, Denise would have rebelled against him, as I rebelled against my own father. As it was, in her second year of college, he died. "He had some kind of cardiomyopathy. It was caused by a virus, I think. Only a transplant could have saved him, and they didn't know how to do those yet."

After Denise's father died, Denise's mother sold their house and everything in it. "She just shut the door and moved away. We couldn't even mention my father's name." At the time, Denise was living out of a backpack, traveling from flat to flat in Europe, and she had nowhere to store her father's things. Aside from some photos, all Denise and her brother had left were their father's stories. "He talked about India all the time. He had a servant there, and when my father left the country, he left this bicycle to his servant, and this was just the greatest gift this man could imagine getting." She also remembers stories about this friend who was convinced her father was related to the shah because Sidney looked so much like him. "I certainly believed the story," she said, "and I think my father did."

Did she still believe the story?

"I guess I still do, because the physical resemblance is

so remarkable." Both her father and the shah had the same strong Semitic features, the same thick, dark hair, the same big nose and chiseled face. (Denise's brother, Brian, told me that as a boy he went to the 1964 *World Book Encyclopedia* and looked up the shah. "It's Dad!" he yelled. "It's Dad!" He went to school the next day, showed his friends the picture, and told everyone he was related to the shah.)

Denise was curious about her family's relation to the shah, but she was even more curious about her father. Her mother's illness seemed to isolate her father. He didn't have many friends. "This is something I've been discovering only recently, that you can find out a lot about a person by understanding who he's close to. Who are your friends? Who knows you? Who *really* knows you?"

My own father knew Denise's father as well as anyone. When I told him that I had talked to Sidney's daughter, I could hear the tears in his voice. My mother got on the phone, and when I related what Denise had said about her mother not allowing Sidney to see his friends, she started yelling: "Abe! Abe! It wasn't our fault that Sidney and his wife never came back to see us," the wound as fresh as it had been fifty years earlier.

Not many days later, Denise called my father at his condo in Boca Raton. They talked a long time, then arranged for Denise to fly to Florida. The week after Thanksgiving in 2001, my parents and I met Denise at the airport. A youthful, dark-complected woman with a blazing smile, she wore her hair in a buzz cut; after my father hugged her, he said that he could see "a little of Sid" in her face. We spent the evening going through my father's dental-school yearbook. ("Sid and I were both shutterbugs," my father said. "We took most of these candids.") Denise owned only a few photos of her father, but most of the shots from India showed him posed against the same background as photos of my dad. Clearly, her father had taken my father's photo, then they switched places; putting the photos side by side was like rejoining the halves of a stereopticon slide. On and on the stories went, until, after midnight, we sat shaking our heads over the resemblance between Denise's father and Reza Pahlavi.

The next morning, Denise jogged around the retirement community while my father and I played tennis. I was glad she didn't play; it would have been too sad, the three of us on the court and her father the ghostly fourth. My dad was eighty-three. I had never beaten him before, and I only won that day because I finally could outrun him. I shook my head at my teenage self, so dismissive of a man who put himself through dental school, fought a war, then raised a family and spent more than four decades relieving other people's pain. Only a teenager would regret that her father hadn't served a more glamorous function in World War II than fixing people's teeth. As if anything could matter more—to me, or Denise, or, I guessed, to Reza Pahlavi—than having your father still alive when finally you were old enough to understand who he really was.

RANCH HOUSE

IN 1954, MY PARENTS drove around Long Island until they found a house they liked. They wrote away to get the plans, then built a similar house in the town we lived in. Bad enough to grow up in a cookie-cutter ranch house on Long Island; how much worse to grow up in upstate New York, in a cookie-cutter copy of a cookie-cutter ranch house on Long Island.

But my parents liked the way the ranch house looked, and the rooms were considered large ("although they wouldn't be anything now," my mother says). The house was completely new—no one had ever died there, no one had been poor or sick. My father worried how he could afford the mortgage of a hundred and five a month, but my mother assured him that his dental practice would only grow and the house would cost less to maintain and heat than an older, cheaper dwelling.

If you are like me and grew up comfortably middle-class, you find it hard to credit the poverty and despair that drove your parents to strive to become middle-class in the first place. My parents' parents all were immigrants. My mother's father died when she was young; her mother went to work selling hats at Macy's, and my mother took a job as secretary for a man who kept trying to pinch her bottom. My father grew up at his parents' shabby hotel in the Catskills, where the family spent the summer hustling to please the guests and the rest of the year huddling to keep warm in the bungalow across the street and living off whatever groceries remained in the pantry at season's end.

My father and the other Jewish men who survived the war used their GI loans to build ranch houses on two streets carved from a pasture that until then had been owned by a farmer named Champlain. Like most fifties parents, mine viewed their role as providing their children with an orderly, hygienic home, the best medical care money could buy, and a college education. I didn't spend much time with either parent and when I did, we didn't discuss our inner lives. One of my few opportunities to feel close to my mother came when I sat outside her bathroom and watched her shave. Her body hair seemed erotic. And I coveted her electric razor, with its sleek turquoise body and the stainless steel blades you popped up with a button and cleaned with a tiny brush.

My most intimate moments with my father revolved around shaving, too. He would lean back and close his eyes while I patted his cheeks with cream, then shaved him with his double-edged chrome Gillette. I was only five, so the razor didn't contain a blade, but I enjoyed the nearness to my father's flesh, the Vitalis he allowed me to smooth through his hair, and the way, when I was done, he would snap his fingers and chant: "Shave and a haircut [snap snap] two bits," then hand me a quarter, which I didn't realize at the time was "two bits."

Then I came upon him finishing a real shave, after which he ejected something shiny and thin into a slot at the back of his medicine cabinet. "What was that?" I asked.

"What was what? The blade? You can't shave without a blade, pussycat. That's what cuts off the beard."

I might have felt cheated, except that when my father showed me how sharp a blade could be, I grew dizzy and nearly fainted. I asked where the used blades went, and my father said they fell to the basement through a space in the wall, leaving me to think about the walls of our house filling up with razor blades.

I think about those razors still.

Whenever my parents left the house, I would open my mother's drawers and riffle through the sachet-scented slips, underpants, brassieres, and scarves. In her closet hung immaculately laundered blouses and skirts; upside down on a rack along the floor were her impossibly narrow shoes, as if dozens of Rockettes lay buried beneath the boards. The same infuriating order reigned in my father's closet. His suit coats hung on shoulder-shaped wooden hangers; each carefully polished shoe lay impaled on a wooden shoetree as jointed and realistic as the ankle and foot of a marionette. This bothered me more than the rifle that leaned in the corner. I wasn't any more afraid of my father's guns than I feared the ammunition belts and canteens he had brought home from the war—I loved to strap these on when I played soldier.

What I found scarier was the label gun in that closet. Why did everything need a label? Was anything so unusual in our house that we didn't know what it was? I would sneak the gun from its shelf and dial each letter of my name, pulling the trigger as a blue plastic tape poked from the mouth like a lettered tongue.

Until, one time, the tape got stuck. Panicked, I loosened the screw that held the halves together, at which the insides came flying out. I spirited the pieces to my room, then spent a wretched hour jamming them back inside, until, in despair, I fit the label gun in its box and replaced it in the closet, not revealing what I had done until forty years later, when my father lay dying in Florida. "So that's what happened to that label gun!" he said, relief washing across his face.

*   *   *

Perhaps the incident with the label gun haunted me because I was so uneasy about my own insides coming out. My parents were obsessed with our bowel movements, the one aspect of our health they felt able to control. Every fifties parent lived in fear of the polio epidemic that crippled so many kids; until the day she died, my mother thought I would be stricken by paralysis if I sat around for more than a few minutes in a damp bathing suit.

My parents were so preoccupied with our bodies that I became hypervigilant as well. It was as if they had erected an electrified fence around our house, and instead of this making me feel secure, I wandered the perimeter, peering out to see what frightened them.

Nothing gave me greater pleasure than going through my father's drawer and coming upon the heavy red pen-light whose beam I loved to shine down my mirrored throat; or the blood pressure cuff I wrapped around my arm and pumped with a rubber bulb until I felt as musclebound as Popeye; or my father's stethoscope, with its deliciously creepy yellow tubes, valentine-shaped earpieces that fit neatly inside my ears, and shiny, cold head that I pressed against my chest to hear my own heart beat (*but-but, but-but, but-BUT*), unless it was thumbing through my mother's gilt-edged *Merck Manual* hoping to find a symptom I might have. (I am probably the last child in America who was able to convince a doctor she had St. Vitus' dance.)

In the bathroom I shared with my older siblings, I took perverse delight in handling the rubber bulbs my father used to remove wax from our ears and both kinds of thermometers, oral and rectal. Despite my terror of the latter, I longed to play with the mercury inside the bulb, an activity I had been introduced to by my dad, who brought home mercury from his dental office so we children could play with the shimmery quicksilver blobs, which would skitter across a mirror, break into ever-smaller blobs, and then, if we coaxed them back, re-cohere in a single blob that slithered inside the vial, except for the remaining particles that adhered to our skin and lungs.

But the scariest aspect of that bathroom was my parents' insistence that at all times there be a roll of toilet paper on the spindle, with the tissue coming from the bottom, and a spare roll on the tank, its appearance disguised beneath the dress of a plastic doll, said dress having been crocheted in hot-pink yarn by my grandmother down in Florida. Whoever used the last sheet of toilet paper was obliged to replace that roll with the spare from on top of the toilet, then retrieve a fresh roll from the closet, jam the doll's legs down the center, pull down her skirt, and place that roll on the tank. Once, my father scolded me so excessively for failing to perform the oblig-atory final step that I took five rolls from the closet, piled them on the tank, and stuffed the doll's legs in the upper-most roll, but purposely neglected to pull down her skirt. Instead, I yanked down the bodice of her dress, dabbed nail-polish nipples on her breasts, and smeared a sensuous leer on her lips. To which my father—no tyrant he—responded by holding up his hands and telling me that I had won.

Although this didn't relieve me from having to obey the rules the next time.

In addition to the rolls of toilet tissue my mother hoarded, the hall closet held towels and sheets she had hung outside to dry, which meant even on the darkest, coldest winter night you could bury your face in the linens and smell a sky-blue summer's day. However, to do so was to run a risk. Beneath those linens lurked the laundry chute, into which my brother threatened to stuff me. I was afraid of getting stuck, and equally afraid of not getting stuck and plunging to the concrete floor below. I was the messy child, the wild child, always tearing my clothes or staining them, and at some level I feared I would get washed and bleached and ironed like everything else that went down that chute.

I still dream about that closet. It was the nexus where time and space converged and did magical, nightmarish things. No one in my family talked about the Holocaust, but I had picked up enough to know that if Nazis banged down our door, I could hide by lowering myself down the chute and hanging on there with my fingers. So central was that laundry chute to my imagination I tried to write a book in which it served as a passage from one realm to the next—like the wardrobe to Narnia, or the rabbit hole to Wonderland—except that I couldn't envision the enchanted world into which my heroine would emerge on the other side.

Perhaps what I craved wasn't an escape from reality so much as a way to burrow from the present to the past and learn what the shiny veneers in my family's ranch house were meant to hide. On nights when my father deigned to show home movies, he would remove the portable screen from the closet and set it up in the living room—the contraption reminded me of a stiff-backed butler who would lean to one side and remove from his pocket a giant handkerchief, which he unfurled before his chest and held patiently while we watched the show. Since I was the youngest, by the time I arrived on the scene my parents had grown tired of taking movies and I felt cheated not to see myself growing up on the screen as my siblings had done. Still, everyone else's lives formed the Old Testament to my New. No wonder my siblings wished I never had come along. How much happier they seemed twirling around the living room at the center of my parents' gaze before their lives were ruined by my late arrival.

In one bit of film, my brother, disguised in an oversized nose, moustache, and Captain Spaulding hat, sneaks around the living room waving a wood machete. (On the wall in his room hung an actual steel machete that my father had brought home from India, where he had been stationed in the war, as well as a sword with a three-foot-long triangular blade inscribed with foreign lettering. Sometimes, my brother would take down the machete, slide it from its scabbard, and describe the damage it might inflict on a human limb. Or he would show me the grooves that ran along the sides of my father's triangular sword. "These are the blood gutters," he would say. "You can still make out the stains.") In the home movie, my sister puts her hands to her mouth and screams a silent scream before allowing herself to be tied to a chair, at which my brother pulls out a magic wand and makes her vanish. He looks around for a second victim and makes my toddler self vanish, too. As much as I enjoyed seeing myself assume this starring role, I couldn't figure out how I had been made to disappear and was troubled by the possibility that my brother truly did have this power and might use it if I disobeyed him.

So much for the private part of our house. On the way to the public spaces, you passed the two closets in the hall—not only the closet with the chute, but its identical and opposing twin, in which we kept our coats, along with the card table on which my mother and her friends played mahjongg (the mahjongg set was a thing of beauty, with its richly colored racks and hand-painted ivory tiles), the bridge chairs, and the accordion-pleated covers my dad hefted down to protect the mahogany table in the dining room. There was nothing worth exploring in that closet. Our public selves were beyond reproach.[1]

Nor was there anything scary about our living room, just the usual French provincial furniture, the tinny Yamaha piano most of us could play with various degrees of lack of talent, the black-and-white television set whose cloth-covered speakers I jabbed with a pencil simply for the satisfaction of watching the point go through—a set replaced much later by a color console that had a stereo, although we owned few records besides *Fiddler on the Roof*, a comedy routine by Myron Cohen, and that album by the guy who could imitate all the Kennedys.

Back when my father still made fires, he might bring up firewood from the basement, then get down on his knees and look up the chimney to make absolutely sure the flue was open, after which he lit the kindling and drew the metallic curtains shut. I loved everything about those fires—the poker my brother used for stirring up the flames, the chenille rug my mother spread across the hearth, the long-handled fork she brought in from the kitchen so we could jab marshmallows into the flames until they lit up like sugary torches.

But my father stopped building fires, his excuse being that if there was a fire in the fireplace, the thermostat, which was situated in the living room, thought the whole house was warm and didn't heat the other rooms, an excuse that made no sense since the only time this happened we were gathered comfortably around the fire and didn't mind the other rooms being cold. I think his edict had more to do with the absurdity of devoting so much care to maintaining a house, only to build a fire that threatened to burn it down. My mother

---

[1] The only scary story about that closet concerns my father's hat. Once, my father came down with the flu, and our neighbor stopped by to see him. Mr. Rothblatt put his fedora beside my dad's, then took my father's hat by accident. The next day, when my father dragged himself out of bed to go to work, he put on what he thought was his fedora and started screaming, "Will! Will!" (My mother's name was Wilma, which is frightening in itself.) "The virus must have gone to my brain and swelled my head!"

put a plastic fern on the andirons, and decade after decade, the wood in the basement grew so dry, it might have burst into flames of its own accord, not to mention it was stacked inches from the furnace.

In the kitchen, every item glowed with the pride and care my mother had bestowed on acquiring and maintaining it. Among the objects I loved were the heavy steel garlic-press, which crushed the soft white bulbs and riced them through its grid in delectable creamy threads; the egg slicer, on whose curved plastic bed you placed the egg before bringing down the wires; the Waring Blendor, which sat like a Siamese cat with its cord wrapped around its base; the potato peeler; the melon baller; the nested measuring cups and spoons; the cookie press; and the flour sifter.

Like every fifties kitchen, ours could boast a plethora of specially designed cabinets and drawers, multiplied by my family's need to keep two sets of everything, one for dairy and one for meat. Every few months, my mother would hold the door while the delivery man stomped inside in his blood-stained smock and deposited crates of freshly slaughtered chickens and cuts of lamb and beef, after which she and my grandmother devoted the day to koshering the meat in brine, reaching inside the chickens and yanking out the liver, the heart, the lungs, scraping the pin feathers off the feet, cutting apart the breasts, snipping off the wings with giant shears, then wrapping each portion in wax paper, labeling the packet with a pen, and ferrying it downstairs to the freezer. We ate parts of the cows and chickens regular Americans never ate. An enormous grainy tongue might boil on the stove all day. My grandmother stuffed intestines with breadcrumbs and sautéed these in a pan. One of my favorite delicacies was chicken skin fried in fat, but I also loved to suck the feet and necks.

That is, until I figured out these were animals we were eating. After that, I cringed whenever I saw my father use the electric knife to slice a breast, felt sick when I saw the taste buds on the tongue, couldn't bear the vertebrae in a can of salmon. I would sit there with a slab of liver on my plate, crying to be excused, while all across America the children of parents who had grown up in the Depression sat in their own ranch houses spurning the meat their parents had worked so hard to put on their own Formica tables.

Not only did everything in our kitchen have its place, the place for it had its place. There were special racks for spices; special drawers for waxed paper, Saran wrap, and aluminum foil; and in a special corner-shaped cupboard, a lazy Susan for our pots and pans (the name struck me as an insult as to whoever this Susan was). The refrigerator came with special compartments for vegetables, fruit, butter, milk, and eggs, but that didn't satisfy my mother, who bought Tupperware in every shape—most notably, a container in which to keep a head of iceberg lettuce (you impaled the core on a plastic spike, then set the head in a lettuce-shaped plastic tub). Often, I got in trouble for failing to close all four corners of the container designed to hold a block of American cheese, the necessity for which eluded me since each slice was already extremely well protected in a hermetically sealed plastic sleeve.

Of course, the main feature of any fifties ranch was the front-facing picture window. When I think of our house, I see my grandmother sitting sideways in a chair, arms resting on the sill as she gazes out at the street, waiting for the occasional car to pass. When my brother and sister and I were young, she helped to cook and care for us, but after we got older there was little for her to do. The few things she owned she kept upstairs, the exception being a brass mortar the size of a man's top hat (the date on the bottom, 5-3-1829, made it older than anything else in the house by 120 years), and the barbell-shaped pestle I used for crushing nuts, although I couldn't imagine why anyone would have schlepped such a cumbersome object all the way from Europe. It was a wonder the steamship hadn't sunk from all that weight.[2]

Like most fifties families, ours changed radically in the sixties. My mother enrolled at SUNY New Paltz, where she majored in English but also enjoyed biology, with its revelations as to how her children had grown inside her and the opportunities it provided to demonstrate her facility at dissection, a talent she attributed to all the years she spent reaching inside those chickens and yanking out their guts. As a result of her being occupied with these courses, my father finally learned where we kept the silverware and how to open a can of soup.

Then my mother redid our kitchen. Before, the cabinets had been plain pink wood, the appliances white, the floor yellow-and-gray linoleum. After, the cabinets were those heavy dark wood monstrosities every kitchen in America now seems to come equipped with; the appliances were avocado green, with an elaborately curved and fluted gilt-edged vent above the stove; and the floor was a spongy vinyl in a darker shade of green to complement the avocado. The only fixture that didn't get updated was my grandmother, who remained staring out the window as before.

I had mixed feelings about the basement. That was where the razor blades went to die. On the other hand, I loved tagging along when my brother and his friends played Ping-Pong,

[2] I recently learned the ship that carried my grandmother to America in 1903 had, four years earlier, nearly gone down in frigid seas. The ship was presumed to have sunk, only to limp into harbor a few weeks later with all forty-seven passengers alive and well, the captain having lost only one crew member and one hundred seven horses, which he had ordered thrown overboard to save the human cargo.

darts, or pool. The pool table was a full-size model I wasn't allowed to play on for fear I would rip the felt. Instead, I hung around and watched and tried not to mind when the older kids twirled the blue chalk cube on my nose.

The coffin-shaped freezer held not only those packets of kosher meat, but the salamis my father had been given as a gift by the butcher, whose son he helped get into dental school. Later, the butcher accidentally electrocuted himself by walking into his own freezer, stepping in a puddle, and touching an electric cord, after which the salamis seemed as eerie and repulsive as his severed limbs would have been.

The shelves above the freezer held harmless odds and ends, or so I thought until my brother asked me to take down a bag and I opened it and saw a human skull, although this turned out to be not the severed head of a murder victim, as my brother claimed, but my father's teaching aid from dental school.

The roaring, whooshing furnace kept us warm . . . until the day the needle on the gauge shot up into the red and my mother managed to get us outside only moments before the whole thing blew up, covering everything in the house with soot.

I never went near my father's table saw, whose shrill whine set my teeth on edge. But I loved to keep my mother company while she sorted and washed our clothes, then stretched my father's trousers on wire frames, or stood ironing his handkerchiefs, shirts, and underwear.

To one side of the laundry area, above the bright blue bottles the Seltzer Man delivered to our house, hung a coconut that my grandmother down in Florida had turned into a hideously leering head with seashells for eyes, a feather for the nose, and (don't ask me why) a shoe tree beneath its jaw. That coconut head scared us all, but it was like some powerful evil idol we were too superstitious to get rid of.

The door to the garage wasn't powered by an opener; someone had to get out of the car and pull it up, a job I hated because I feared the driver might—accidentally or on purpose—gun the gas while I was standing between the bumper and the door. Beside the car hung our shovels, rakes, picks, and hoes, as well as a lethal-looking axe and pruning shears with the wingspan of a condor. My terror of insects made me shirk most outdoor chores, but I begged to be allowed to ride the mower (a request my father vetoed because I might cut off my hands or feet), and I couldn't get enough of the blood-red plastic tube with the three-inch spring-loaded needle that my father would fill with poison and pay me to use to kill dandelions by stabbing them at the heart of their pointy, saw-toothed whirls and injecting the poison home.

The exterior of our house was as fastidiously maintained as the interior. The grass was perfectly mowed and raked, and each willow's branches hung as neat as a starlet's bangs. If one of the maples needed to have a limb sawed off, my father painted the socket black.

We also owned a plum tree, whose enticing purple fruit my parents forbade us to eat because the plums were poison. You can imagine our horror when our uncle from New Jersey, who had driven up to see my grandmother, walked over and picked a plum. "Uncle James!" we cried. "Those plums are poison!" At which he laughed and said, "Poison? Who ever heard of a poison plum?" and took a bite. When he suffered no ill effects, we ran outside and ate a few plums ourselves.

The attic was divided into a single long playroom for us kids and a bedroom for my grandmother. The floors were made of some waxy brown substance that reminded me of melted crayons (this provided the perfect surface on which to slide on stocking feet, though you had to be careful not to slam headfirst into the radiators at either end), and the walls were a mottled fake-wood pasteboard I could have punched through with my fist. On either side of the playroom you could open a dwarfish door and step inside the eaves, which we were forbidden to do because we might fall through to the rooms below.

In the closet nearest the stairs, my parents kept albums of crumbling photos, woolens protected by icy nuggets of para-dichlorobenzene (the camphoraceous scent, like gasoline, skunk, or farts, begged to be inhaled), and the blond Shirley Temple curls that had been clipped from my mother's head when she was a child, as if she might yet pursue the acting career she had wanted to pursue in high school, before her father and brothers laughed her out of it.

Beside the closet stood a bookcase in which my parents kept the requisite ranch-house set of Reader's Digest con-densed novels, along with my father's anatomy texts (from which I learned what a syphilitic chancre on a penis looks like), and a history of World War II that I must have read twenty times (had the world really gone so mad only a few years before?).

In the playroom, we kept the Monopoly and Scrabble boards, along with newer games like Operation, in which you tried to remove the patient's funny bone or appendix without setting off an alarm and killing him. Someone had given my brother a chemistry set and, despite my fear of what he would do to me if he discovered this violation, I couldn't resist weighing out and mixing the bilious powders, filling the burner with alcohol and lighting the flame, and peering through the black plastic funnel that contained a lump of radium, which I held to my eye to see the atomic sparks (no doubt starting a chain reaction that will manifest itself as a tumor in my optic nerve).

My grandmother's windowless bathroom was scarcely bigger than a telephone booth. The only furnishings were a vinyl-covered stool, a canister filled with a laxative called Senekot, and a bright pink rubber enema-bag that often had been used on me. It didn't contain a shower or a bath, but in all the years she shared our house, I don't recall seeing my grandmother carry her towel and soap downstairs to use in our first-floor bathrooms.

Despite everywhere I had to play, I brought my friends here, because where else did it get so dark? One of us would hide an object, then the rest would shut the lights and go in and find it. Or I ordered my friends to play Concentration Camp, in which the loser had to do whatever the winner ordered.

Growing up—and for most of my adult life—I assumed my grandparents' families hadn't left anyone behind when they emigrated to the United States prior to World War I. I didn't find out until recently, when I was doing some genealogical research on the internet, that my grandmother lost her brother, his wife, their son, and the son's entire young family to the Nazis. I don't know exactly how they died, but given the accounts I unearthed of the butchery inflicted on the sixteen thousand Jews who were living in Czortkow when the Germans took the city in July 1941, my grandmother's relatives might have been burned alive in their houses by their Ukrainian neighbors, with the Germans looking on in approval, or shot in the streets by the Gestapo, or marched into the woods, executed, and buried in a mass grave somewhere on the road to Jagielnica, or worked to death in a forced labor camp, or herded into a ghetto where they fell victim to typhus or starvation or the final *Aktion* against the Jews in October of that year, or if they managed to join the underground and escape to the forest, betrayed by the Ukrainians and wiped out by German soldiers in the spring of 1943. I knew none of this until last year; nor, it seems, did my mother. Most likely, my grandmother knew only that her brother and his family perished in the war. And yet, something prompted me to play Concentration Camp in her bathroom. That is, until the only Christian girl in the neighborhood objected to my ordering her to wear her underpants on her head and went home and told her mother.

Other than the items in that bathroom, my grandmother owned a container for her dentures, as well as her passport and citizenship papers, a photo of her mother, her father's Sweeney Toddish razor—which she used to trim her corns, a procedure that terrified me since the razor was so sharp and my grandmother's eyesight so bad—and a yellow dish she kept filled with Hershey kisses in case anyone came upstairs. Once, my friend Wendy and I dressed up like Eskimos to fool my grandmother into thinking we weren't the same children to whom she had just given two chocolate kisses, and lo, the disguises worked!

Somehow, this scarcity of possessions meant my grandmother's only real role was to shower her love on me. I would wake before dawn and trundle upstairs with a book, then stare at her until she opened her eyes and saw me. Without her glasses, her eyes were watery, deep, and dark, like the pond behind our house. "*Mameleh*!" she would cry, then grope for the glasses and put them on, a moment as thrilling as my father's declaration that the ice on the pond had frozen and was now thick enough to skate on. "Come," she would say, then pull me up and read the book.

I am not saying my grandmother loved me more than

anyone else, but I was the youngest and by far the neediest, and I gave her more opportunities to show her love than anyone else did. "The Old Country?" she would say. "Mud, mud, and more mud. That's what I remember about the Old Country. *Feh.*" Nor were her early years in America all that great. Not knowing she needed glasses, her teachers smacked her for not being able to read what was written on the board. At thirteen, she got pulled out of school and sent to work sewing buttons on ladies' coats.

No, the good days were now, living in the attic of the ranch house that her daughter and dentist son-in-law had invited her to live in. Her only complaint was that whenever we had a storm, the thunder sounded loudest in the attic, a complaint my family laughed at. How could thunder sound louder on the second floor than on the first? I laughed along with them, but the thunder in the attic sounded louder to me as well.

Then my grandmother began to ask the same questions over and over. She forgot to shut off the stove, or she wandered away, only to be found in a neighbor's yard. My mother was teaching school by then, and I was rarely home. We couldn't find anyone to stay with her and watch her. And so, one afternoon, my mother and I drove my grandmother to a nursing home.

"I know where you're taking me," she said. "I would rather you just left me beside the road to die." It was a beautiful nursing home, but my grandmother kept saying, "I know where I am. I would rather you give me poison." When the time came for my mother and me to take our leave, my grandmother flung herself against the elevator doors, yelling, "Take me home! Take me home!" I had nightmares about that for years.

*   *   *

Like me, most of the young people in my neighborhood went to college and moved away. We bought Cape Cods in Boston, Colonials in Atlanta, condos in Manhattan, fake adobe townhouses in Arizona. In the past few years, my gay friends have started to buy ranch houses and redecorate them in such an inviting way that I might consider moving in, if not for my fear I would drive up and see my grandmother's face framed in the picture window.

Not long ago, I went back to my hometown and took a walk around my neighborhood, ticking off the misfortunes of the families who used to live there. There was the neighbor who was agoraphobic (how had we failed to notice she never left her house?). The neighbor who was bipolar. The neighbor whose father ran off with a girl my age. The mentally ill neighbor who came back to live with her mother, then picked up a pair of scissors and stabbed her in the neck and killed her. The neighbor whose son joined the Marines, sustained an injury, contracted AIDS from his transfusion, and died. And the neighborhood cleaning lady, Helen, who was found dead in her apartment down the street, possibly the victim of abuse by her husband and/or their daughter. The secrets in my own family turned out to be minor—an unusually high incidence of gay uncles, aunts, and cousins, and one or two relatives who served brief stints in jail. There were only those razor blades in the wall, the rolls of toilet tissue in the closet, and all that Tupperware in the fridge.

Our neighborhood, like our town, has gone downhill since I lived there. My house is the only property that looks better instead of worse. The family living there now is Indian; the father is an executive at the bank. The yard is even more fastidiously maintained than when my father was in charge. When I explained to the owner that I used to live there, he took me on a tour, although his children and wife and in-laws kept retreating as we advanced. In the living room, the decor was a combination of American bourgeois and Indian, everything in its place, the house as obsessively neat as it used to be. The kitchen had been redone in white.

I didn't ask to see the attic, but the father ushered me to the basement, which he had finished to provide a playroom for his kids, a laundry room for his wife, an office for himself, and a shrine to the family gods to whom he and his wife and in-laws no doubt prayed that the walls of their lovely ranch house would keep their children safe from the poverty, disease, madness, despair, and death their ancestors must have suffered. The temple roof looked familiar, but I needed a moment to realize he must have salvaged it from the kitchen when his wife tore out and replaced the elaborately fluted avocado-green vent from above our stove.

A FRIENDLY BOOK OF FACTS
FOR BOYS AND GIRLS

WHEN I MOVED TO Ann Arbor to teach creative writing, one of my graduate students told me that his wife wanted to meet me. "She says it's eerie, but she feels as if she knows the characters in your stories, especially the teachers at your school." As it turned out, my stories seemed familiar because my student's wife, Jill, had grown up in the same tiny town in upstate New York as I had, in the building behind my house. Even though Jill is ten years younger, nothing much had changed between her childhood and mine, including the favorite sayings and peculiar behaviors of our teachers.

Another coincidence: Jill dated my mother's best friend's son. After they broke up, the boy's mother continued to act as Jill's surrogate parent. Thrilled by this connection, Jill and I grew close. One night, she and her husband invited my son, Noah, and me to dinner, a generous act, given I was trying to survive the lonely, depressing days after a divorce. When Noah and I showed up at their house, Jill handed me a book with a faded but eye-catching turquoise cover. *Being Born*, the title read. Above the title was a photo of a tomboyish girl—who strangely resembled Jill—and a clean-cut, *Leave-It-to-Beaver*ish boy marveling at a nest of eggs.

"I know that book!" I cried. "That's the same book my mother gave me to teach me the facts of life!"

Jill smirked. "You're right. It is the same book." She opened the cover and showed me "Pollack fmly, 55 Willey

Ave., Liberty, N.Y." inscribed in blue ink in my mother's pristine hand.

I jumped back. Not only was this a book I had last seen in 1965, when I was nine years old and living halfway across the country, it was a book I had tried my hardest to avoid. Imagine if an ugly, scary dog had bitten you as a child, then followed your scent for thirty years, only to spring, snarling, from a friend's front door.

"How did you get this?" I demanded. Jill pointed to the piece of notepaper protruding from the book.

> *Hi Jill—*
>
> *Bob and I were cleaning a bookshelf and found this book that Eileen Pollack's mother gave me for Dean & Mike. I thought you might be able to use it and, eventually, give it back to Eileen. She may like to have it, since she probably read it as a child.* ☺
> *Love, Terry*

If not for the smiley face, I would have wondered at the woman's sanity. Could she honestly think Jill would use *Being Born* to teach her children about sex and love? The book had been published in 1936, then re-issued in a "revised and enlarged 35th printing" in 1952, four years before I started being born myself, and even though the facts of life hadn't changed, I assumed someone must have invented a more up-to-date and engaging way of presenting them.

What intrigued me was trying to remember why I had refused to do much more than open and shut the book. I was the kind of child who couldn't *not* read. If I was on my way to the bathroom, I would grab my father's dental journals so I wouldn't be restricted to reading the toothpaste and deodorant. Had something about this particular book put me off?

Or would I have balked at reading anything whose cover assured me that it was A FRIENDLY BOOK OF FACTS FOR BOYS AND GIRLS THAT IS THE STANDARD WORK ON THE SUBJECT, *friendly* being the fakey adjective teachers used to describe policemen and doctors, who, despite what grownups said, had the ability to haul you off to jail or jam a needle in your arm. Nor would I have reacted well to the author's sexually ambiguous first and middle names, Frances Bruce, or the unpleasant connotations of her last name, Strain, with its implications of a difficult bowel movement.

"Blech," my son said. "What *is* this thing? The pictures are *disgusting*."

I figured he was saying this because the human reproductive system will always disgust a child of eight. But when I took back *Being Born*, the images returned to me with frightening clarity. The hideous black-and-white diagram of "the mother's reproductive system" resembled a disapproving, big-nosed secretary in hideous cat's-eye glasses, while the map of "the father's reproductive system" reminded me of an evil alien with testicles for eyes and a penis and foreskin for the nose. (Are any words ickier than "scrotum," "testicles," "penis," "seminal vesicle," "epididymis," "erectile tissue," and "urethra"?)

I quickly set down the book, at which the pages fell open to the photos that spanned the center seam. "Blech!" I said. And you would have said "Blech," too, if you had seen those grainy clay models of cross-sectioned human wombs splayed across a table like cuts of spongy, gray organ-meat. If that wasn't enough to make you retch, you could have turned the page and found a series of illustrations that, despite the floral imagery of the captions ("Hands and feet blossom from tiny buds"), resembled the severed limbs of a plastic doll some malicious child had held to a flame and melted.

Still, given how ignorant I was of grown-up life, you would have thought I would have studied *Being Born* with a microscope. It's not surprising a girl of nine wouldn't have known what a penis looked like. But I didn't know what a penis *was*. When I was in third grade, one of my piano teacher's cats gave birth, and I asked how she could tell which kittens were boys and which were girls. Well, she said primly, you could tell boy and girl kittens apart the same way you could tell boys and girls humans apart. Oh, no, I said. The only way you could tell human boys and girls apart was by the length of their hair, and boy cats and girl cats all had the same length hair, so how could a person know?

That's when *Being Born* appeared on my bedside desk. And, when I didn't pick it up and read it, appeared on the sink beside the toilet, then elsewhere around the house, until my mother gave up and put it inside her drawer.

Only to take it out a year later when I asked my brother to show me his circumcision scar. You might think this proves I knew what a penis was. But I had read somewhere that circumcision involved cutting a baby's foreskin, and I had no idea what a foreskin was. In Hebrew School, we recited a prayer about Jews carving God's words on the doorposts of their houses and keeping them as "frontlets between their eyes," and I had decided circumcision involved carving the Hebrew letter *chai* on a baby's forehead, but I couldn't see my brother's *chai*, so I figured the scar had faded and asked him to point it out.

At which my mother put *Being Born* back beside my bed, then on the table in the living room, then back inside her drawer, where it must have stayed until she handed it to her friend.

I opened to the inside jacket . . . and immediately was struck by the discovery that only fifty short years earlier, adults were out of their minds. While it made sense that Mrs. Strain would include an endorsement from the *Journal of the American Medical Association*, how could she have been clueless enough to boast that this was "a book to arouse enthusiasm." *Arouse?* Nor was I persuaded by the good doctors praising Mrs. Strain for being "unemotional and scientific" while remaining "friendly and personal" when any kid could guess that reading *Being Born* was going to be as friendly and personal as listening to a doctor ask you how things were going at school while sticking a thermometer up your butt.

Even the author's assurance that the answer to "Where was I before I was born?" is "as fascinating as the story of *Treasure Island* or *Robinson Crusoe*" struck me as inappropriate, given that *Treasure Island* is about a fatherless child being abused by a one-legged pirate and Crusoe spends a significant portion of his adult life with nothing but his own hand as a means to sexual gratification.

Nor would it have escaped my notice that *Treasure Island* and *Robinson Crusoe* are boys' adventure stories. In Frances Bruce Strain's universe, boy fetuses might be allowed to live on tropical islands, but girl fetuses are required to spend those nine long months sitting quietly in tiny pink padded cells. She can't describe an egg without chiding it for not fitting the acceptable dimensions of femininity. "Curiously," she writes, "the egg cell or ovum is many, many times larger than the sperm cell. Being a lady, you would expect her to be small [a curious grammatical ambiguity, that dangling participle], but instead of being smaller, she is larger."

In refusing to read *Being Born*, I was clinging to what little pride the world allowed me. If I didn't know what penises were, how could I envy boys for having them? I didn't want to *be* a boy. For years, I had been stealing looks at my older sister's pamphlets about how to stay neat and fresh even when coping with "the curse." As inane as those booklets were, with their tips for washing cashmere sweaters so they wouldn't lose their shape and making boys feel special by asking them questions about themselves, the booklets heralded an era when I would be able to go places in cars with boys and enjoy exciting adventures without my parents. If getting my period was the price I needed to pay, so be it, and I appreciated the way the authors of those pamphlets didn't whitewash (so to speak) the way cramps could keep a girl curled up in bed all day or send an embarrassing gush of blood through the bottom of her shorts.

But that same girl could have picked up *Being Born* and read the entire section on *men-stru-a-tion* ("such a long word and such a personal one for girls") without figuring out that blood would come streaming out her vagina and she better be prepared. As to cramps, Mrs. Strain's opinion was any healthy girl could entirely prevent cramps, if only she took care never to catch a chill or think gloomy thoughts!

The author applied this same evasive approach to her male readers' questions about their "seminal emissions." Despite two-and-a-half pages of explanations, a reader would never have guessed such emissions had anything to do with sexy dreams. As to the reasons a boy's penis might become erect, such erections likely had been caused by "excitement over a ball game or fire, or over an examination, or punishment." Now, I have never had an erection, so for all I know a boy might find himself with a hard-on from catching a pop-up fly, toasting a marshmallow, or studying for a difficult math test. But if Mrs. Strain truly wanted to assure her readers that getting an erection while being spanked was normal, she might have tossed her readers a hint that thinking about a girl (let alone another boy) might produce an erection, too.

All she has to say on *that* score is that when we are "really stirred up," we get stirred up "all over," and if readers want to know more than that, they should turn to page thirty, where they will find this maddeningly elusive bombshell:

> When the two mates are ready to unite and the sperm fluid is to leave the father's body, the penis becomes hard and straight like a finger, though much larger in size. Erect, it enters more readily into the long narrow passage of the mother that leads up into the place where the egg may be found.

I am all for an approach that is "devoid of emotionalism and sentimentality," but you can't tell me Mrs. Strain is showing a "sympathetic understanding of youth" by refusing to acknowledge that if you tell a boy one day his penis is going to grow as hard as a finger (only bigger!) and he is going to stick it up a woman's narrow passage, he is going to want a few more details as to *how* his penis is going to become hard and straight, and his female friends are going to be left dangling, so to speak, as to whether this isn't quite a painful activity to engage in.

Making fun of a book like *Being Born* is like shooting giant ova in a barrel. I can hardly express surprise that a book written in the middle of the previous century by the widow of a Congregational minister would have taken a sexist view of sex. I was happy to discover that at the end of a long, bizarre discussion of interracial coupling, Mrs. Strain issues a heartfelt plea that each of us accept everyone else, no matter his race, color, creed, or nationality. What I object to is that the author presents sex in such a frightening and repulsive way while pretending there is nothing the least bit frightening or repulsive about what she is saying. How else to explain the passage in which Mrs. Strain tells her readers that "[o]nce in a great, great while, the soft down coat on a human [baby] does not disappear." Such a baby grows up to be covered with thick dark hair. But not to worry! Some circus will pay the child "a good price to be exhibited before the public as the Wild Man or Wolf Man."

A woman who sees nothing unpleasant about life as a sideshow exhibit will be all too willing to illustrate her account of childbirth with a nightmarishly distorted Karl Rove-headed baby being extracted from yet another grainy cross-section of a female torso by a pair of disembodied hands in white rubber gloves. And if you are going to admit that little girls are bound to hear stories about childbirth so disturbing they announce, "I don't believe I shall want any babies when I grow up," you can't brush off such worries with a fairytale about how the stories "got started long ago when there were no hospitals, no doctors, no nurses who were especially trained in the care of mothers" and how giving birth in a hospital has become a piece of cake. I gave birth at one of the best hospitals in Boston, attended by a team of doctors and nurses so well-trained even their ova and sperm had degrees from Harvard, and I can tell you some pretty disturbing stories about the mistakes everyone made and the pain and misery I was in for two days of labor and the emergency C-section the doctors needed to perform to save my baby's life.

Not that I disagree with Mrs. Strain's testimony that the contentment of nursing a newborn is worth every bit of the pain and mess, or that feeling a fetus kick inside you is "like the flutter of a bird in the hand," or that it is very exciting to "hear the little heart beat," or that some people say you can even hear a baby hiccough inside its mother. I am here to testify nothing is more bizarrely miraculous than feeling another human being hiccough inside you.

What drives me nuts is the way the author of *Being Born* seems unable to accept that sex and birth (and love) can be beautiful as well as ugly, wondrous as well as painful, enticing and mysterious as well as frightening and repulsive. Not only does Mrs. Strain seem unable to convey such complexities to a child (who is perfectly able to understand that one might both love and hate one's parents, or that it feels wonderful to run and play even if one becomes hot and sweaty in the process), she subscribes to the delusion still prevalent today—cross reference Martha Stewart and a host of influencers on the internet—that everything can be made beautiful and pleasant if only the lady of the house dresses it up in the right décor.

You can see this in the chapter in which Mrs. Strain goes on about the differences between animals, who eat and reproduce by instinct, and human beings, who have conquered their wild, instinctual natures by relying on good manners. While lions and monkeys kill other animals and eat them raw, human beings make a social occasion of eating. "There is a lace or linen cloth on the table, pretty china, bright silver and glass, flowers. Everyone talks and laughs, tells the events of the day, and enjoys the good warm food. . . . Sit down alone and try to eat your dinner on a newspaper with an iron spoon from an iron pot, and see what would happen to your appetite."

According to Mrs. Strain, the same is true of that other human appetite, "mate hunger." Animals might run around showing each other their brightly colored buttocks without so much as an introduction, but human beings have learned to wear clothes and mate in private. Instead of using bodily colors to attract each other, "men and women use color in dress, personal decoration and hair arrangements, voice, gesture, words, songs, smiles, gifts—all sorts of things." This allows them to find partners who match their "heart's picture" of the ideal mate—at which point, if Mrs. Strain's illustrator is to be believed, they marry and take off their clothes, revealing themselves to be as pure and airbrushed as the hairless, breastless "modern statue of a young woman" reproduced near the end of *Being Born*, and the "ancient Greek statue" of a young man equally devoid of pubic hair, with genitals so tiny and dark I couldn't have made them out if I had tried, which I don't remember doing, because I never reached that far in *Being Born*.

Then again, I went overnight from being completely ignorant about sex and birth to being the font of wisdom for the other kids. In seventh grade, when I was finally forced to sit through a movie called *From Boy to Man*, the penis on the screen provided the final piece in a puzzle I had been filling in all along.

That same week, I saw *Butch Cassidy and the Sundance Kid* and was aroused to the point of sexual obsession by the scene in which Robert Redford surprises Katharine Ross in her bedroom and orders her, at gunpoint, to take off her clothes, at which they have passionate sex and the viewer understands that the rape was only a game the couple had been playing all along. One of my classmates also had seen the movie, and she and I became so exhilarated by our discussion of the rape scene that I ran over my fingers with the sewing machine and just kept talking.

Which was as good a sign as any that I was ready to understand the facts of life.

Maybe all we need to do is wait until our children's psyches are developed enough to accept that something can be exciting and painful—both—and then confess sex is as weird and gross as they think it is, but eventually they are going to want to do it anyway, and when they do, please use a condom. After that, they are on their own. I like to think I was as enlightened and hip about discussing the facts of life with my son as any parent could be, but I am sure he couldn't wait until our conversations were over and remains as baffled by love and sex as I am.

No matter what anyone says or does, kids are going to pick up the facts of life from other kids, or if they are lucky, from reading novels. Now that I think about it, I became a writer precisely because I wanted to get down in words how pleasurable and painful life can be from the moment we inhale our first breaths to our first experience of love and sex, with the astonishing opportunity this provides to give birth to very small people who will grow up to be as thrilled, confused, and terrified by love and sex and birth as we are.

THE HOUSE OF THE WORLD

BETH OLEM CEMETERY LIES within the fenced-in grounds of a General Motors manufacturing facility larger and more sprawling than many college campuses. The company allows the public access only twice a year, from ten until two on the Sundays before Passover and Rosh Hashanah. On the Sunday before Rosh Hashanah in 2002, my friend Marian and I drove around and around the deserted factory, searching for a gate that wasn't locked. The landscape around the plant is a wasteland of now-defunct factories that once produced automobile bodies, airplane engines, military helmets, radiators, and cigars. The first commercial property Henry Ford ever owned now houses General Linen and Uniform, one of the few functioning businesses in the area. ("Ford would turn over in his grave if he knew that the guy who owns it and sits at his old desk is Jewish," Marian said as we passed the building.) Millions of square feet of factory space do little but shelter decaying machinery and the trees that have grown inside, pushing through cracked foundations. The windows are boarded up or smashed, the cinderblock walls spray-painted with graffiti (THOU SHALT NOT SCAB). If your car broke down on a Sunday afternoon, you would need to search for miles before you found a soul.

On my own, I wouldn't have dared to come. Even on a mellow, late-September day, this section of Detroit is a nightmarish vision of a metropolis fallen prey to some mysterious catastrophe—apocalyptic riots, atomic holocaust, cureless plague. But my friend Marian—all right, my boyfriend,

Marian—grew up in the Polish neighborhood where the GM plant now stands, and a person tends to be less fearful of the decomposing ruins of something he knew while it was living.

The child of Polish parents who spent time in Nazi jails and barely escaped the Communists, Marian was born in Munich, where his mother and father lived in a camp for displaced persons. They made it to Detroit in 1951, when Marian was three. His father had been trained as an architect but didn't speak English and found it difficult to get a well-paying job. The family, which by then included Marian's younger brother, barely got by, moving from flat to flat in east Detroit. In 1966, Marian left for college in Ann Arbor. The following year, Detroit erupted in riots. Most of the city's white residents—and most middle-class Blacks—left for the suburbs. Marian's parents stayed in Detroit longer than most white residents, but in 1972 they moved to a suburb, too.

I didn't arrive in Ann Arbor until 1994. I drove into Detroit a handful of times to visit the museums, but the city could boast few neighborhoods in which an out-of-towner simply could park and walk around. Although Detroit is less than an hour's drive from Ann Arbor, most people I met bragged about how long it had been since they had last gone in, if they had ever been there at all.

Then I met Marian. Like many middle-aged Detroiters, he is nostalgic for the neighborhoods that were destroyed by the riots and the decades of mismanagement and indifference that followed. He laments the loss of the companies that made the city the hub of American manufacturing, as well as the many races and nationalities that mingled on its streets. What makes Marian different is he is trying to re-create that vanished world. He is not a trained historian—during the day he runs a community and economic development program at the University of Michigan and in the evenings he sees clients as a social worker—but in his spare time he records the oral histories of people who lived in the Polish neighborhood centered on Chene Street, to the south of what is now the GM plant, and collects artifacts and memorabilia the residents saved. Bit by bit, he is loading all this information onto a website that will allow viewers to click on an address and find out what businesses operated there in a given year, which families lived above the store, who dropped dead while drinking at the New Elk Bar, how much a pastry cost at the American Bakery. Click on Chene-Trombly Recreation and you will see a photo of Babe Ruth and Harry Heilmann, the Tigers' Hall-of-Famer, consorting with local fans and street kids; click on the Chene-Ferry Market and you will hear what it was like to slaughter chickens for the housewives who shopped there; click on Central Savings at the corner of Chene and Harper and you will hear the story of "Big Stack" Podulski, who shot Cass Kaliszewski, a Detroit policeman, in a bungled attempt to rob the bank; click on Edna's Cozy Corner and you will hear about the Canadian airman who asked for a date with one of the beautiful women at the bar and got clocked because he didn't know Edna's was a lesbian hangout. The idea seems ripe for science fiction: someday a person will be able to step into a computer-simulated re-creation of their childhood and revisit a favorite theater, ice cream shop, or playground, stopping to talk to long-dead shopkeepers, teachers, relatives, and friends.

As someone who grew up in another vanished world—the Jewish Catskills in upstate New York—I couldn't help but be attracted by Marian's dream of re-creating Chene Street. But his Polish Catholic background scared me. Like most New York Jews, I am the grandchild of men and women who were born in a part of Eastern Europe that at various times was ruled by Russians, Ukrainians, Lithuanians, Austrians, and Poles. Rarely was this association happy. I like to joke that my grandparents fled Poland to get away from Marian's grandparents. When I told my parents I was dating a Polish Catholic, visions of pogroms—in the past and yet to come—caused their end of the telephone line to fall silent. Knowing what I know of history, I couldn't dismiss their fears. As interesting as I found Marian's stories of east Detroit, he was rebuilding a world in which I would have felt uncomfortable. He told me many Polish Jews used to live and work among the Polish Catholics on Chene Street and he was interviewing as many as he could find, but I assumed relations between the Catholics and Jews on Chene had mimicked the antagonisms between Catholics and Jews in Poland. Whenever he drove to Detroit to take photos of the few buildings left on Chene or to interview Catholics who once had lived there, I usually declined to come. He knew I wouldn't be able to resist an invitation to see a Jewish cemetery inside an auto plant. But even as we drove there, I couldn't help but think Beth Olem would be yet another mute reminder of the Jews' abuse at Polish hands. In Jewish cemeteries around the world, the tombstones offer moving yet immovable testimony to the eviction or extermination of the Jews who used to live there. Maybe, deep inside, my growing affection for Marian scared me so much I was hoping to find evidence that would justify my ending it.

Because he had grown up in the neighborhood, Marian had long been aware of Beth Olem's existence, but he only recently had learned GM permitted visitors. An article in the *Detroit Free Press* revealed the date and time the gates would be open but not how to get inside. Few landmarks remained from the old days, so Marian found it hard to get his bearings. Finally, we found an open gate. The pleasant, rotund security guard told us she wasn't allowed to escort us to the cemetery, but we might reach it on our own if we kept driving to the left. We let her write down our license plate, then continued along a road that snaked behind a blacktopped lot full of shipping containers, dumpsters, loading docks, and ramps. We passed the looping, paved track on which GM tests the Allanté Cadillacs it produces at this plant. A copse of trees rose incongruously in the distance. Driving closer, we could see the trees were surrounded by four brick walls, like animals in a zoo. Even then, we might not have known what lay beyond those walls if we hadn't thought to drive to the other side, where an apron of macadam provided space for a dozen cars and a caretaker in a pickup truck kept a watchful eye.

A wrought-iron arch embroidered with BETH OLEM CEMETERY spans the entrance to the graves. Standing inside those walls, a visitor views the headstones against an incongruous backdrop of enormous above-ground pipes, the cars of a rusty freight train, a row of squat white fuel-tanks, a red-and-white-striped smokestack, a water tower, an upraised hoe. In Hebrew, *Beth Olem* means "House of the World," but the grounds are barely larger than the yard of a suburban home. About eleven hundred bodies lie within the plot, with only seven hundred stones to mark them. Orthodox Jews must be buried beneath the earth, so the cemetery is unadorned with mausoleums. Most of the monuments are modest slabs engraved with the person's name, their dates of birth and death, a brief inscription in Hebrew, maybe a star of David or those splay-fingered hands TV viewers of my generation know as the Vulcan form of greeting offered by Mr. Spock on *Star Trek*—hardly an accident since Leonard Nimoy stole the gesture from the Jewish men he remembered greeting one another at his father's shul.

As Jewish cemeteries in America go, this one is old. The first bodies were interred here in 1868. The original wooden markers have decomposed. Even the granite stones have been effaced by wind and acid rain, and many inscriptions are hard to read. As is true in any graveyard, a visitor can discover unintended irony—the plot for a Jewish family named Shellfish—along with loss and grief—Ida Kaufmann, daughter of Abraham and Rachel, who was born on December 1, 1880, and died on July 14, 1881; the son of S. H. and Gusta Markas, who passed away in 1904, nine months and six days after his bar mitzvah; Jacob D. Wolf, who was born on Christmas Day, 1887, and "Drowned at the Flats, Aug. 3, 1905"; and Regina Brasch, "beloved wife and mother," who died in 1907 at thirty-six ("In love she lived/In Peace she died/Her life was craved/But G-d denied").

Regina Brasch's age indicates that, like many women at Beth Olem, she probably died in childbirth. That first time Marian and I visited the cemetery, we met an elderly mourner who told us she had been four years old in 1911, when her mother, Sarah Saperstein, died from this very cause. Dorothy Glass had last stood by her mother's grave in 1947, the year before the cemetery closed. Dressed in black, bent at a right angle to the ground, she was escorted across the root-pocked terrain by her granddaughter, Sheila, who lives in a predominantly Black and Jewish suburb called Southfield, to the north. Following Jewish custom, Sheila and her grandmother set pebbles on Sarah Saperstein's monument to indicate they had been there. Then Sheila took her grandmother's arm and guided her in tiny, hobbled steps back to their waiting car.

There were few mourners besides the Sapersteins, but amateur historians wandered among the graves. When I asked how Beth Olem had come to be imprisoned within an auto plant, one of the men handed me an article from *Michigan Jewish History* written by Milton Marwil, an elderly member of the Jewish Genealogical Society of Michigan. According to Marwil, Beth Olem was founded in 1862, when two members of the Orthodox Detroit congregation, Shaarey Zedek, got in a buggy and drove three miles beyond the outskirts of Detroit to buy land from some German farmers. The plot was so far outside the city the congregation figured Beth Olem would remain a pastoral site for years to come. But two major railroads laid their tracks beyond the cemetery's walls, and this easy access to transportation brought with it a clump of factories. In 1910, Dodge Brothers built one of the largest auto plants in the world a few hundred yards beyond Beth Olem's gates. Other auto companies grew up around Dodge Main. The Jews of Shaarey Zedek found more picturesque sites to lay their dead. The last burial at Beth Olem took place in 1948. The cemetery sat untended. The earliest tombstones crumbled. Vandals and animals took their toll.

In 1966, Chrysler, which had come to own Dodge Main, bought two adjacent blocks to build a parking lot for its plant. Smith Street, which provided access to Beth Olem, was absorbed by the new construction. To permit visitors entrance to the cemetery, Chrysler built a ninety-foot driveway from the next block, Clay Avenue. The company also paid Shaarey Zedek $10,000 for property rights to the streets around Beth Olem, money the congregation spent repairing the rundown grounds. At that point, Chrysler razed the surrounding properties, leaving Beth Olem, as Marwil puts it, "a green island in a vast sea of a concrete parking lot."

So yes, Beth Olem did resonate with the presence of Jews who had lived and died in places you might not expect to find them. But that didn't seem the whole story. It was one thing for a cemetery to end up inside a parking lot, but how did it come to lie inside an auto plant?

Marwil's article struck me as strangely coy about what happened to Beth Olem next. "Around 1980, General Motors acquired a parcel of land encompassing much more than the old Chrysler possession, for a Cadillac Motor assembly plant. Even Clay Avenue was swallowed up, leaving the cemetery imprisoned within the vast holdings of the auto company." I showed Marian the article.

He shook his head. "All this was part of Poletown. GM wanted to build the plant. They got the city to use eminent domain and kick everyone out. They knocked down all the houses. When I was a kid, my family lived on Lyman Place. The house was somewhere over there—" He pointed to a depression of marshy land not far from the gate where the guard had let us in. "This is all that's left. The only part of Poletown that GM couldn't destroy was the Beth Olem Cemetery."

Marian had been telling me about Poletown's destruction since the day we met, but I hadn't understood. Maybe I hadn't listened. I suppose I hadn't cared. This section of Detroit wasn't destroyed by riots. It was knocked down by GM. I asked Marian to drive me around the neighborhood and repeat what he had said before. And this time, I listened.

The parcel of land General Motors "acquired" was still, in the early 1980s, a vibrant working-class neighborhood that covered four hundred and sixty-five acres of land and was home to thirty-five hundred residents. GM's desire to build its Cadillac assembly plant where the antiquated Dodge Main factory stood was understandable—after all, it owned the property, and the railroads were conveniently placed to bring in supplies and move out cars. Unfortunately, to make way for this new facility, GM decided it needed to condemn and tear down fourteen hundred houses, as well as dozens of family businesses, a hospital, schools, and churches, including the regal brick Immaculate Conception, which served as the house of worship for most of the Polish immigrants who lived around the plant.

In its prime, Poletown offered its residents tens of thousands of jobs, not only at Dodge Main but at auto manufacturers and suppliers such as Plymouth Huber, Chevrolet Gear and Axle, Packard Motor, Studebaker, Hudson, Hupp, Fisher Body, Murray Body, Briggs, Bulldog Electric, McCord Radiator, and Bohn Aluminum (Marian recited the companies' names with the reverence due a prayer). Grocery stores and bars grew up around the plants. Most of Poletown's residents lived in cheap two-story frame houses kept tidy by babushkas who washed the windows and swept the steps. ("Every day they'd be out there, sweeping and dusting and trimming," Marian remembered. "These were poor people. They didn't have much. But they kept the neighborhood spotless.")

If the area around Dodge Main could be considered Poletown's head, the neighborhood farther south, on either side of Chene, could be considered Poletown's spine. At various times, Marian and his family lived in both sections. As we drove around the potholed streets, he pointed out the weedy lots where he had lived while he attended first grade at Saint Hyacinth Church—he didn't speak a word of English and was one of sixty-five students in a class taught by beautiful Sister Mary Andrew, a kind young Felician nun who never had taught before—or the Butzel branch library, designed by Albert Kahn, where Marian once read novels by Zane Grey and dreamed of going west and living as a cowboy—or the soda fountain where he bought comic books and pop. The longer we drove, the more I came to see that even though relations between Catholics and Jews in Poland had been strained by mutual animosity off and on for centuries, when members of both groups emigrated to Detroit, they chose to settle side by side on Chene Street, with a considerable number of working-class Blacks living among them in a stable if uneasy peace.

The first blow to Poletown came in the 1950s with the building of the Edsel Ford Expressway, which severed the neighborhood at the neck. The businesses up and down Chene, deprived of their customers farther north, shriveled and died. Many of the Jewish shop owners moved to suburbs north and west. But even in the late 1960s, when Detroit was torn by racial strife and its white inhabitants fled, Poletown clung to life, populated by working-class Polish Catholics, African Americans, and a smattering of stubborn Jews.

Then, against its inhabitants' fervent wishes, the city allowed GM to tear it down. Didn't just allow. Got down on its knees and begged. Detroit was hemorrhaging jobs. Coleman Young, the city's first Black mayor, might have been expected to understand the agonies of a neighborhood threatened with being razed—his father's tailor shop had been destroyed when the state seized the district known as Black Bottom to make way for Interstate 75. But Young was rabid about keeping factories in Detroit. What good was it to preserve a neighborhood if there were no businesses to employ the people who lived there? If the city could retain GM, maybe other companies would stay or move back. So Detroit used its right of eminent domain to acquire Poletown, then gave the land to GM, along with millions of dollars' worth of tax concessions.

The residents couldn't believe the government would force them to leave their homes, let alone tear down their church. Many of the men had served in World War II, Korea, or Vietnam. Maybe in fascist countries a person could be evicted from his house, but that couldn't happen in Detroit. And how could the city use the taxes paid by Poletown to subsidize its own destruction? The mayor portrayed anyone who opposed the plant as racist for preferring to save a white Polish neighborhood rather than provide jobs for the city's Blacks, but many Black families lived and worked in Poletown, and most of these families, especially their older members, were as dismayed by the city's decision to seize their homes as their Polish neighbors.

Whatever their race, the majority of Poletown's residents didn't oppose the plant; they wanted jobs. But they didn't believe GM needed to destroy their neighborhood to find enough land to build it. Architects submitted plans for vertical parking structures instead of sprawling lots for employees' cars. At the least, the company could have spared the Immaculate Conception Church. But GM refused to consider any such suggestions. And by threatening to build the plant elsewhere, the company could have its way.

A city acquiring a plot of land for a public project like a highway isn't so unusual. A city acquiring an entire neighborhood, razing the buildings, and donating the land to a profit-making company is putting the principle of eminent domain to such questionable use that Poletown's seizure is studied in many law schools; Marian's elder son, Marek, called one day to say his professor at Columbia Law had just discussed the legality of the destruction of his father's hometown.

To justify the evictions, the city and GM portrayed the neighborhood as a slum. But Marian remembers it as no shabbier than Hamtramck, which borders Poletown to the north. (Hamtramck, an integrated island in the middle of nearly all-Black Detroit, is now considered hip, a destination for tourists who favor cutting-edge music, funky coffee shops, and kitschy Polish restaurants serving pierogis and pickle soup.)

No one would help Poletown fight GM. Rather than save the Immaculate Conception Church, the archdiocese used the opportunity to sell GM the building—which the parishioners had paid to build—as part of its program to close as many ethnically identified inner-city churches as it could. Only Ralph Nader came to Poletown's aid, and Nader, who already had stuck it to GM by writing *Unsafe at Any Speed*, was seen by most Detroiters as an outside agitator who hated the auto industry simply for producing cars. Many of Poletown's residents refused to accept the city's modest offers to buy their homes. But their initial disbelief at the government's collusion with GM and the Catholic Church kept them from mounting a strong opposition until it was too late. Entire blocks began to burn, and the police did little to stop the arsonists. Demolition workers hauled away the statues from Immaculate Conception, then, as horrified parishioners watched, knocked down the church. Several elderly residents died of the stress, as did Father Joseph Karasiewicz, one of the only priests who tried to save it. The city bulldozed the remaining houses. GM put up its plant.

But few of the thousands of jobs GM promised ever came to be. The company used the chance to experiment with robotics. Most of the men and women who work at the factory now drive in from the suburbs. Instead of buying sandwiches from the hundreds of vendors GM predicted would gain business from the plant, the majority stay inside the fence and eat in the cafeteria. Chene Street is so nearly devoid of life that Eminem used its blasted remains in his movie *8 Mile*. (Marian and I went to the movie to catch sight of the sign for Chene Street that is visible through the window of the bus Eminem rides to work. "Look!" Marian whispered as the bus passed an abandoned concrete hulk. "That used to be the Wel Com Inn bar!") Although the merchants up and down Chene once sold more merchandise per frontage foot than any commercial district except Fifth Avenue in Manhattan, the street now looks bucolic; the few remaining residents could graze sheep in the grassy lots.

In an attempt to erase the story of how it acquired the land on which it produces Cadillacs, GM insists its facility be referred to as the "Detroit-Hamtramck Assembly Plant." Older Detroiters call it Poletown anyway (ironically, no one called it Poletown before GM threatened to tear it down; the name started as a catchphrase by reporters and a verbal rebellion by people who used to live there). But as those older Detroiters die, the only reminder of Poletown's existence will be the graves at Beth Olem.

So Beth Olem isn't the testament to anti-Semitism I expected it to be. Rather, it is a monument to the complexities of religion, class, race, and ethnicity in America. Jewish and Catholic Poles have ended up in proximity more often than can be explained by mere coincidence, just as it is no coincidence Marian and I ended up together amid the graves of Beth Olem, a few hundred yards from the industrial slough where his family once lived. As my colleagues at the university like to say, there is an erotics of the Other, a thrill in making love across the rift of the forbidden, although there is also, I think, an urge to heal that rift. If I hadn't fallen in love with a Polish man, I might feel little compassion for the inhabitants of Poletown. Given the destruction of most synagogues in Poland during World War II, not to mention the complicity of many Poles in the annihilation of the Jews who worshipped at those synagogues, I might be less than sympathetic about the demolition of a Polish Catholic church. Yet I have come to understand that Polish Catholics and Jews share a common culture as well as a common past.

Beth Olem is a concrete manifestation of such ironies and inversions. Unlike most Jewish cemeteries in Eastern Europe, Beth Olem was not destroyed. The Jews here died at peace, their remains honored and taken care of. The Jews who lived in Poletown, unlike the Jews who lived in Poland during the pogroms of the nineteenth century and the atrocities of World War II, left this part of Detroit more or less willingly. It was their Polish Catholic neighbors who were forcibly uprooted. I spent my first eighteen years living in a comfortable fifties-style ranch house in a largely Jewish enclave of upstate New York. My grandmother's brother and his family were murdered in the Holocaust, but otherwise my relatives came through relatively unscathed. Marian's parents spent time in a Nazi jail. Not long ago, when he made a pilgrimage to Auschwitz, he saw a memo the Nazis had printed with a list of one day's dead. By a macabre coincidence, there, on the page tacked to the museum wall, was his grandfather's sister, Maria Krzyzowski, whose name differs from Marian's by just one letter.

After that first visit to Beth Olem, I wondered why GM, which was powerful enough to buy and raze the houses of thousands of living residents, wasn't willing or able to move a few hundred graves. Maybe Beth Olem's survival was a sign of our reverence for the dead as reminders for the living. Rather than bury those we love in isolated plots, we consecrate a common ground and commemorate our dead together. *We have been here*, the markers say, the way Orthodox Jews leave pebbles to mark their visits to a grave. The inscriptions on those markers testify to a more tangible reality than the version of our lives that governments and corporations want us to believe.

At some basic level, that theory might be true. The dead are there; the living aren't. But the deeper I dug into the story of Beth Olem, the more I came to see GM would have moved those bodies if it could have. Jewish law considers it a desecration to exhume a body and therefore forbids it. But GM wasn't obliged to follow Jewish law. Most of the articles written about Beth Olem assert that GM was stopped from moving the graves by a Michigan law that prohibits moving a body without the descendants' consent. But that isn't strictly so. Moving a dead person is hard, but not impossible. You need to obtain a permit from the local health department. You need permission from the dead person's next of kin. A funeral director must supervise the exhumation. And whoever moves the grave must pay all the costs. Moving Beth Olem would have been a headache for GM. But a company that had gone to all the trouble of acquiring and destroying an enormous section of Detroit probably wouldn't have let a bunch of dead Jews stop the project.

For a long time, I couldn't find anyone who knew what prevented GM from moving Beth Olem. Finally, a member of Shaarey Zedek put me in touch with Andrew Phythian, who took part in the negotiations between the Jewish community and GM in the early 1980s and supervised Beth Olem for Shaarey Zedek. According to Phythian, GM had no "hard plans" to move Beth Olem, but the company "speculated on the possibility." An article in the *Detroit News* of September 22, 1984, backs up Phythian's claim. GM wanted to move the graves, but "horrified Jewish leaders told the company, as well as Detroit and Hamtramck officials and the governor's office, that Jewish law considered the removal of the bodies from their graves a form of desecration. The leaders said the cemetery probably also contained prayer shawls, Bibles, scrolls and paraphernalia which under Jewish law must be buried, not burned or otherwise destroyed." Although the article maintains the protests of these leaders prevented GM from carrying out its plans, Phythian told me Shaarey Zedek held a card GM couldn't trump even with eminent domain. The congregation retained the rights to a perpetual easement the width of a two-horse carriage leading from the cemetery to Joseph Campau Street in Hamtramck to the east. GM couldn't build its plant without that strip of land. After three years of negotiations, the Jewish community agreed to give up the corridor in return for GM's promise not to disturb the graves and to allow the public access. GM preserved Beth Olem not out of generosity or religious spirit or reverence for the dead, but because it had no choice.

On the Sunday before Rosh Hashanah in 2003, when Marian and I visited Beth Olem a second time, the same jovial round security guard let us in the gate and the same caretaker lounged in his pickup outside the cemetery entrance. Both the caretaker and the guard were Black, which caused me to marvel at the way white people shy away from predominantly African-American cities in fear, yet hire Black people to protect their property, their children, their elderly relatives, and their dead. A man from the Jewish genealogical society asked us to sign the guest book on a pedestal beside the arch. He showed us a bucket full of golf balls the caretaker had collected from the cemetery grounds: apparently, the employees at the plant spent their lunch breaks driving golf balls toward the giant cup formed by Beth Olem's walls.

As had been true the previous year, the only mourner was an elderly woman who had come to pay her respects at her mother's grave. This woman and her two middle-aged companions sat on a marble bench beside the stone for

Hattie Wedes, who died on January 21, 1919, at the age of twenty-nine. Hattie's daughter, Anna, now in her nineties, laid an orange rose on her mother's stone and sat smiling at the antics of a little boy whose exact relation she couldn't quite explain except that "he is the love of my life."

I knelt beside the bench to speak to Anna and her companions, one of whom was deaf. Although this was the first time Anna had been back to Beth Olem since her mother's funeral, she remembered her mother's death "as if it happened yesterday." Soldiers returning from the killing fields of Europe in World War I brought with them the Spanish flu. The disease struck Anna's mother. Her family brought down her bed from the second floor and put it in the parlor. Everyone wore canvas masks. The doctor ordered the family to stand away and give Anna's mother air. "'Open the window!' the doctor shouted. Can you imagine?" Anna shook her frail head. "It was January, my mother had the flu, and he said to open the windows and let in the cold!"

The little boy ran up, and Anna smiled at him and kissed him. "I will never forget," she said. "I could see my mother's eyes over the top of her canvas mask. I was seven at the time. I was standing in the door. My mother looked at her sister— my aunt. Then she looked at me. She was worried who would take care of me when she died. My aunt nodded, as if to say that she would take me in, and then my mother allowed herself to die."

One of Anna's companions told me when GM decided to build the factory, Hattie Wedes's descendants considered moving her remains to another cemetery. But in the end they decided she was at peace at Beth Olem, and they left her where she was.

The three women stood to go. As Anna placed her feet beside the bench, I noticed a golf ball the caretaker must have missed and grabbed it before she could step on it and trip.

After we left Beth Olem, Marian and I drove to Hamtramck, where we stopped for lunch at one of that city's many Polish restaurants. With its Polish eagle above the door and the painting of the pope hanging in the dining room, the restaurant was hardly welcoming to Jews; my parents would have starved rather than step inside. If I hadn't been with Marian, I wouldn't have found the nerve to eat there either.

But the rye bread was the hard-to-find variety I missed from my childhood. Everything on the menu, from the borscht to the stuffed cabbage, was food I had grown up eating, under slightly different names. As we waited for our meal, we passed the time, as we often do, comparing Polish and Yiddish words and guessing whether people we know or various celebrities might be "one of yours" or "one of ours." For dessert, we both ordered the seven-layer chocolate cake we both loved eating when we were kids.

On our drive back to Ann Arbor, Marian took his usual nostalgic detour south down Chene, where little remains except a TV repair shop, a shooting range, several bars, and a restaurant called the Polish Yacht Club, although neither yachts nor water can be found on this burned-out block. One by one we passed the magnificent Catholic churches— Saint Stanislaus, Saint Hyacinth, Sweetest Heart of Mary, and Saint Albertus—that (along with Immaculate Conception) once formed the heart of Polish east Detroit. In front of Saint Albertus, which is open only once a month, stands a forlorn statue of Jesus.

"One of your guys," I joked to Marian.

"No," he reminded me, "one of yours."

Postscript: On July 30, 2004, the Michigan Supreme Court

responded to a plea from a Wayne County landowner whose neighborhood was threatened with being destroyed to make way for a high-tech industrial park by unanimously overturning the 1981 decision that allowed Detroit to bulldoze Poletown and give the land to GM. The attorney for the landowner, Ed Hathcock, argued that large-scale development projects such as the Poletown plant or the industrial park planned for Wayne County rarely if ever deliver the jobs and added tax-revenue that would justify the use of eminent domain to seize private land for the public good. Given the verdict in *Hathcock v. Wayne County*, the 1981 Poletown decision no longer can be cited as precedent in similar disputes around the country, and the new ruling can be retroactively applied to cases in which a plaintiff still is challenging the city's right to tear down Poletown.

I TRIED TO RAISE A JEW AND
HE TURNED OUT A COMMUNIST

I WAS RAISED IN AN Orthodox Jewish home, but I studied physics in college and stopped believing in God. The universe seemed wondrous enough without inventing miracles. I married a biologist who believed in Darwin. He didn't object to raising our children Jewish, as long as I didn't expect them to take the Bible literally. When our son, Noah, was born, I decided the wisest approach to his education—both secular and religious—was to teach him to rely on empathy, logic, common sense, and love. Above all, I vowed never to lie to him or expect him to put his faith in anything I didn't trust myself.

At first, this approach seemed to bestow some real advantages on our son. A rational little boy, he knew monsters weren't real and so didn't fear them. Once, when a giant yellow creature came toward him in a video store, Noah collapsed to the ground and started screaming. The man inside the Big Bird suit removed his head; when I was able to persuade Noah to look up, he saw that the apparition was now explicable, at which he brushed himself off and asked why any grownup would want to go around scaring kids like him.

Another time, Noah summoned me in the middle of the night to ask if he needed to worry that an alien would get in his room. I could have lied and told him no. Instead, I said I was pretty sure there were creatures on other planets. But the chances such a being would visit Earth were very small. If aliens did manage to travel such great distances, they would need to have developed a very advanced civilization, which meant they were likely to be peaceful. Besides, I said, wouldn't it be exciting to make contact with a creature from another planet? It sure would be, Noah said, and he tried to stay up to meet one.

The only time I lied was when he started losing teeth. I am not sure why this one aspect of childrearing caused me to indulge in make-believe, but my father had been a dentist, and anything to do with teeth seemed laden with tradition. Like my parents before me, I told Noah that if he put a tooth under his pillow, the Tooth Fairy would visit him in the night. Sure enough, the next morning, he found a Susan B. Anthony dollar in place of the tooth. "See?" I said. "The Tooth Fairy left you a coin. It even has her picture on it." I didn't think he would believe me, but he did.

"How could I *not* believe you?" he told me later. "You said the Tooth Fairy would leave me money, and she did. If God had left money under my pillow, I would have believed in Him."

I might have stretched the truth when it came to the Tooth Fairy, but I wasn't about to lie about anything as important as God. When Noah asked if God was real, I told him I believed God was whatever positive force had caused the universe to exist. God was the reason there was something rather than nothing, the reason human beings love each other and work toward making the world a better place for everyone rather than a paradise for just a few and a miserable, unfair swamp for so many others.

For a while, this seemed to satisfy him. But one night, Noah woke up sobbing. "Mom!" he said. "God doesn't care about anything we do! The universe doesn't care who we love, or who loves us!"

I wanted to lie and say the universe *does* care. I wanted

to say that even though we die, our spirits continue living. "Sweetheart," I said, "everyone has nights like this. Usually, when this happens, they ask someone they love to hold them." I took him in my arms. "The universe might not care, but I do. Your father cares. Your grandparents care." I remembered the Beanie Baby I had bought earlier in the week. "And you know what? I have a Beanie Baby I've been meaning to give you. It's not much. But it's better than nothing."

Noah stopped shaking. He dried his eyes. "All right," he said. "I'll take it." And he cuddled the penguin to his chest and went back to sleep.

Of course, a Beanie Baby can stave off existential despair only for so long. One day, I was driving Noah to school when he announced glumly he had decided it didn't matter what he did with his life. Luckily, I had felt this way often enough that I was prepared to tell my son what I told myself. "Just because there's no God to order you what to do with your life doesn't mean you should throw it away. If you found a million dollars, but it didn't come with instructions for how to spend it, would you toss it in the trash?" No, he said, he wouldn't. "Of course you wouldn't. You would think a long time and figure out the best way to spend it. You would keep some of the money so you would have enough food to eat, and a nice place to live, and enough money to go to college. You would buy some fun stuff for yourself. Maybe you would take a trip. And you would probably give the rest to poor people, so they wouldn't have such hard lives."

Noah's eyes lit up. "You're right!" he said. He would definitely use some of it for himself, but he would give most of his money to other people.

"Well," I said, "think of your life as a million dollars you just happened to get for no good reason. Just because there's no God to tell you how to spend it, doesn't mean you can't figure it out for yourself."

That conversation kept my son satisfied for another few years, until he started preparing for his bar mitzvah. The rabbi at our ultra-Reform temple in Ann Arbor is a feisty, iconoclastic intellectual, and he wasn't offended by Noah's skeptical questions. Between us, we managed to keep him on track. But a few weeks before the big event, Noah told me that he felt like a hypocrite going through with the ceremony. He had started reading Karl Marx and considered himself a communist. He didn't believe in God. He didn't believe in organized religion. The best I could do was extract his promise that he would go through with his bar mitzvah, in return for which I would never require him to attend religious services of any kind.

I shouldn't have been surprised. If you raise your kid to believe it's up to him to decide the right way to spend his life, you can't express shock when he announces he has become a communist. I guess the bigger surprise was how disappointed I was that he didn't consider himself a Jew.

Then I got an idea. My mother's father had been an ardent socialist, and I showed Noah the card that documented his great-grandfather's membership in whatever branch of the party he belonged to. It was no coincidence, I said, that so many communists and socialists were Jews. "You know how you want to bring about a better, more perfect world?" I said. "That's pretty much the same as the Jewish principle of *tikkun olam*."

Noah smiled. "I know, Mom. I thought of that, too. I don't believe in God. I don't believe in being Jewish. But my not believing in God, or in religion, or even in being Jewish, is my way to be a Jew."

RIGHTEOUS GENTILE

WHEN I TOLD MY MOTHER I was dating a Polish Catholic, the abyss that opened in our conversation was so deep and dark I could see three generations of our family tumble in. Hadn't my grandparents fled Poland to escape the brutish peasants who got drunk and murdered Jews? Didn't all Poles rat out their Jewish neighbors, or nod approvingly as the Nazis led them to waiting vans?

My boyfriend fit none of my mother's stereotypes. The director of an economic development institute at the university where we both worked, Marian was far better read than most writers I knew. When the High Holidays rolled around, he donned his *kippah* and accompanied me to services, then suggested we walk to the river and toss in our sin-laden crumbs for *tashlich*. The local Hadassah awarded him the designation "Righteous Gentile" for organizing the yearly Holocaust symposium and editing a magazine in which he took his fellow Poles to task for their anti-Semitism. In one of our first email exchanges, I admitted I couldn't help but be turned on by the idea of kissing a Righteous Gentile.

And yet, I shared my mother's fears. Marian had been raised by parents who viewed the Jews as conniving financiers and communists. His parents had been imprisoned in Nazi jails, yet his father sat in the basement listening to an anti-Semitic Polish radio station and was anything but pleased to see his son dating a Jewish divorcee. When Marian took me to a Polish fair in suburban Detroit, the sight of the towering steel crucifix, the sour smell of kielbasas and Okocim beer, and the oompah-pah of the accordion to which the fairgoers were dancing a polka induced a panic attack.

Even so, I was determined to prove my mother wrong. As Marian and I spent more time together, I saw a side of Polish culture few Jews encounter. Whenever a Polish writer or musician visited Ann Arbor, the auditorium filled up with the local intelligentsia. I learned to pronounce Polish names, and even to spell them. (Once, when Marian and I showed up at a resort in northern Michigan, he fumed at the way he was registered at the desk—until I confessed that I had been the one to misspell his last name.) On Wigilia, I stood with head bowed while Marian's mother recited the Lord's Prayer in Polish. Then I took one of the Styrofoam-light *oplatki* crackers embossed with the Holy Family and shared pieces with Marian's brother and father.

Finally, he asked me to travel with him to Poland. He had been born in a Displaced Persons camp in Germany after the war and brought to America by his parents in 1951, when he was three. But he traveled to Poland often. During the Communist years, he smuggled assistance to Solidarity. (We joked that he single-handedly brought down the Iron Curtain.) Now, he spent several weeks a year visiting his relatives, keeping up his fluency in the language, and immersing himself in Polish culture. I had no desire to visit Poland. But I knew if I wanted to remain his partner, I would need to accompany him on future trips. What I was less sure of was whether I could directly confront the reality that the man I loved was a Catholic Pole.

The journey started well. Marian's friends picked us up at the airport and drove us past the dismal Soviet-era apartment blocks that surround Warsaw to a house so modern and luxurious my friends in Ann Arbor, or even New York, would have coveted it. Walking the cobbled streets, I felt that pressure behind my eyes that nothing but a quaint, graceful European city seems able to evoke—an effect intensified by the knowledge that eighty percent of the buildings I saw were replicas of the originals, Warsaw having been dynamited by the retreating Germans.

I was surprised how many Polish words I understood, the equivalent of their Yiddish counterparts. Ditto the tastes and smells of the heavy, fatty, fried, dill-and-garlic-seasoned foods, which, with the exception of the kielbasa, could have been found in the dining room of my grandparents' Catskills hotel. In fact, my inability to stop shoveling in all that familiar and enticing Polish food almost spelled my doom. I previously had undergone three abdominal surgeries, and my intestines were knotted by scar tissue. Often, when I travel, my digestive system shuts down and I become what my father would have called *ongeshtopt*, which in Yiddish means "all dammed up."

The condition is made worse by stress. Marian had already visited Auschwitz six times—his family had lost many relatives there—and we agreed it wouldn't do our relationship any good to turn our trip into the death-camp march most American Jews follow. But how could I not visit the Warsaw Ghetto—or rather, the residential neighborhood where the ghetto once stood? The Poles weren't the ones to create that ghetto. But they didn't come to the aid of their starving, disease-ridden fellow citizens, even when the Jews staged a suicidal uprising against their common enemy.

As if my intestines weren't knotted enough, I kept noticing the Jewish stars embedded in the town's graffiti. When I asked Marian to translate a slogan etched on a bus, he admitted a citizen was venting his frustration with the prime minister, Donald Tusk, by labeling Tusk's economic policies "Jewish chicanery," a telling gripe considering Tusk is not a Jew. On our drive to Krakow, we saw spray-painted slurs accusing the players on rival soccer teams of being dirty Yids—an odd complaint given that virtually no Jews remain in Poland. It was as if enemies of the Detroit Tigers defaced the team's posters by spray-painting an N over the T and adding a second G, even though no Black people played for the team or remained anywhere in the United States.

In Krakow, Marian and I checked into the quaint apartment he had rented. Guilty about bypassing Auschwitz, I requested we spend the few hours before dinner touring the Jewish Quarter. The Kazimierz was even eerier than the Warsaw Ghetto; here, the shops, apartment buildings, and synagogues still stand, though creepily devoid of Jews. In recent years, Judaism has become trendy. Poles who once would have cursed you for intimating they had a drop of Jewish blood now go to great lengths to claim Jewish ancestry. The busloads of American Jews who visit Auschwitz stop in Krakow, so a bustling business in Jewish kitsch has grown up in the Kazimierz. Tourists can dine at Jewish-style restaurants owned by non-Jewish Poles. They can attend Jewish cultural festivals, study Yiddish, and listen to Klezmer music played by non-Jewish musicians. They even can buy hand-carved wooden dolls in the shape of davening rabbis and pious old *balabustas.*

I told myself we in the United States had done much the same thing to Native Americans—tried to wipe them out, then turned them into objects of fascination. And yet, the kitschy Jew-dolls pissed me off. For one thing, I had seen exactly such a doll in Marian's bedroom back home. Bought on a previous trip, it had been carved by a craftsman with higher artistic standards than most of his fellow hucksters. Also, Marian knew a graduate student who was writing her dissertation on these figurines, which have a long history in Polish folk art (apparently, a big-nosed rabbi holding a sack of money might bring the owner his own good fortune).

And yet, here in a Jewish Quarter devoid of Jews, the sight of these dolls, combined with the memory of having seen one on Marian's shelf back home, made me feel like a doll myself, something to be fetishized and collected. How could Marian not have noticed the graffiti on Poland's walls? How could his father believe the Jews caused Poland's downfall? And the question I couldn't stop asking: If we had lived in this country three quarters of a century earlier, would Marian have saved me from the Nazis? Would I have saved him? Would I have risked my life to protect a Pole, even if he had been my lover? It wasn't as if I expected the Nazis to rise again. But I needed to know the person I loved wouldn't have blindly gone along with the crowd. Easy enough to earn the designation "Righteous Gentile" in Ann Arbor. I needed to be sure Marian would have been one of the very few Poles who disobeyed the Nazis to save the Jews.

I refused to eat at the fake Jewish restaurants, and I was afraid another bite of Polish food would kill me, so Marian treated me to an Italian bistro. We strolled back to our apartment. Exhausted from our long day, Marian conked out. I tried to sleep, but the cramps I had been ignoring all week grew so excruciating I hurried to the bathroom, only to pass out on the floor. Near dawn, Marian came in and found me barely able to breathe. He ran to the street to call an ambulance, then came running back and led me from our apartment down the narrow alley past three locked gates to wait. Crippled by pain and convulsed by the most intense nausea I ever experienced, I slumped to the cobblestones and lay curled on my side until the ambulance came.

Deducing I was an American, the driver promised he

would take me to "best hospital in Krakow." I was grateful for this consideration, but I couldn't help but be dismayed when the facilities turned out to be as primitive as something in *Doctor Zhivago*. The emergency room was so crowded that even though I was screaming in pain, the admissions clerk told Marian I would need to wait. "Scream louder," Marian whispered, and finally, the orderlies rolled me into a vast room filled with cots occupied by heavyset older men, many with their privates hanging out. The doctors spoke little English. If not for Marian, I wouldn't have been able to make myself understood. I begged for drugs, but I was informed no medications could be administered until the cause of my pain had been determined. A nurse wheeled me through a maze of primeval corridors to a cavernous exam room, where an alarmingly somber gynecologist jammed her ultrasound probe up my vagina and studied the images it produced on a computer that resembled my ancient Apple IIe. A boy who looked young enough to be in elementary school translated her instructions.

"Has anyone ever say you have very advance cancer of uterus?" the boy inquired. When he saw my expression, he added cheerfully: "Not to worry! Very, very serious cancer, but we surgery you tomorrow, and you maybe live many month!" I tried to convince the gynecologist she was seeing a benign fibroid my doctor in Ann Arbor had been ignoring for years, but she pooh-poohed my diagnosis. "She know is difficult to believe," her sidekick said, "but very sad is true."

When I promised I would have my uterus examined the moment I got back to the United States, the surgeon said she couldn't allow me to leave the hospital. She would "surgery me tomorrow," she repeated. Then she pointed me in the direction of the ER and instructed me to walk back to wait.

Bent ninety degrees and shivering, I wandered the desolate corridors until I found my way to the waiting room, where I begged Marian to swear he wouldn't allow the doctors to operate on me for cancer.

"Cancer?" he said. "You have cancer?"

"No, no," I said, "I *don't* have cancer. They only *think* I have cancer. Swear to me you won't let them operate!" I could see he wasn't sure. How many of us would believe a layperson, even a layperson we love, rather than believe the doctors? Only when I had extracted his promise that he would, under no circumstances, allow the doctors to "surgery me" for cancer did I head back to the hellish ER.

Hours later, Marian convinced the doctors to move me to a ward for patients with gastrointestinal disorders rather than the ward for patients dying of uterine cancer. My room housed five other women, each of us assigned to a metal cot against a wall. Whoever had occupied my cot before me had tacked above it two images of the Black Madonna, an icon that graced the nearby monastery at Czestochowa. An object of veneration for Poles, the six-hundred-year-old painting reportedly had saved the country from invading Swedes. Another legend had it that she rescued the church from a catastrophic fire, which is how she and Jesus ended up with black skin. Marian asked if I wanted him to take down the cards. But with my five Catholic roommates watching, I told him no. I didn't really think my roommates would turn me over to the Gestapo. But I decided not to tempt fate by removing the images of a woman everyone believed to be the mother of God and the most powerful healer in the universe. Besides, she and her son were the only two Jews in the room but me.

At last, the nurses hooked me to a morphine drip. The drugs allowed me to sleep. But in the middle of the night, the laxatives in my IV started to work. The nurse on call unhooked me from my tubes, but she indicated it was up to me to make my way to the bathroom. Barefoot, half blind without my glasses, I wobbled down the infinitely long corridor, only to reach a communal bathroom so filthy I could barely withstand the stench. Despite my lack of slippers, I made my way across a floor puddled with urine and feces and sank to the toilet, where I remained for hours, convulsed with diarrhea. When I discovered the bathroom had no toilet paper, I sat weeping until dawn, when a kindly older woman came in and took pity on me by sharing hers. As I later found out, the hospital couldn't afford luxuries such as toilet paper, soap, or paper towels. Patients were expected to bring their own.

You can imagine how overjoyed I was to see Marian, who ran out to purchase my supplies. He helped me to wash my face and brush my teeth. Then, as I lay recovering from this ordeal, he chatted to my roommates in Polish, explaining who I was and how I had come to be in such a sorry state. Goodness! they said. Wasn't I lucky to have been admitted to one of Poland's finest hospitals! They had made their appointments months in advance and were looking forward to a vacation from all the cooking and cleaning for which they normally were responsible. Several of the women patted their heads and motioned in my direction, and Marian said they envied my curly hair.

"You mean my Jew hair?" I whispered.

Yes, well, he said, these women had never seen a Jew. But they wished they could get their boringly straight Polish hair to look like mine.

The weather grew unseasonably hot, and the nurses opened the windows. Not only did the flies buzz in, but anyone could have climbed in from the street. Without curtains, the cots were exposed to view; when a doctor conducted an exam, the rest of us could hear and see whatever there was to hear and see. After visiting hours, when everyone's boyfriends, husbands, sisters, mothers, and children left, my roommates passed the time comparing maladies in Polish, watching Polish soap operas, and reading Polish magazines. The reservation on our apartment had run out, and Marian needed to hurry around Krakow to find another place to stay; reluctant to ask him to run more errands, I made do with the glossy English-language edition of a fan magazine about Michael Jackson one of the women had found for me to read.

After three or four days, I managed to choke down a few bites of bread and drink a few sips of water. The doctors interpreted this as a sign I was strong enough for the surgery to remove my uterus, while I tried to use my newfound ability to eat and drink as evidence I was healthy enough to check out of Hospital Dostoevsky. After heated negotiations, Marian persuaded the doctors I could leave, but only if I agreed to undergo an endoscopy. Sadly, the hospital could afford to provide the services of an anesthesiologist only on Thursdays, and today was Monday.

I have a terrible gag reflex. The thought of a doctor jamming a length of metal tubing down my throat all the way to my intestines made me shake. But I was even more frightened of staying in a hospital where toilet paper and soap were luxuries and everyone seemed determined to "surgery me" for a cancer I didn't have. I don't mean to imply the Polish doctors and nurses were sadistic or incompetent. I was getting far better care than most Poles. And I had suffered equally appalling misdiagnoses at the hands of American doctors. Yet lying helpless in a city that once had been home to sixty thousand Jews, of whom only two thousand survived the war, I couldn't help but grow more paranoid.

Marian supported me through the corridors to the wing where I would undergo my endoscopy. We took our place at the end of a very long line of patients, many of whom were elderly, frail, or both. At last, it was my turn to enter the tiny room where the doctor and his assistant waited. I tried to relax, but as they lowered me to the table and inserted the thick metal snake in my mouth and began unwinding it down my throat, I panicked. The doctor and his assistant pinned me down and kept jamming in the tube. I flailed my arms, attempting to throw them off, but Marian joined in and held me.

That's when I lost all self-control. He was no better than the rest! If his fellow countrymen wanted to torture me, he would take their side and hold me down! I struggled harder. Finally, Marian saw the terror in my eyes and ordered the doctor to remove the tube. Then he lifted me in his arms and carried me from the room. It was his fault I had come to Poland. But it wasn't his fault that I had gotten sick or that the best hospital in Krakow was so poorly equipped. For a while, he had taken his countrymen's orders. But in the end, he had fought for me and saved me.

As we passed the line of feeble old people waiting their turn, I could see how frightened they were. If the healthy young American needed to be carried from the room in the arms of her strong Polish-American partner, how would they, so much older and frailer, be able to endure whatever was in store for them?

I doubt the endoscope descended low enough to allow the doctors to make out anything in my intestines. But they told me I could check out—so long as I paid my bill. By American standards, the amount I owed was laughably small. (If I had been a Pole, I wouldn't have owed anything.) And my insurance back home would reimburse me. (A week later, my gastroenterologist confirmed I had been suffering from an intestinal blockage, while my gynecologist looked at the grainy ultrasound and said there could have been an old shoe in my uterus and the doctors wouldn't have been able to determine what it was.) But the hospital demanded we pay in cash, and so, on a sweltering afternoon, Marian ran from one ATM to the next to extract enough zlotys to pay my ransom.

At last, the time came to pack my few belongings. I surprised myself by taking down one of the cards of the Black Madonna. When Marian asked why, I couldn't say. I didn't want a reminder of my ordeal. But the Madonna had endured ordeals of her own, and seeing her above my bed had brought me comfort. In the old days, I might even have credited her for my miraculous cure from what the doctors assured me was a fatal case of uterine cancer. But mostly I took the card because it would offer me a false identity in a world in which it is still sometimes dangerous to be a Jew.

Marian carried my bag and held my arm as we preceded step by tiny shuffling step down a long street to a corner where we could find a taxi. He helped me up the stairs to our new apartment, then sat beside my bed while I took a nap. When I awoke, I was ravenous. The doctors had warned that trying to consume anything fatty or spicy or fried would land me right back in the hospital. Eat boiled chicken, they advised, along with the broth in which the chicken had been boiled. I laughed. Chicken soup! Exactly what my much-loved and long-deceased grandmother would have prescribed. But where in Krakow might we find boiled chicken? As we hobbled past the cafés lining the main square, we saw nothing but couples dining on French, Italian, Indian, and Chinese food. At the more traditional Polish restaurants, the menus listed the usual sausages, fried cabbage, potato pancakes, and pierogis.

In an alley off the main square, I stopped, so exhausted I needed to slump against the wall. I was about to tell Marian that he should go on without me when he noticed a plaque on the wall. There, in the basement of the building against which I leaned, a division of the Polish underground called the Zegota had schemed to provide Polish Jews with false documents and hiding places. Because of the Zegota, some four thousand Polish Jews had survived the war.

"Look," Marian said. "There's a restaurant around the back. This building used to be good to the Jews. Do you want to go in and try it?"

The shabby café looked as if it hadn't changed since the 1930s. The waitresses were cleaning up from the evening meal. But Marian said a few words in Polish, and the hostess nodded and held up one finger. They did indeed have boiled chicken on the menu. But there was only a single serving left. Did we want the cook to save it?

"Tak!" Marian told her. Yes! Thank you! *"Dziekuje!"*

The waitress ushered us to a seat, then brought out a cup of chicken soup so comforting it brought tears to my eyes. When the soup was gone, she returned with a domed silver plate such as the ones we used to use in the dining room at my family's hotel. When I lifted the lid, I saw exactly what I would have seen when I ate there as a child—the same breast of boiled chicken, the same boiled potato, the same waxy white beans. It was the blandest, whitest, most delicious meal I'd ever eaten.

"So," Marian said, "was I right? Is this building good for the Jews?"

"Yes," I said. "This building is good for the Jews." I took another bite. "And so are you."

THE YOUNG FRIENDS
PLEASURE AND BENEFIT SOCIETY

I HAD NEVER VISITED the cemetery where my mother's parents lie buried. My grandfather died before I was born. My grandmother helped to raise me; I loved her dearly, but she died while I was living abroad, and I didn't attend her funeral. All I knew was that the cemetery was called Mount Zion, one of those never-ending seas of graves you glimpse to one side of the BQE or the LIE as you are hurrying to LaGuardia.

"Promise you will never go there," my mother said. She seemed to believe if I attempted to find it, I would end up lost, or dead, or both. But how could I live my life without once visiting my grandparents' graves? And how could I die without knowing I had said goodbye to my beloved Grandma Pauline? Every time I traveled to New York, I vowed I would find Mount Zion. And every time, I chickened out.

Then my mother turned eighty-six, and her Parkinson's got so bad she wouldn't last much longer. Despite her fear for my safety, I was fairly sure she would want to know her parents' graves were still well tended. When I googled "Mount Zion," I discovered all I needed to do was take two subways and a bus. Oddly, the directions came with a review, as if the cemetery were a restaurant or Broadway show. "Waste of fuckin' space" was the considered judgment.

From the website, I also learned Mount Zion had been established nearly one hundred and twenty years ago to the day I was due to visit, in what was then a rural expanse of

Queens. Its seventy-eight acres provided space for two hundred and ten thousand dead Jews, including Lorenz Hart, the five-foot-tall closeted homosexual alcoholic who gave the world some of its most romantic love songs, and Nathaniel West, author of *Miss Lonelyhearts* and *Day of the Locust*, two of America's grimmest yet most moving novels. But most of the Jews buried at Mount Zion were working-class immigrants, their plots divided among burial societies whose membership was determined by which village in Europe the person's family came from or the labor union or political faction to which he or she belonged. For the most part, these were secular lefties who had little patience for their parents' traditional religious observance. People joined burial societies not so much because they wanted to know their bodies would be properly cleansed and shrouded, but so their survivors wouldn't be impoverished by a funeral. Being buried at Mount Zion might not assure eternal life, but as the president of one society put it, those who remained would "do everything in their power to prevent the name of a member from being erased from the memory of the living."

And so, two days before May Day, 2013, I took two subways to Queens Plaza, then stood in the rain to wait for the Q67 bus, which, I had been told, would take me to Mount Zion. As I rode, I watched neighborhoods of modest two-story buildings give way to a wasteland of factories, warehouses, distribution centers, and steel-and-concrete structures whose purpose I could not identify. In one lot, Coca Cola trucks stretched forever; in another, Hazmat vehicles. Living as I do in Michigan, I couldn't help but be amazed these factories and warehouses still were operational. When the bus let me off, I passed an auto-body shop redolent with the smell of paint, then another fenced-in lot protecting endless rows of NYPD vehicles. Overhead, a giant bloodstained

1-800-Cop-Shot billboard promised a reward to anyone providing information leading to the arrest and conviction of anyone who had shot a cop.

And there, beyond the gates of Mount Zion, thousands of dowdy tombstones rose on gloomy knolls, dwarfed by the ominous waste-disposal facility sprawling across the hill above them. Staring up at those smokestacks, I couldn't help but think the Jews buried in these plots had the good sense to immigrate to America rather than remain in Europe to be incinerated in Nazi ovens. I also was reminded of the reviewer who condemned these acres as wasted space; the furnaces seemed to be biding their time until someone hatched a plan to dispose of all these idle dead to make way for some more lucrative enterprise.

In the main office, a nice, middle-aged woman in a brassy beehive provided me with a map. "See?" she said. "Your grandparents are buried in the plot for the Young Friends Pleasure and Benefit Society." Really? I said, marveling at the name. She also revealed the cemetery held a monument to the victims of the Triangle Shirtwaist fire, fifteen or twenty of whom lay within its walls. The monument was located just up the road from the Young Friends Pleasure and Benefit Society, in the section for the much more popular Workmen's Circle.

I set out in the rain. Not a single blossoming tree or flower brightened my way. The only relief was provided by the photographs of the dead burned into the porcelain on some of the stones, startling me with this evidence of what impressive hats the women wore after they gave up their *sheitels*, how amazingly assimilated these immigrants had grown in such a short time, how many of them died so young.

Then, there it was, Path 31, and off to the right, the arch spanning the entrance to the YOUNG FRIENDS PLEASURE

& BEN. SOC. Searching for my grandparents' stones was like making my way through a crowded party, trying to find two people I used to know well but wasn't sure I would recognize. Finally, I found them: Joshua Davidson, who died on November 29, 1946, age 64 years, and Pauline (Pesha) Davidson, Beloved Wife, Devoted Mother, Grandmother, Great-Grandmother, who died May 12, 1979, at 91. Standing before their graves, I experienced the satisfaction that rewards anyone who finds the treasure she sets out to find. I felt I had glimpsed my grandparents in their native surroundings—not the cemetery, but a room filled with the tired but happy members of the Young Friends Pleasure and Benefit Society.

My grandmother wasn't a beauty, but I had seen a photograph of her as a young woman, posed in one of those enormous hats, and she gave off the same aura of self-effacing warmth and generosity I recalled from when I knew her. In her earliest years, she had worked in a sweatshop, sewing buttons on ladies' coats, and even though my grandfather was a widower with two young sons, he must have seemed a catch—he had gotten a degree from Cooper Union (which, from the time of its inception until a few days before my visit to Mount Zion, charged its students no tuition) and found a job as a patent agent. Although my grandmother was a conventionally religious Jew, my grandfather was a freethinking Mason (a Jewish Mason!) and a card-carrying member of the Socialist Labor Party. My grandmother would light the candles on Friday nights, and when my grandfather got home from work, he would lick his fingers and pinch them out.

Working in a patent office, he enjoyed regaling my mother with predictions of the rocket ships that would change *Buck Rogers* from fantasy to reality, and the magic box that would bring into your living room not only the actors' voices but their images. And yet, he could not predict his early death from the clogged arteries that run in our family; when he died, my grandmother was forced to go back to work, selling women's hats at Macy's, and my mother resigned herself to continuing her secretarial career, at least until she married.

I inherited my grandfather's scientific mind; I don't believe a skeleton can hear what a living person says. And yet, I stood there in the rain, telling my grandmother how much I missed her, how sorry I was I hadn't understood why, when dementia clouded her mind, she began to ask the same questions over and over, how I wish I hadn't lost my temper. I told her that her youngest child, my mother, had had a good life, but now she was dying. I thought of the way my grandmother, who hated to startle my mother awake for school, would slip my mother's socks on her feet to wake her. I thought of my mother's feet now, and how I sat beside her in the nursing home massaging her gnarled toes. I told my grandmother I would be sure to slip my mother's socks gently on her feet before we buried her.

And then I told my grandfather that, like him, his great-grandson was a socialist. "He's like a twenty-first century Joe Hill," I said, picketing what needed to be picketed, occupying what needed to be occupied. In July, when Ann Arbor fills with tourists eager to buy what passes for art at Art Fair, my son sits for hours beneath a banner that reads ASK ME ABOUT SOCIALISM. "Everyone thinks he's nuts," I said. And yet, if not for all the crazy socialists and labor radicals buried in New York, who knew but that millions of Americans would still be stitching away their lives in filthy, crowded, windowless sweatshops. When I teach courses on Jewish-American literature, I remind my students most Jews who immigrated to America were lefties. You would think the students would take this fact for granted. But many of them seem surprised, if only because so many older Jews strike them as so conservative.

I stood there in the rain and cried. Then I took out a pair of scissors and tended the graves. My grandparents' cozy plot—barely the width of a double bed—was mounded with a neat coverlet of ivy. A few wild onions sprouted around the edges. Scallions had been among my grandmother's favorite foods, so I allowed those weeds to flourish. But an ugly, spiked vine was invading the plot, so sticky and stubborn, I almost felt as if it were trying to pull me under.

I couldn't find any pebbles to leave on my grandparents' graves, so I used fragments of an older stone. I don't know why the gesture mattered. Who would ever come here to notice? Then again, who would visit my grave? I was fifty-six and single. I had only one child. If Noah didn't think it important to return to whatever cemetery might hold my remains, who would? Maybe the message I was sending was not to my grandparents, but to my son.

Finally, I said goodbye and went in search of the Workmen's Circle plot. The rain was really coming down now, and I hurried past a large, water-stained monument with a single name, GREIF, as if the inhabitants of this city were so beaten down by sorrow they couldn't even label their pain correctly.

I had known for years about the Triangle Shirtwaist Factory, which had occupied the eighth, ninth, and tenth floors of a building in what is now Greenwich Village. On March 25, 1911, just before quitting time, a fire broke out in a bin of fabric. Most of the exits were locked. The one rickety fire escape collapsed under the weight of the twenty girls who tried to climb down it. The one hundred and forty-six victims, most of them Jewish and Italian seamstresses between sixteen and twenty-three, either died in the blaze or jumped screaming to their deaths.

What I hadn't known was that the tragedy sparked three

days of protests, after which the Workmen's Circle, a Jewish fraternal organization, erected a monument to the fifteen or twenty women who were buried at Mount Zion. The longest living survivor, Rose Rosenfeld Freedman, was later buried here, too. She had been hired at sixteen to fill a position vacated by a worker suspected of union organizing. A few years later, when the fire started, Rose was working on the ninth floor. Unable to escape by running down the fiery stairs, unwilling to follow the girls who were jumping to their deaths, Rose made her way to the tenth floor "to see what the executives were doing." But the executives already had fled. Pulling her long skirts above her face, Rose ran up a smoky stairwell to the roof, where a fireman carried her to safety. Although she had once enjoyed the independence of earning her own wages, the fire convinced her to go to college. She found a job with the Cunard cruise line, then married and raised a family. She lived to be one hundred and seven and spent most of that very long life fighting for workers' rights.

"Hundred forty-six people in a half an hour," she once said. "I have always tears in my eyes when I think. It should never have happened. The executives with a couple of steps could have opened the door. But they thought they were better than the working people. It's not fair because material, money is more important here than everything. That's the biggest mistake—that a person doesn't count much when he hasn't got money. What good is a rich man and he hasn't got a heart? I don't pretend. I feel it. Still."

Searching for Rose Rosenfeld Freeman's grave, I couldn't help but think of the news I had woken to that morning. In Bangladesh, rescue parties were shifting through the wreckage of the eight-story building that had collapsed on the three thousand garment workers who had been laboring inside. Already, the dead numbered more than four hundred; eventually, the toll would rise above one thousand. As Bangladeshis rioted to protest the abysmal conditions in their country's factories, rescuers worked frantically to save a woman named Shaheena, who was trapped in the building's bowels. Just as the rescuers were about to free the Bangladeshi version of Rose Rosenfeld, the electric saw they were using threw off a spark that set fire to the rolls and scraps of fabric that surrounded her. After she died, the rescuers gave up hope of finding anyone else alive (they eventually did pull one more miracle-survivor from the wreckage, but that morning, the news was as grim and hopeless as the weather).

The woman in the main office at Mount Zion had said that when I went looking for the Workmen's Circle plot, I should keep my eyes open for two statues whose arms were raised to form an arch. What she hadn't said was the statues had been vandalized. The young male worker stood to one side of the gate, a hammer in his right arm, his left arm amputated at the elbow. The young female worker held a torch in her left arm; her right arm, raised to meet her brother's, had been snapped off at the wrist. The distance between the stumps was greater than two arms' lengths, so the workers must have been holding something between their hands. A banner? Some object that marked the triumph of the workers of the world, who finally managed to unite?

Beside the statue of the man stood a small granite slab inscribed with the following tribute: "We remember the victims of this tragic event and strive to achieve safe working conditions and dignity for all in a *shenere un a besere velt*—a better and more beautiful world." I admired that the workers who had erected this slab hadn't confined their sympathy to their fellow Jews, or even their fellow New Yorkers, but expressed their desire to create a better, more beautiful world for everyone. I doubted they would be pleased to learn that their fight for better wages and safer conditions had led to their jobs getting shipped overseas so laborers in Bangladesh could suffer much the same danger and hardship that our grandparents had found to be intolerable.

By the time I left, the factories were letting out. The Q67 bus filled with dark-skinned workers, some of them quiet with fatigue, others carrying on in languages I could not identify. Then everyone got off, except for a kind Hispanic man who seemed very concerned that I find the subway back to Manhattan, where I obviously belonged.

Two days later, in a nursing home outside Philadelphia, I told my mother about my trip, rightly predicting that once the adventure was in the past, she would be comforted to know her parents' graves were receiving the perpetual care for which she paid. I asked if she remembered Joshua and Pauline receiving any pleasure from the Young Friends society or only the benefit of a decent burial, and she said they used to get dressed up and go out to society events all the time. I showed her the photos I had snapped on my cell phone, and my mother, who rarely bestows compliments on anyone, remarked that her father would have been proud to know my son, a remark that lessened the sting of the derogatory jibes he has suffered sitting beneath his ASK ME ABOUT SOCIALISM banner.

After the visit, as my brother and sister and I sat around discussing the inevitable arrangements we would need to make to have our mother buried beside our father, my brother said he already had told his kids to just burn him up and put his ashes in a box. I suppose I understand his sentiments. But I can't help thinking burials are worth the expense, and cemeteries aren't wastes of space. Even with real estate so expensive, there are reasons to dedicate acres to the dead. How else to be reminded who our ancestors were, if only one or two generations earlier? Where else can we erect perpetual monuments to our GREIF? And where else but a cemetery can we be inspired to rededicate ourselves to experiencing the few pleasures our lives afford, even as we work to bring about a benefit for our survivors, a *shenere un a besere velt* for all?

ALL OF US, WE ALL ARE ARAMEANS

I MUST HAVE BEEN the oldest Jew in America who never had been to Israel. During the Six Day War, when I was eleven, I was determined to defend my people's homeland. I doubted I would be able to take aim at an enemy who reminded me of my beloved Danny Thomas, the only Arab I knew and the star of my favorite television show, *Make Room for Daddy*. But I could pick oranges at an Israeli kibbutz and thereby free a sabra to fight off the invaders. At the least, I could sit at the piano in my parents' living room and pump out a rendition of "Exodus" so heartfelt that even the pious, sad-eyed rabbi I had painted in art class looked ready to cry.

But after I got out of college, I never seemed to find the time or the money to go to Israel. When my son was born, I decided we should celebrate his bar mitzvah in Jerusalem or on Mount Masada. But by the time he turned thirteen, Noah had shifted his allegiance to that famous branch of Judaism known as Marxism, and he refused to accompany me to Israel unless we spent an equal amount of time touring the West Bank and Gaza. I might have traveled to Israel on my own, but I couldn't figure out why I should visit a place where I couldn't ride a bus or sit in a café without fear of getting blown up, even as I despaired of my hosts' mistreatment of their Arab neighbors and fellow citizens.

Then, as a Christmas gift, my Polish Catholic boyfriend bought me a ticket. Marian had been to Israel and loved it, and he couldn't understand why I had never gone. What kind of Jew didn't want to go to Israel?

I tried to explain I felt the way an adopted child must feel about the prospect of meeting the woman who had given birth to her. Either I would learn my biological mother was a terrible person, in which case, what did that say about me? Or I would discover I loved her even more than I loved the mother who had raised me, in which case I would need to disrupt my life to join the mother I barely knew.

But Marian was determined to show me Israel. He spent six months planning our itinerary. Then, two weeks before we were supposed to leave, our relationship fell apart. I will spare you the intimate details—I still love the man and wouldn't want to embarrass him or bring him pain. As much as we loved each other, even a couples therapist couldn't help us overcome our incompatibilities, one of which had to do with his insistence that I share his pleasure in sampling cultures not my own—Black Evangelicals in Ypsilanti, Michigan; Navajos on their reservation in Arizona; white Pentecostal missionaries in Indiana; and yes, Polish Catholics in east Detroit and Warsaw. Marian's boldness in taking me places most middle-class white Americans rarely go was one of the attractions of our relationship. I shared his curiosity about other cultures, the longing for connection across boundaries most of us are too lazy or afraid to cross. And yet, I had grown weary of pretending to fit in with people who might come out with a disparaging remark about Black people, Jews, or homosexuals, or who believed a divine being had created the universe and planted dinosaurs in the rocks to test our faith. After struggling for half a century to find my place among people for whom literature, art, justice, and compassion trumped any narrow devotion to religion or nationality, I had become loath to give up that comfort. Worse, I didn't want to tour Israel with a non-Jew who idealized my people in ways I couldn't or wouldn't.

And so, when Marian and I broke up, my first thought was: Thank God I won't need to go to Israel! Then we had a fight about whose fault it was that he had spent three thousand dollars to buy two airline tickets we weren't going to use. I settled the argument by writing him a check and, having just bought a ticket to Israel I could barely afford, decided I might as well go alone.

Unfortunately, paying for the ticket left me with virtually no money to spend once I got there. I might have asked my friends on Facebook if anyone knew a cheap place I could crash. But if I posted my destination, at least a few of those friends, or those friends' friends, would express outrage at Israeli politics. Not that I didn't often share such outrage. But if I were traveling to China, would any of them make a peep about the government's oppression of Tibet? If I were traveling to Sri Lanka, would anyone but my one Sri Lankan friend urge me to register a complaint against the Sinhalese-dominated government's mistreatment of the Tamil minority?

I lived in a town where I couldn't shop at the Food Co-op without getting hectored to boycott Israeli products. I couldn't attend services at the Conservative synagogue without crossing a picket line whose protestors (more than a few of them Jews) demanded I denounce Israel before I went inside to pray. I couldn't show up at a rally for any cause without seeing a colleague holding up a sign that asked what Israel has done for peace, a sentiment I might not object to if I ever saw a sign that asked what North Korea, Russia, Syria, or Somalia has done for peace. Many of my undergraduates had no idea that most Jews who live in Israel are descended from refugees who fled the killing grounds of Europe rather than, say, Long Island, or that there would have been two states right from the beginning if the armies of Egypt, Syria, Lebanon, and Iraq hadn't launched an attack to wipe Israel off the map the day after its independence, or that Israel did not start the wars in which it ended up acquiring the West Bank or Gaza. But the idea of arguing any of this on Facebook made me ill.

I wasn't so crazy about revealing my plans to my friends who love Israel either. "This will so change your life!" they gushed. "You have no idea what it's like to walk around in a country where everyone is a Jew." To which I wanted to respond that I had grown up in the Catskills, where nearly everyone was a Jew, and I couldn't wait to leave.

Finally, a friend of a friend of a friend agreed to rent me a room in the trendy Jerusalem neighborhood known as the German Colony. I boarded a plane in Detroit expecting it to be packed with Hasids. But I was flying on a Friday night, so nearly all of my fellow passengers were fundamentalist American Christians, most of whom fell asleep, leaving me with an empty seat where my partner of the past ten years ought to have been sitting, a bad case of food poisoning from an airport taco, and my usual airplane-induced insomnia.

To pass the long hours when I wasn't throwing up, I tapped the screen in front of me to select a movie. *Ben-Hur*! What a perfect way to kill some time. I had always been embarrassed not to have seen this classic, which wasn't exactly required viewing in my parents' Orthodox Jewish house. And I figured Hollywood could provide me with a relatively quick and beautifully costumed introduction to the history of the region to which I was now winging my way at four hundred miles an hour.

At first, I found pride rising in my chest that a Jewish prince could be as ruggedly handsome as Judah Ben-Hur.

Even when I remembered Charlton Heston wasn't really a Jew, I couldn't help but be impressed by his determination to survive three tortuous years as a slave on a Roman galley so he could rescue his mother and sister from their nightmarish Roman jail and exact revenge on the consul who destroyed their family. *Ben-Hur* was the most riveting drama I'd ever seen—for all the advancements in special effects, Hollywood has never topped the chariot race. But the movie also brought the unexpected benefit of helping me to understand Christianity. How appealing it must have been to be a poor, downtrodden Jew listening to a handsome young rabbi assure you it was better to love than hate, better to forgive than seek revenge, better to be a Jew than a Roman—even though the Romans had all the power.

Not until the final scene, in which the rain that falls on a bleeding Jesus also falls on Ben-Hur's mother and sister, washing them clean of leprosy, did I think twice about converting. That's where any religion loses me, when I am expected to believe that blood or suffering can wash anyone clean of anything. Besides, within no time at all, didn't those blood-drenched, long-suffering Christianized Jews become the Romans?

Americans who travel to Israel, especially Americans as old as I am, usually do so on a tour. When my sister and her family took my parents, they booked as their guide a native of our hometown (I tell myself the man's suicide a few months later had nothing to do with carting my mother around Israel in his van for two weeks). My nephew had visited on a free tour sponsored by Birthright, whose buses you see traversing the country in carefully controlled attempts to instill a love of Eretz Yisrael in young American Jews who are less interested in experiencing a political or spiritual conversion than they are in getting laid. I wondered if I was crazy to be stumbling around such a dangerous part of the world with no one to protect me. But to do so seemed less insular than touring the country in the sort of protective bubble that allows you to return home believing exactly what you believed before you left.

If I was going to see Israel, I wanted to see as much of it as I could, and I wanted to see it on my own terms. I had only ten days—eight, if you subtracted the time required to travel there and back—and the budget of a backpacking teenager. But I wanted to figure out what I thought and felt about this so-called homeland of mine. If I wasn't one of those Jews who defend Israel no matter what, and I wasn't one of those anti-Semites who attack Israel no matter what, then what did I think and feel about Israel, and what was I going to do about whatever I thought and felt?

Exhausted by the long flight, I took a shared van—a sherut—from the airport in Tel Aviv to the neighborhood in Jerusalem where I would be renting my room. I schlepped my bags up three flights of stairs, the last two in the dark because Shabbat wasn't yet over and the automatic timer didn't give me enough time to reach the top. All I knew about the woman from whom I was renting a room was she was a reporter for one of Israel's English-language publications, so when the door was opened by a tanned, zaftig young woman in black Spandex shorts, a tank top, and a tattoo, I figured she must be my host.

Oh no, she said, she was only another visitor. She introduced me to her son, a heartbreakingly androgynous six-year-old with ringlets of long dark curly hair—he might have been King David as a child, strumming on his harp. Excited to have a visitor, the boy led me to the rooftop patio, where we stood surrounded by the pointy tops of slender firs davening in the breeze. Looking down, I saw the cemetery I assumed must hold the remains of the brave German-Jewish pioneers who had settled the neighborhood—why else would it have been called the German Colony? The sky turned indigo, and the woman in Spandex shorts counted one, two, three stars now visible over the Old City, which meant Shabbat was over. My feet lifted from the roof, as if I were one of those gauzy brides in a lithograph by Chagall. Declaring the Sabbath over by counting three stars over Jerusalem felt like figuring out which direction was north by gazing out your igloo door at the candy-striped North Pole.

Then my host—let's call her Rivkeh—came in. Having rested on the Sabbath, she needed to stay up all night to write her story. All I had the chance to find out was that she had grown up in New England and attended college in Massachusetts. I wanted to ask what she thought about the government allowing so many settlements in the Occupied Territories, but something told me that I couldn't assume, as I might in the United States, that a journalist would share my lefty politics.

I soon realized I couldn't predict much of anything about anyone I met in Israel. The woman in Spandex shorts turned out to be a rabbi. The cemetery harbored the remains of the messianic German Christians who had settled the neighborhood and lived there for half a century before they got booted by the British on the eve of World War II for throwing in with the Nazis.

The first thing I did when Shabbat was over was figure out a way to get to Masada, the desert fortress where nine hundred and sixty Jews committed suicide in AD 73 rather than surrender to the Romans. The obvious choice would have been to take one of the luxurious state-run buses. Most visitors to Israel combine their excursion to Masada with a visit to Qumran, where the Dead Sea Scrolls were discovered, and Ein Gedi, a stunning oasis on the Dead Sea. But I knew if I saw Masada with a bunch of American Jews piously intoning "Never again!" I would grab the microphone from the guide and make certain everyone knew that the martyrs who died at Masada were fanatics prone to assassinating any moderate Jews reluctant to risk extermination by attempting to over-throw their Roman rulers. These fanatics, the Sicarii, jabbed a dagger into the heart of anyone who so much as suggested negotiating with the Romans. They set fire to the food supply so their fellow Jerusalemites would be forced to fight rather than wait out a siege. The Sicarii didn't flee Jerusalem to escape the Romans; they left because their fellow Jews kicked them out.

Not only that: Before the Romans surrounded them at Masada, the Sicarii sneaked down and wiped out seven hundred presumably Jewish inhabitants of Ein Gedi so they could steal their supplies. (Recently, a group of ultra-Ortho-dox extremists in Jerusalem renamed themselves the Sicarii and began harassing women and girls who wouldn't comply with their idea of modest female dress or who refused to sit at the back of public buses so the men in front wouldn't be forced to see them.) I knew I would hear none of this on an Israeli-sponsored tour. Besides, I had noticed a much cheaper excursion advertised in *Lonely Planet*, the catch being that I would need to stop by the company's office the next day to pick up my ticket.

And so, early the next morning, I put on the one long-sleeve, calf-length dress I had packed to avoid offending any of the Christians, Muslims, or Jews whose places of worship I might want to enter, and I set off up the hill to the Old City. Sweating furiously, I entered the Jaffa Gate, and within minutes was lost in a maze of alleys and stairways so baffling I was sure I would end up like one of those desperate, haunted pilgrims in a Paul Bowles story.

Finally, I stumbled on the headquarters of the company whose tour I had signed up to take—and immediately understood the price was low because it didn't include admission to any of the sites we would be visiting. I might have walked out, but I noticed the tour included Jericho. Jericho? Wasn't Jericho in the West Bank? The young woman answering the phones seemed to be speaking Arabic. A courtly old man appeared from a back room with a Dixie cup of lemonade, which he handed me with a bow. The woman told me to be waiting at seven the next morning outside the Jaffa Gate, where Sam the Driver would pick me up. I didn't mention I was Jewish. No one asked. I walked out clutching my ticket and wondering why I had signed up to visit the Jews' greatest symbol of resistance with a Palestinian as my guide. If Marian had booked us on such a tour, I would have raised holy hell. If my son had demanded we visit Jericho, I would have told him no. Even when a person thinks she is traveling alone, she is accompanied by so many invisible companions she might as well be traveling on a bus.

The tour wouldn't begin until the next day. In the meantime, I walked the Old City, getting my sense of its four quarters— Jewish, Arab, Christian, and Armenian. My heart lifted at the sight of the spectacular desert valleys that sloped away to the south, the towering high-rises to the west, the quaint, low-slung Arab neighborhoods to the east. Who could have guessed that Jerusalem would be the most beautiful city I ever visited? And really, what had prevented me from coming sooner?

Now that I had my bearings, I explored the Jewish Quarter. Years before, my ex-husband and I had entered a cave in southern Spain and stared in reverence at a twenty-five-thou-sand-year-old painting of a fish. After my divorce, Marian had taken me to see the cliff dwellings at Mesa Verde and the great stone pueblos at Chaco Canyon. Now, the ruins were the ruins of my own people's civilization, and I couldn't help but be even more deeply touched. In the charred basement of a priestly family's dwelling I saw the iron spear and the bone of a woman's severed arm that had been discovered beside the fireplace. Is that where I would have been, cooking at my hearth, when the Romans came thundering in? And Noah, would he have been out trying to talk universal brotherhood with the soldiers? Most likely, he would have been cut down in the streets or, like Judah Ben-Hur, carried off as a slave. Did that mean I should be willing to defend this city against anyone who, even today, might attempt to wrest it from us Jews? Or should I make it my life's work never to allow the soldiers of any country to burst into anyone's house, cut off the women's arms, and carry the children away as slaves?

All I know is after I left the Burnt House, I reconsidered my vow never to visit the Western Wall. One reason I hadn't wanted to come here with Marian was I knew he would insist I accompany him to watch the Hasidic men dancing in front of the one remaining section of the Second Temple. When Marian sees an Orthodox Jew, he thinks of the shtetl Tevyes his ancestors tormented for centuries before the Nazis wiped them out. When I see that same black-hatted, black-coated Hasid, I think of the narrow-minded fanatics who took over my hometown in the Catskills, literally turning their backs on Jews like me when we passed them on the street, or stoning our cars if we drove by their bungalow colonies on the Sabbath. If I went to the Western Wall, I would be enraged by the barrier between the men and women's "sides." I had experienced enough such segregation attending my parents' synagogue as a child. (When I was very young, the women had been forced to sit upstairs in the balcony. Later, in the newer, more modern building, an aisle down the center of the sanctuary kept the sexes apart.) I had never been bat mitzvahed; in an Orthodox shul, women and girls aren't allowed to read from the Torah. Why would I want to put up with such misogyny? I certainly had no intention of writing a prayer on a scrap of paper and stuffing it in a crack, as if the rabbi who cleared that day's slips might play Santa and fulfill my dreams.

And yet, I allowed myself to be patted down at security. I covered my head. I closed my eyes and laid my palms against those ancient limestone blocks, at which an electric jolt of images shot through my brain, carrying with it generation upon generation of poor, bedraggled Jews, female and male, who had struggled and survived so I could be standing there lamenting that we weren't treating our enemies with a kindness that never had been shown to us. I kissed the stones. I cried.

But why should a person be moved only by her own mistreated ancestors? The Old City is set up like a theme park, and after I had seen all there was to see in Jewland, I wandered over to experience the thrills and chills of Christianland. Entering the Church of the Holy Sepulchre and watching the pilgrims kneel and kiss the slab where Jesus had been taken down from the cross, I saw a woman press to the stone a bag of what appeared to be potpourri. I was tempted to shake my head and whisper, as my parents would have done: "Only the *goyim*."

And yet, if there really was a Jesus, if he really was crucified, then his poor, broken body must have been taken down and kissed and wept over by his mother. Maybe not at this exact spot. But given how tiny Jerusalem used to be—and how small it still is—could the actual slab have been more than a few yards to the left or right? Something must have happened, and the repercussions of that something still were being felt all these millennia later, passionately, by these pilgrims. If I left the church before I visited every site within its walls, it was only because, with the interior so stifling and so many pilgrims pressing in from every side, I figured the last thing anyone in Israel needed was for a Jew to pass out in Jesus' tomb.

Outside, shawl still tenting my head, I moved on to the Arab Market, where I maneuvered through a labyrinth of stalls whose contents included a colorful display of melons, pottery, tablecloths, pastries, grilled meats, spices, underwear, plastic toys, T-shirts, candlesticks, pickled vegetables, and glass beads. Unable to find the entrance through which non-Muslims are allowed to enter the Temple Mount, I consulted a map. As I was standing there, head bent, a handsome young man grabbed my hand and kissed it.

"I love you," he said. "Where you want to go? I take you." I tried to yank back my hand, but he pulled me through a dizzying array of alleys. "There. I take you where you want, now you give me big tip."

"Are you crazy?" I said. "Leave me alone!" I hurried away, stopping to catch my breath only when I was sure he was no longer following.

"Where you want to go?" a shopkeeper asked, taking my hand and kissing it. "I will help you get out if you buy my earrings. I love you, but I will love you even more if you buy my earrings."

*　　*　　*

An hour later, I discovered the entrance to the Temple Mount and passed the checkpoints necessary to gain access to one of Islam's holiest sites. I marveled at the exquisite turquoise, gold, and white tiles of the stunning mosque known as the Dome of the Rock. I admired the reverence with which a succession of Muslim families shepherded their wide-eyed children toward the entrance. I wished those families well. And yet, I couldn't help but think about the oceans of blood spilled on this very plaza. This was where Abraham had bound his son and nearly obeyed God's command that he slit the young man's throat. This was where the Romans had sacrificed their pigs to Jupiter. This was where my own ancestors had burned pigeons and goats as offerings to their god—to my god. This was where the first Jewish Temple, Solomon's temple, had been destroyed by the Babylonians. This was where the Second Temple had been rebuilt, then desecrated and reduced to rubble by the Roman legions. This was where Israelis and Palestinians had clashed during the Intifada. No non-Muslims were allowed to pray here now. But I offered a silent wish that each and every human being on the planet might, at that exact moment, stop believing in God. Or stop using God as an excuse to kill his fellow humans.

And yet, as I passed a sign forbidding Orthodox Jews from walking where I was walking because they might trod the stones beneath what once had been the Holiest of Jewish Holies, where only the High Priest could enter, I nearly dropped to my knees in awe. I don't believe any single site on this planet is holier than any other. And yet, there really had been a Temple. There really had been a High Priest. There really had been, before the Romans ransacked and destroyed it, a Holiest of Jewish Holies.

*   *   *

At dawn the next day, I was heading back up the hill to meet the van for our excursion to Masada when four mangy dogs leapt from the park and charged me. Their leader snarled and bared his teeth. Darting across the street, I barely avoided being run down by a sherut. Distracted, the dogs shot off across a rubble-filled lot and disappeared.

Later, an American friend exclaimed: "The wild dogs of Jerusalem! I assumed they were a myth!"

And I thought: No. In this city, nothing is a myth. In this city, the myths are so real that if you are not careful, they will chase you, snarling, and bite you on the ass.

At the Jaffa Gate, I noticed a tall blonde with the same ticket I was holding. This was Effy, although she pronounced her name as "Iffy." A German fashion photographer, she was visiting Israel because she had met some really, really cool Israeli guys in Germany, and she really, really liked them. I wanted to ask how it felt to be a German traveling in Israel, but I was afraid she would meet my question with a blank stare. I don't think she even realized our driver was a Palestinian.

At the Damascus Gate, we picked up two dark, Semitic-featured sisters, who, I was sure, would turn out to be fellow Jews but who revealed themselves to be penniless Christians from New Zealand. "We can't believe it!" one of the sisters said, pulling a Bible from her straw bag. "We are going to be walking the same paths that Jesus Christ, our Lord and Savior, walked!"

The van was a shabby, beat-up affair. The dusty polyester curtains made it hard to see out the windows. Effy's seat belt didn't work. But none of us said a word—my companions were too young to be worrying about dust or seat belts, and I didn't want our driver to peg me as a whiny American Jew. Maneuvering through the chaotic one-way streets, Sam seemed too distracted to offer the commentary a tourist expects. But even when we were clattering along the highway out of town, he remained silent. Then again, surrounded as we were by sand and rock, there didn't seem to be much upon which to comment. The only sign of life came when we passed a rough-looking encampment of huts and shacks. "Bedouin," Sam muttered darkly, as if these former nomads, oppressed less by government decree than by the cities and highways that had ended their wandering, were the only safe objects of conversation.

I expected the drive to take hours, but in minutes we reached Qumran. From the United States, it is easy to picture a vast land in which Muslims and Jews go about their business sequestered behind their respective walls, lobbing rockets at each other. In reality, the two groups live intimately intertwined in an area barely larger than New Jersey. At the turn-off to Qumran, Sam stopped to pick up two young women who opened the exhibits for us. Qumran is in the West Bank, but the site is administered by settlers at a nearby kibbutz. Was this a marriage of convenience—the women got a free lift, while Sam and his employer were assured the Israelis' goodwill—or had a friendship sprung up between them? For the first time, I missed Marian. Engaging in suppositions as to other people's ethnic or religious affiliations had drawn us together. Then again, if Marian had been in Israel, I wouldn't have been traveling with such odd bedfellows in such a *farkakteh* van.

The truth was, the longer I remained in Israel, the more baffled I grew. I had wanted to visit Qumran since I was a child, reading in my parents' *National Geographic* about a sect of super-observant Jews who, around the time of Christ, had written a bunch of scrolls and hidden them in clay jars, which, thousands of years later, a Bedouin shepherd found. I imagined myself arrayed in pure white linen, walking up the stark cliffs to the caves where the sacred scrolls were stored, astounding my elders with the strictness of my observance. Lonely and inward, I heard God speaking to me often, assuring me that even though I was a speck on a speck, He Who Created Everything cared what I thought and felt. Awed by the improbable complexity of my own existence, ignorant of the science that would allow me to retain my awe but do away with its author, I believed the purpose of life was to bring about *tikkun olam*—that is, to repair and perfect the world.

Now, squinting to make out those same caves, I was reminded the Essenes were celibate men who wouldn't have allowed a woman to enter their commune even to do the cleaning. They were so fanatic about their purity—they saw themselves as the Sons of Light, preparing for an apocalyptic battle against the Sons of Darkness—they wouldn't defecate on the Sabbath. The plateau on which they lived rose from a landscape so forbidding I couldn't imagine crossing it for any reason. Who in his right mind would have valued such isolation? The purity that once made me long to join this sect now struck me as repulsive.

Effy and the New Zealanders snapped photos in front of a sign that read "Ritual Bath." When Sam asked if we wanted to stick around or head to Masada, I eyed the caves, which turned out to be accessible only to experienced climbers with the hardiness to resist parching heat, stinging scorpions, and venomous snakes. This might be my last chance to see them. Not only was I growing old, but if the West Bank became part of a Palestinian state, Qumran might be prohibited to Israelis and more difficult to reach for American Jews. I shrugged, then followed my less-conflicted companions to the van.

*   *   *

On the way to Masada, we stopped at an Israeli checkpoint. I froze, fearing the soldiers might hassle Sam or demand to know what a Jew was doing in a van driven by a Palestinian. Instead, they indicated two attractive but bedraggled young women who sat beside the road, slumped against their Goliath-sized backpacks. Trying to hitchhike in such brutal heat seemed suicidal—if no one picked you up, you would sizzle and combust in the noonday sun. Sam nodded. Either he genuinely didn't mind being of assistance, or the soldiers presented him with no real choice. The women hefted their packs into the back of the van with us and then squeezed in the front with Sam. At the turnoff to Masada, they hopped out with barely a nod to Sam and stood waiting for another lift.

By then it was noon, and Masada was deserted. Most tourists who visit the ruins do so at dawn, in part because it is a ritual to watch the sun rise above the Dead Sea, but mostly because the middle-aged and elderly American Jews who make up the majority of the paying customers would drop dead from the heat later in the day. The afternoon we visited, the snaking footpath from the visitor center at the bottom to the fortress on top was closed because the government did not want to be responsible for anyone, even tourists as young and healthy as the two sisters from New Zealand, keeling over on the grueling climb. The New Zealanders claimed not to have enough money to buy a ticket to ride the cable car, which meant they would need to spend the next two hours hanging around the museum. I considered paying their fares, but Jesus never visited Masada, so neither sister seemed to care.

That left Effy and me. I had been curious what our guide might say about this desert fortress to which young Israeli soldiers traditionally have been brought to take an oath that "Masada shall not fall again." But Sam handed us each a pamphlet and drove away. (For the record, the pamphlet did say Masada "symbolizes the determination of the Jewish people to be free in its own land.") I wasn't about to tour Masada with a German, especially a German who didn't have a clue why I might be uneasy touring Masada with a German. As soon as the cable car disgorged us at the top, I darted through the gate and lost her.

Unfortunately, I hurried away so fast I didn't notice the booth where I was supposed to pick up earphones. I had been afraid if I made it to Masada, I would need to listen to a bunch of American Jews clucking about how brave our ancestors were to commit mass suicide rather than be taken as slaves, while the theme song from *Exodus* wafted from loudspeakers in a rendition even schmaltzier than the one I used to bang out on my parents' piano. But the fortress was deserted; the only barrier to imagining myself as a member of that desperate band of Zealots came from the small signs informing me that this pile of stones had been the synagogue, or that pile the storehouse, or that pile the dovecote.

One sign explained I was standing on the exact spot where archaeologists unearthed eleven small shards, each bearing a Hebrew name, which the men at Masada used to determine who would be the last alive after the other ten had killed their families. I felt overwhelmed with pity. But I also wondered why so many American Jews wanted to hold their children's bar and bat mitzvahs at Masada. Would I have really wanted my son to perform the rituals that marked his entrance to Jewish manhood on the spot where so many Jewish mothers had comforted their Jewish children whose Jewish fathers were about to kill them? If I had been here at the time, would I have been comforting Noah as I prepared him to be slaughtered? Or would I have been one of the two women who, according to the historian Josephus, took their children and hid, preferring to throw themselves on the mercy of their captors rather than submit to their husbands' knives? As dangerous as it is to predict what one's earlier incarnation would have done under such extreme conditions, I feel safe in saying I would not have allowed myself to end up under those conditions in the first place.

I took the cable car down. Effy and the New Zealanders were waiting in the museum. No one said a word. Sam drove up, and we four women climbed in his van. What did I care about the mass suicide of a band of religious fanatics who had lived and died on this mountaintop two thousand years earlier? In what way could I identify with Jews who killed their own children rather than continue to live under another nation's rule? Then again, didn't someone need to stand up to Rome? Didn't I admire the Jewish partisans who assassinated their co-religionists for collaborating with the Nazis? The back of the van was stuffy, and as Effy and the New Zealanders nodded off, I wished I had taken my vacation in a country where I was so ignorant of what I saw that I could enjoy myself—and take a nap—like any normal tourist.

We passed the exit for Ein Gedi.

"Wait!" I cried. "I thought we were going to stop at the Dead Sea!"

"Dead Sea, yes," Sam grumbled. "Ein Gedi, no."

It dawned on me that Ein Gedi was in Israel proper, while the beach to which Sam was taking us was in the West Bank. As I later discovered, the beach at Kalya is administered by the same kibbutz that runs Qumran. Settled in 1929 by a Jewish engineer from Siberia, Kalya was built to house the workers at a plant that produced potash by solar evaporation from the briny lake (Kalya means "potassium" in Latin and is an acronym for the Hebrew phrase "the Dead Sea has returned to life"). Because the plant employed Arabs as well as Jews, the kibbutz was spared the anti-Jewish rioting of the 1930s. But when Jordan conquered the region, the kibbutz was destroyed, only to be rebuilt and resettled after the Six Day War. For years, Israel prohibited Palestinians from bathing anywhere along the west bank of the Dead Sea. Recently, though, the beach at Kalya had become one of the few places where Arabs and Jews could relax and take a swim in each other's company. Was I more virtuous to be bathing at a beach that allowed Palestinians to swim there, even though it was administered by a kibbutz illegally situated in the West Bank, or should I have stuck to a government-sponsored tour that avoided the West Bank altogether?

All I knew was I was caked with dust and sweat, and a dip in the Dead Sea was so tempting a prospect I would have bartered my birthright to achieve it. Effy and I paid the extra shekels to be admitted; Jesus had never taken a swim at Kalya Beach, but even the New Zealanders coughed up the admission fee. We changed into our bathing suits, then made a dash across the foot-scorching sand, only to slip on the slimy mud that lined the shore and tumble headlong into water so hot we might have been trying to cool off in a pool of lava.

Earlier that morning, knowing I would be swimming for the first time in weeks, I had remembered to shave my bikini region; now, my crotch stung so badly I yelped. As my companions covered themselves with the silky black glop that is reported to have healing properties, I looked around at the other bathers. Coated with mud, everyone, even uber-Aryan Effy, looked black. But as each bather emerged and stood beneath the showers, I was shocked to see how many of the swimmers remained black. Even more wonderful: When those same bathers went back to their chairs, the men put on their skullcaps. Black Jews! I was aware that lighter-skinned Israelis sometimes discriminated against their fellow citizens from Yemen and Ethiopia. But I nonetheless felt as comforted as if I had just taken a dip in a soup of briny, molten brotherhood.

As we prepared to depart for Jericho, I asked Sam if I could sit in the front of the van with him. The ride from Masada to Kalya Beach had made me carsick. And I couldn't help but hope some interfaith camaraderie might spring up between us. Sam was a secular-looking young man, neither friendly nor hostile, and in my naïve American way, I figured every time a Palestinian and a Jew made genuinely human contact, the decades of hostility between the two groups would be eroded. But he didn't say a word. And as we approached our next stop, I grew more nervous. As recently as a few years earlier, Israelis and Palestinians had been killing each other in Jericho. Now, the city was controlled by the Palestinian Authority, and most Israelis weren't allowed to go there. The woman at the tour company had reminded me to bring my passport. Nothing on that document identified me as a Jew, but anyone could have guessed.

At the checkpoint, the guard grilled Sam in Arabic. Then he stuck his head inside the van, nodded approvingly at Effy and the New Zealanders, glanced with indifference at middle-aged me, and waved us all through.

A sign proclaimed the road leading to the city had been reconstructed with USAID dollars. Surely I wouldn't be kidnapped by people who could see that my country wished them to have good roads. The sign also reminded me of my theory that if only Israel would respond to the Palestinians' demands for statehood—and yes, even to their terrorist attacks—by entering the West Bank and Gaza to build roads, schools, parks, hospitals, universities, swimming pools, and power plants, an equitable peace might be achieved. Of course, if I had mentioned that idea to most Israelis, or even most American Jews, I would have been greeted by derision. And yet, that's what I would have done if I were Netanyahu.

Not surprisingly, the deeper we drove into Arab-controlled territory, the more our driver relaxed. Jericho may be shabby, but it seemed to be a thriving metropolis compared to, say, Detroit, or the Pine Ridge reservation in South Dakota, or even my hometown in upstate New York. Of course, the Indians at Pine Ridge and the Black residents of Detroit don't need to pass checkpoints to leave their cities. But I couldn't figure out why the protestors in Ann Arbor cared so much more about the conditions here—or even Gaza—than they cared about the poverty and despair in cities much closer to home.

I stuttered out a question about whether "things" seemed better now in Jericho than they had been in the past, but Sam shrugged. Was he reluctant to start a debate, or stymied by his lack of English? Did he suspect I was a Jew? Or did he prefer to keep his mouth shut, earn his living, and stay out of politics?

"We stop here," Sam said. He parked beside a walled church and pressed a bell. We had no inkling of the significance of the glass-enclosed stump Sam showed us in the church's inner court, but I learned later it was all that remains of a two-thousand-year-old sycamore in which a rich but dwarfish tax collector named Zacchaeus once perched to get a better view of Jesus. I also learned that a second sycamore, sixty feet tall and thriving, stands near the city's main square, competing with the stump at the church for the honor of that same heritage. Why Sam went to all the trouble of getting someone to open the church rather than driving us past the sycamore in the square I'll never know; apparently, in Israel and the Occupied Territories, even the sycamores have their partisans.

After that, Sam chauffeured us to the foot of a mountain from which we stared up at the magnificent monastery that had been built over the cave where Jesus fasted for forty days before the Devil tried to tempt him into leaping from a cliff and relying on his father's angels to break his fall. Effy asked me to take her photo in front of a sign that read "To the Mount of Temptation." And then (how could I resist?), I asked her to take my picture in front of the same sign.

Later, we spent a blistering but enjoyable half hour traipsing the ruins of a palace built in the eighth century by an Umayyad caliph. In one room, off the swimming pool, we encountered a magnificent mosaic of two gazelles grazing peacefully to one side of a tree, while, on the other side, a third gazelle was being torn to bits by a raging lion—an apt metaphor for life in the Middle East.

At the time, I didn't know enough to ask Sam to take us to see Jericho's other famous mosaic, the one that shows a menorah, a shofar, and a lulav and bears the Hebrew inscription *Shalom al Yisrael*, "Peace Be Upon Israel." That mosaic decorates the floor of a sixth-century synagogue whose remnants were discovered in 1936 on land owned by an Arab family. The family built a house atop the ruins but, for a small fee, allowed visitors to see the mosaic in the basement. After the Six Day War, the Israelis took control of the site, but they permitted the Arab family to continue living in the house and administering the museum. Then Jews started coming there to pray in greater numbers, and the government confiscated the property. Later, the Israelis handed it over to the Palestinian Authority, which promised to protect the synagogue. When vandals desecrated the building, the Palestinians repaired the damage. At the time of my visit, the PA and the IDF were allowing Jews to pray at Shalom al Yisrael the first day of each month, an arrangement religious Jews consider to be a denial of access to a house of worship located in a city that has been central to Jewish history since the beginning of recorded time and most Palestinians no doubt see as an act of goodwill and cooperation. I like to think if I had asked, Sam would have taken us to see the mosaic at Shalom al Yisrael, or the synagogue at Wadi Qelt, which archaeologists believe to be the oldest synagogue ever found. Never having asked, I can continue to believe he would have.

Even without the synagogues, I couldn't help but think how prosperous the West Bank would have been if not for all the fighting. When Sam pulled into the lush oasis at the center of town, I was stunned to read a tiled sign above a fountain that proclaimed Jericho to be the oldest city of the world. Beyond the fountain rose a rocky mound that held the remains of nearly two dozen civilizations. The walls surrounding the excavation lie strewn in such a way that it is impossible not to start humming the song about Joshua blowing on his horn and causing the walls to come tumbling down, although the plaques make clear that a succession of earthquakes were responsible for the damage.

It was even hotter in Jericho than at Masada. I was the only member of our party who chose to tour the ruins, and who should be the only other visitor but a young man who attended the same university as my son and "kind of" knew him! How could I not laugh? Eight years earlier, Noah had refused to be bar mitzvahed in Israel unless we spent an equal amount of time visiting the Occupied Territories, and here I was touring the West Bank with a young man the same age as my son who attended the same university but wasn't him. Why hadn't I listened to my son's request that we visit Israel together, as long as we spent equal time exploring the West Bank? Instead of being in Jericho with this young man who wasn't him, I could have been here with Noah.

Of course, if Noah *had* been here, we would have been arguing politics. As frustrating as those arguments tended to be, I often felt I was arguing with myself. What else was Noah's Marxism but my own weak concern for the poor and oppressed taken to extremes? Maybe Noah was an atheist, but he was an atheist who devoted his life to bringing about the utopia that devout Jews refer to as the Age of the Messiah. As much as I love Jews and feel disappointed my son doesn't share that love, or rather, doesn't love Jews more than he loves other people, both he and I believe no single group has a monopoly on justice. Like Noah, I want the Palestinians to have the same rights and opportunities as anyone else. On what, then, do we disagree?

The young man who looked like my son joined me in exclaiming at the world's oldest wall. We marveled at the world's oldest set of stairs. Then I started to feel faint from the heat and went inside. Bypassing the souvenirs, I headed upstairs to the sweltering cafeteria, where the odors from the buffet made the air intoxicating and too close to breathe. A plate of heavy food was the last thing I wanted, but the spices wafting from the chafing dishes lured me to pile my plate with meats swimming in sauces I couldn't identify. A sign said the restaurant welcomed American dollars, so I handed a twenty to the pleasantly rotund and nattily mustachioed Palestinian behind the register. He murmured something and pressed a few quarters in my palm. My change ought to have come in bills—the meal, in American dollars, was ridiculously underpriced.

"Wait!" I said. "I gave you a twenty!"

Behind his mustache, the man's smile grew stiff. "Yes," he

said. "And I asked you please to wait because I must be going to get more change." His gaze lingered, as if to say he knew I had been thinking that because he was an Arab, he must be trying to cheat me. *Oh no!* I wanted to say. *That isn't what I was thinking at all!* But I realized with shame it was.

"I am so sorry," I said. "Really. I am very sorry."

The man patted my arm. "Please," he said. "I will go and get your change. In the meanwhile, you must return to the buffet and take a dish of the rice pudding, which is included in the price and is especially delicious."

And what can I say, it was.

On the way home, Sam detoured through Arab East Jerusalem and parked on the Mount of Olives, where we stood looking west across the Kidron Valley—the Valley of Dry Bones from the Bible, the Valley of Jehoshaphat, the valley where Jews have been burying their dead for three thousand years and where Arabs now live in a spreading village called Silwan. I held no love for the Palestinian vandals who routinely defaced those tombs. But what about the rest of Silwan's residents, some of whom were being displaced by Jewish settlers and by an archaeological dig that seeks to uncover the foundations of the original walled city of Jerusalem, including King David's palace? Shouldn't the needs of the living trump the respect that we show our dead? Or maybe it's vice versa. History helps to make us what we are. But wouldn't cultural amnesia be preferable to all this bloodshed? (Later, I took a tour of the site and waded through the icy spring that still flows through the deep subterranean tunnels dug by the workers of King Hezekiah twenty-seven hundred years ago to prepare Jerusalem for a siege by the Assyrians. Some of my more lefty acquaintances cautioned me not to go, but the tour was thrilling.)

Sam dropped us at the Jaffa Gate. Effy and the New Zealanders started to walk away. "Wait!" I said. "I know you don't have much money, but you need to tip the driver." Grudgingly, they pulled out a few coins. To make up for their delinquency, I handed Sam a larger bill than I had intended. Frustrated because in nine hours in his van, I hadn't been able to connect with him in a human way, I could barely restrain myself from adding: Oh, and by the way, if you haven't figured this out, I happen to be a Jew!

The next morning, the only sign of my host, Rivkeh, was the latest edition of the newspaper for which she wrote. Exhausted from my excursion the day before but reluctant to waste any of my remaining time in Israel, I slathered on yet another layer of sunscreen, refilled my water jug, then slogged back up the hill to sightsee.

Hours later, after viewing another few millennia's worth of examples of one nation's brutality to another, I felt beaten and dazed. I might have gone back to the apartment, but I had heard the Israel Museum would be open late that night and decided I could cram two days of sightseeing into one.

I left the Jewish Quarter. Even at four, with the light that radiant honey-gold you find only in Jerusalem, the sun was hammering on my head. In my five days in Israel, I had walked or taken a bus wherever I needed to go. This time, I raised my hand to hail a cab. A taxi crested the hill behind me, but the driver zoomed past. A second cab. A third. No one seemed willing to stop. Finally, a cab pulled over. "Where you want to go?" the driver asked. He was a dignified man my age. Clean-shaven. Dark. I assumed he must be a Jew, but he wasn't slick or brash like most Israeli men; something about him seemed more European. Years before, I had been kidnapped and mugged by a pair of fake cabbies in London, so I am very careful about which automobiles I do or do not get into. But the markings on this taxi seemed identical to the markings on every other taxi in Jerusalem, and the driver struck me as a mild, trustworthy man. We settled on the fare—everyone had warned me cabbies in Jerusalem will rip you off—and off we went.

We didn't get far. We were driving a narrow, one-way, walled street when the car ahead of us stopped and a bearded older man in a white shirt, black trousers, and *tsitsit* got out. I waited for his car to pull away. When it didn't, I waited for the driver of my cab to honk. Israelis honk because they like the sound of their own horns, so I was surprised to see my driver sitting ramrod straight, both hands on the wheel, staring ahead as if nothing lay beyond his windshield.

"What's the matter?" I asked. When he shook his head, I turned and saw another cab pull up behind us, and two or three cars behind that. The silence ticked. Then, suddenly, we were surrounded by men gesturing at the driver, banging on his window, shouting what seemed to be curses, although who could tell? As a child, I had spent four afternoons a week in Hebrew school, but my teachers had been refugees from Eastern Europe, and the only Hebrew they knew was the language of study and prayer. If there had been a State of Israel and a modern Hebrew language for those men to know anything about, they wouldn't have been cowering in front of a bunch of ten-year-old savages, drilling us in our prayers. Despite all my years in those classrooms, I knew only three Hebrew phrases: "Mother comes"; "Father comes"; and, for reasons I can no longer recall, "the monkey's head," and if the men outside our cab were shouting anything about mothers, fathers, or monkeys' heads, they were using those phrases in such idiosyncratic ways I couldn't decipher what they meant.

The man with the beard—although really, all the men

except my driver had beards—began banging on my window, motioning me to get out. "What is it?" I said. "Someone tell me, in English."

By now, another five or six men—and several women—were gathered around our car, yelling at me to get out. Seeing that the driver of the taxi behind us was one of the angriest in the crowd, I wondered if my own driver was some kind of scab. "Is this a union thing?" I asked. My driver continued to sit with his hands on the wheel, ignoring our attackers. I rolled down my window an inch or two and demanded to know what was going on. Rather than answer, the man with the beard jammed his arm in the cab, jerked open my door, grabbed me by my wrist, and pulled me out.

I don't want to exaggerate my fear. These were my own people—what were they going to do, gang rape me? Cut off my head? But I distrust anyone who yanks me out of my car and starts dragging me toward his car. "Stop!" I shouted. "Someone tell me right now what this is all about!"

Disdainfully, one of the women hissed in English: "He is an Arab. He will cheat you. We don't want our women driving in cars with their men."

I wish I could say I admonished my co-religionists with a speech worthy of Martin Luther King Jr. But my guilt over accusing the nice Palestinian cashier in Jericho of trying to cheat me leadened my tongue. The best I could come up with was: "That's disgusting!" I yanked back my arm, climbed in the cab, rolled up my window, locked my door, and told the driver, "I am so, so sorry. I didn't understand. I'm not going anywhere. I will sit here as long as it takes. I am from America. All I want is for everyone to get along."

As an American, I still hoped for a happy ending. The driver would sob with gratitude at my heroic display of solidarity, and somehow this would lead to Netanyahu and the

Palestinians making peace. In reality, he remained staring out his windshield at the men who had resumed pounding on the glass and cursing him. "I don't say anything to them," he said. "I say nothing to you. You must do as you wish."

Judging by his forbearance, this happened to him all the time. Worse, his own co-worker—the driver of the taxi behind us—must have been in cahoots with the driver of the car in front; how else could they have planned their ambush? Still, how could my driver just ignore me? Wasn't he concerned for my safety? Did he lump me in with these hateful lunatics because I was a Jew? How was that different from my thinking he must be dishonest—or a terrorist—because he was an Arab?

Another fifteen minutes went by, and the mob gave up and left. "You still want to go to the museum?" my driver asked.

"If you will take me there," I said.

He nodded and drove the few miles in silence. At the gate, a guard inspected our trunk for bombs and let us in. I paid the amount we had agreed on—I wish I could say I doubled it as a tip, but trying to compensate the man for what he had just suffered with a few extra shekels struck me as an insult. Shaking with anger, I went inside the museum to view the magnificent cultural displays of a nation I still loved but whose policies I wasn't sure I could continue to defend when I got back home.

After that, I lost confidence in my plan to rent a car and drive north to the Galilee. If such craziness had taken place right here in Jerusalem, what might befall me if I set out through a country whose geography and politics were so confusing I could take one wrong turn and, because of the color of my license plate, or the day of the week, or the length of my hem, get attacked by a *meshugenner* Arab or an ultra-religious right-wing Jew?

Then again, I didn't want to leave Israel having seen nothing but Jerusalem. And I have never been one to wimp out on an itinerary. I packed a bag and traipsed up the hill yet again, skirting the park where the not-so-mythical wild dogs of Jerusalem had sprung out to attack me. The rental agency where I was picking up my car turned out to be across the street from the King David Hotel, which is famous for having been blown up by terrorists. Jewish terrorists. In 1946, members of the Irgun disguised themselves as Arabs, planted explosives in the basement and, after issuing a warning that the British ignored, triggered the bombs and killed ninety people.

I buckled myself in my car and set off to find the entrance to the highway we had taken with Sam. The aggressive habits of the local drivers didn't faze me, but the streets bore no relation to their counterparts on the map, and nothing seemed marked by signs. Within minutes, I found myself driving through a town in which the writing was in Arabic. Stunned, I turned around and headed back. Four times I made this same hectic loop; four times, I ended up in that Arab village. I wondered how two groups living in such proximity could be so different. Then I remembered Michigan, where I live. There is Detroit, which is almost entirely poor and Black, and the affluent white suburbs that surround it, which are Christian and Jewish, except for the Arab enclaves like Dearborn, and the mixed-race, working-class towns like Ypsilanti, and the lefty college towns like Ann Arbor, Lansing, and Kalamazoo, and the conservative, fundamentalist Christian towns like Dexter, Howell, Pinckney, and Wolverine, some of which boast their very own anti-government right-wing militias. On a good day, everyone gets along. But many of my white neighbors consider a trip to Detroit to be suicidal (I used to go there all the time with Marian, and we never experienced the slightest problem), while my Black friends wouldn't dream of visiting Dexter, Howell, Pinckney, or Wolverine. If the civil rights legislation of the 1960s hadn't been enacted and the Black Panther movement had grown to be a national insurgency, or if the Oklahoma City bombing hadn't convinced many of the militias to pursue a less militaristic path, or if the events of September 11 had been followed by other bombings by Islamic radicals, who knows whether driving around Michigan today would be as hazardous as driving around Israel and the West Bank.

On my fourth try, I turned on an unmarked street and found myself heading east on the main thoroughfare out of Jerusalem. At the turnoff to Highway 90, which Israel built to provide a timesaving route through the West Bank, I shushed my guilty heart and traveled north. For long stretches, I had reason to ponder the shared linguistic roots of the words "desert" and "deserted." I had brought an extra liter of water, sunscreen, and a hat, but if my crappy rental car broke down, I would be sitting there, helpless, in the middle of the West Bank, a stone's throw from Jordan, with which Israel maintains an awkward peace. Like most Americans who visit this part of the world, I needed to reconsider the visuals I summoned to accompany spirituals in which the singer longs to cross the River Jordan. The poor singer didn't need a chariot; all he needed to do was take a very big step.

And so, with great relief, I entered the small, working-class town of Beit She'an. Not that the city had much to offer. Most of it seemed to be a maze of public housing inhabited by Russian and Ethiopian immigrants who couldn't understand my repeated questions in English—or even in phrasebook Hebrew—as to how I might find the national park for which the town is famous. But my sister had cautioned me not to miss the ancient Roman ruins at the city's heart. More than a dozen civilizations—Canaanites, Israelites, Assyrians,

Egyptians, Scythians, Seleucids, Romans, Muslims, Christian Crusaders, Mamluks, Ottomans—had built their settlements on the site. If an international peacekeeping body were to apportion Beit She'an according to who made the most convincing claim, each grain of sand would need to be apportioned to a different owner.

As had happened at Masada and Jericho, the site was so blazingly hot I was the only tourist there. A park employee transported me in his long, empty train past the amphitheater where gladiators once fought and, for all I knew, Ben-Hur raced his chariot. Then, slowly, I walked along the colonnaded main street, past the temples and shops of the Romans who used to live and work there. Not a creature disturbed the peace; I might have been the first archaeologist who stumbled on the ruins. The theater was magnificent; the seats could have held my entire hometown, and then some. The bathhouse, with its swimming pool, exercise facilities, and public toilets, resembled the gym where I work out in Ann Arbor. How intimidating it must have been to wander in from the desert and see people living in such luxury that even their shit and piss got washed away. As much as I like to think I would have accepted Jesus' message that it was better to be a poor Jew than a wealthy Roman, I am not so sure I would have.

I trudged back to the visitors' center, where a guide was asking her group of young charges what language they were speaking.

"It is Aramaic," a woman said. "All of us, we all are Arameans."

"Arameans?" the guide marveled. "I didn't know there are still any people living who call themselves Arameans!"

I, too, was taken aback. The only Arameans I had heard of were the ones in the Passover Haggadah. After God leads the

Hebrew people into the Promised Land, He cautions them to remember: "Once, your father was a wandering Aramean," by which He means: Never forget that before you became a powerful nation, you were a bunch of homeless nobodies.

The Aramean laughed. "Oh, no, I assure you, Arameans are very real. We grew up in a village in Syria. Now, we live all over. But no matter where we go, we still say we are Arameans."

Sweaty again, dying of thirst, I spent more money than I had budgeted to gain access to the beach along the Sea of Galilee. The tan, muscular, uniformed young men who guarded the entrance flirted with me shamelessly and begged me to remain at the booth with them. I was taken aback. At home, men rarely came on to me this way. Maybe my sunglasses and hat obscured that I was twice their age. Maybe they were bored. I wouldn't have been averse to passing time with an Israeli man. But I had yet to meet an Israeli man who exhibited the soulful, neurasthenic air I find attractive.

"Thanks for asking," I said, "but you have no idea how much I want to get in that water."

I parked and staked out a space. The Israeli side of the lake was built up with hotels, but if you looked east, toward Jordan, you could imagine yourself wading in the same fresh, sweet waters in which Jesus must have fished, and if not Jesus, then Jews like him. Recently, a simple wooden fishing boat from Jesus' time had been uncovered on this very shore; if I'd had another hour or two before dark, I would have stopped at the nearby kibbutz to see it.

As it was, standing there in the water, I could see the Mount of Beatitudes to the north. The image of Jesus preaching his sermon about the meek inheriting the earth and the peacemakers being the children of God was still fresh in my mind from *Ben-Hur*—it was the scene I had found so moving. If the Jews and Muslims wanted to argue that ownership of a given piece of land should be determined by how much it meant to each religion, shouldn't the Galilee be ceded to the Christians? Then again, the Christians seemed to think if all the Jews returned to Israel, the Apocalypse would arrive and Jesus would bequeath everything to them anyway.

Fresh from my baptism in the water where Jesus walked, I drove up the winding mountain road to Safed. Cool, green Safed has been the center of Jewish mysticism since the late 1400s, when Spain kicked out anyone who wasn't Christian and many of the leading Kabbalists ended up here. In the centuries that followed, the Jews of Safed survived earthquakes, plagues, and the occasional Arab pogrom, until the War for Independence, when they claimed the city as their own and thousands of Muslims fled. In college, I had discovered the Kabbalah—at least, in the form popularized by Martin Buber and Gershom Scholem—and become intoxicated by the idea that our task in this fallen world is to liberate the sparks of divine light hidden in each person and object we encounter. Now, I was inspired to walk the same cobbled streets where the fathers of Kabbalah once walked. But I also felt uneasy that Safed had been taken over by Hasidic mystics and New Agey Americans, who had turned the town into an Israeli version of Sedona—apparently, Madonna and her boyfriend (whose name was Jesus) had sneaked into Safed one night to visit the tomb of the Kabbalah's founder.

As darkness fell, I paid my own respects to Rabbi Luria, then made my way through the medieval alleyways of the Hasidic ghetto. In the twilight, everything glowed, and it was easy to imagine that if you laid a finger to this leaf or that stone, a spark of divine light would rise up to join all the other sparks hovering above the town. I browsed the artists' colony, but it bothered me that the galleries were housed in what once had been the Arab quarter. In Spain, I had found it hard to enjoy the quaint *Juderias* of Cordova and Seville, knowing the original inhabitants had been exiled by the Inquisition. In Krakow with Marian, I had been unable to stomach lunch in the "Jewish style" restaurants in the Kazimierz district or buy the figurine carved in the shape of a rabbi, knowing that neither the owners of the restaurants nor the carvers of the figurines were Jews and the original inhabitants of the district had been transported to nearby Auschwitz. I had no idea if the Arabs who once lived in Safed had been more or less deserving of their fate than the Jews who had been exiled from Cordova, Seville, or Krakow. All I knew was that most people who lose their homes during a war aren't the same people who started the war, or who stand to gain if their side wins.

Tired, I stopped at a café where a bunch of bored American teenagers sat listening to a white-bearded man in a fakey Kabbalah get-up trying to convince them that every time they went to the mall, they lost a part of their souls. "The stores and their advertisements incite within you a desire for something where no desire existed," the man intoned in a pretentious accent. "If you buy this item, a part of yourself goes out of you with your money." I couldn't disagree with the impromptu sermon, but I can tell a canned spiel when I hear one, and if there is one thing mysticism isn't, it is canned.

Disgusted, I got back in my car, drove to the top of the mountain, hit a dead end at a military base, then found the bed-and-breakfast at which I had booked a room. The proprietor, an American-born Jew who looked like Mama Cass, had been living in Safed for decades and complained the influx of Kabbalah nuts was ruining her town. When I told her about the ultra-Orthodox Jews who had pulled me from the taxi in Jerusalem, she was furious. "My family lost everyone in the ovens," she said, "and I can tell you, the Nazis should have taken those guys, too."

After dinner, I soaked in an outdoor hot tub while a multiracial couple wrote postcards at a picnic table and their multihued children kicked a soccer ball around the yard, which was fragrant with the scents of flowers I couldn't identify. For the first time since arriving in Israel, I felt at home.

Then again, everyone around me was American.

As it turned out, I felt at home everywhere in northern Israel. Driving from Safed to Akko was like driving through wine country in California. Akko itself is a beautiful port. As I walked along the harbor, I imagined myself one in a long line of important visitors, from Alexander the Great and Julius Caesar to St. Francis of Assisi and Marco Polo. The fort had changed hands so many times, from the Arabs to the Crusaders, I expected to see Saladin ride up on his camel, only to be overtaken by Richard the Lionheart on an armor-plated horse. Akko is one of the few cities in Israel where Muslims, Jews, and Christians live in relative peace. Making the picture even rosier is the location of Baha'i world headquarters in nearby Haifa, Baha'i being a religion whose main tenet is the unity of all religions.

Sadly, I looked up Akko on my laptop and learned riots had erupted there not long before, set off by an Arab father and son driving into an ultra-Orthodox Jewish neighborhood on Yom Kippur to pick up the man's daughter, who was baking pastries at a relative's house. Jews mobbed the car. Young Palestinians joined the fray. Ever since, Israeli extremists had been using the riots as an excuse to move in and scare off the Arabs.

I drove south along the coast. Why hadn't I realized how

stunning Israel is? If not for the violence, everyone in the world would be clamoring to live there. What other country has a Mediterranean climate, deserts and oases, huge inland bodies of water like the Dead Sea, the Red Sea, and the Sea of Galilee, history-rich sites like Jerusalem, Qumran, Masada, and Beit She'an, artsy mountain towns like Safed, farms that produce oranges, dates, and figs, a thriving high-tech industry, orchestras, museums, first-class universities, and a cosmopolitan beach-side city like Tel Aviv?

I parked the car, then wandered happily through the stylish but invitingly shabby downtown. Who knew? Tel Aviv has all the charm of Paris or New York, but with a scruffy informality—used bookstores on every corner, a bustling open-air market with vendors selling colorful fruits, vegetables, underwear, toys, and fish. The women's skirts were short. The men weren't even wearing yarmulkes. After a walk along the sea, I went for a swim, then ate shawarma at a café and sipped a smoothie.

At fifty-five, I often find my mind wandering to retirement. In America, most cities with warm weather and proximity to a beach are populated by people who hate to read. How could I have guessed the ideal city in which to spend my golden years might be Tel Aviv? I thought about one of my former students, Ayla, who had moved to the Negev, where she taught writing to engineers and volunteered to help the Bedouin, and two other students, Nava and Ilana, who lived in America but spent a significant amount of time in Israel, working to bring about peace between Arabs and Israelis. Their relative youth allowed them the freedom to live as expatriates. Maybe my age would allow me to do the same. Now that Noah was in college and Marian was no longer my partner, to whom did I have to answer? I even found the men in Tel Aviv attractive. Or I would have, if they hadn't been wearing Speedos.

I went for another swim, then hung out on the beach. On my way back to my car, I detoured through a neighborhood famous for its Bauhaus buildings. When I found the aptly named Rothschild Boulevard crammed with tents, I experienced the thrill of discovering not vestiges of the past, but history being made. For days, I had been reading about Israel's version of the Arab Spring. And here I was, in the middle of a street jammed with protestors my son's age who were fed up with the high cost of housing, along with stroller-pushing couples fed up with the high cost of child care, and Israelis my age fed up with the high cost of food relative to their salaries and pensions. The movement promised to bring together secular and religious Jews with Israeli Arabs, all united in their dismay at how hard it was to eke out a living in a country where such a huge proportion of the budget was allocated to the military and the construction and defense of settlements rather than to human services for those citizens, Arab and Jew, who live inside the Green Line. The tents stretched for blocks; the sidewalks were so crowded I finally gave up and stopped.

From America, the view of Israel doesn't include Jews like these. Then again, viewed from anywhere else, America often seems to be populated exclusively by Tea Partiers in tricorn hats. I wished the protestors well. I blessed their tents. *Please*, I thought, *take back your country from extremist crazies on both sides who are trying to destroy what so many worthy people built*. I doubted the protestors would succeed in time for me to retire to Tel Aviv. I only prayed they would succeed at all.

I made it back to Jerusalem and returned my car. The next morning, I slept late, then trudged up to the Old City yet again, this time to shop for gifts. If Marian had been there, he would have insisted I buy candlesticks or a mezuzah. Once, in Santa Fe, we saw a ceramic plate painted with a Jewish star, and Marian said I ought to buy it, to which I replied it was in bad taste to put anyone's religious symbols on a plate. In fact, seeing the plate with the star on it reminded me of the time Noah painted a University of Michigan maize-and-blue block M on a massively overgrown zucchini and used it to decorate his lemonade stand, only to discover that a fan on his way to the football stadium was willing to pay five dollars to buy the vegetable. Well, Marian said, he probably would have bought that zucchini, too.

After browsing all four quarters of the Old City, I bought some hand-painted icons of the Virgin Mary for my Christian friends back home, some Armenian pottery for the neighbors who had been watching my house and, for everyone else, bright blue glass charms to ward off the Evil Eye. That left only my son. I lingered over the nicest handmade yarmulkes, admired the finest Kiddush cups, ran my fingers along the fringes of the most elegant *talisim*. Even if Noah remained a Marxist, he might marry a Jewish girl and want to share wine with her from the kiddush cup his mother had bought for him in Jerusalem. At the very least, he might want to put on a yarmulke and *talis* to say Kaddish at my funeral. That I was fairly certain none of these dreams would come to pass made me inexplicably sad. Then again, what did I care whom my son married, as long as she made him happy? What did I care what he wore on his head or draped across his shoulders when I knew he would be sobbing out his eyes beside my grave?

With the markets about to shut for the Sabbath, I passed an elderly Arab merchant using a hook to take down the keffiyehs above his stall. Before my trip to Israel, I had seen keffiyehs only on the news, adorning the head of

Yassar Arafat as he vowed to wipe Israel off the map or tied across the faces of rock-throwing Palestinian youths. But the cloths hanging above this stall, some in the traditional black-and-white-checked pattern, others in red and black and white, looked like nothing so much as beautiful scarves and shawls. Most of the keffiyehs sold in Israel come from China, but these, the merchant said, had been manufactured in the last factory that still wove keffiyehs in the West Bank. The cloth was thick and richly dyed, yet light enough to carry home. The old man quoted a fair price, so I said yes, please pack up the shawl and I would buy it.

For a few minutes, I was pleased with what I had done. Then I thought: What kind of a Jewish mother goes to Israel and brings back a keffiyeh for her son? I hadn't bought it out of love. I had bought it to teach Noah a lesson: *Here I am in Israel, and what do you make me do? You make me buy you a keffiyeh!* If a security agent at the airport were to ask why I was bringing home a scarf associated with Yassar Arafat and rock-throwing Palestinian youths, what would I say? Besides, if I had bought Noah the yarmulke or the kiddush cup, I might not have detected the disappointment I noticed in his eyes when I gave him the keffiyeh.

That night, Rivkeh, the woman from whom I was renting my room, and her friend the rabbi in Spandex shorts invited me to a Shabbat dinner. Marian would have welcomed the opportunity to celebrate a genuine Sabbath meal with genuine Jews in a genuine apartment in Jerusalem. But the last time I observed the Sabbath, I had been attending a "Shabbaton" for Orthodox middle-schoolers. I thought religious girls might be nicer than the mean secular girls who made my life hell. But the girls at the Shabbaton all had crushes on a handsome young man named Irving, and when Irving paid slightly more attention to me than he did to them, one of the girls filled my shoes with chopped liver.

As an adult, I had several friends who made it a point to celebrate the Sabbath. I admired their decision to set off one day each week to go for a walk or read a book rather than check their e-mail. But sanctity has a way of slipping into sanctimoniousness. Religion often seems to me a game people play because following a set of rules sets them apart from the other poor shmoes who stumble through life with no rules to follow. What, really, is so admirable about observing a set of commandments that people who were living in caves five thousand years ago scratched on the skin of a sheep and preserved in a clay jar? If adhering to our ancestors' beliefs is so important, why not demolish the Dome of the Rock, rebuild the Temple, and resume sacrificing pigeons and unblemished heifers—which some of my co-religionists want to do?

That said, as a divorced Jewish woman who had just broken up with her partner of ten years and bought her son a keffiyeh, I had no business criticizing any Jewish family that managed to enjoy a Friday night together, lighting candles, blessing their food, and singing psalms. Not to mention that observing the Sabbath would provide me with an excuse to stop racing around the country in a vain attempt to experience everything a person in Israel might experience instead of walking around my neighborhood and spending time with the people who actually lived there.

Our hosts, who recently had emigrated from Canada, took us on a tour of the condo they had bought and renovated, and I couldn't help but think of the young Israelis camped out in Tel Aviv to protest the high cost of housing, which, they claimed, had been created by the influx of wealthy Jews from abroad. On the other hand, the meal our hosts served was delicious, their teenage son and his young friend were respectful and well informed, and no one slipped chopped liver in my shoe. The rabbi told us about the time she and her son had gone swimming in Tel Aviv and had all their possessions stolen. The Palestinian taxi driver who picked them up took them to the rabbi's friend's house to see if the friend could help, and when the friend wasn't home, lent the rabbi a hefty sum to pay for two seats on a sherut to Jerusalem.

Unfortunately, that wasn't the only story we heard that night. One of the guests was an itinerant Kabbalist from St. Louis who had been invited to give the dinner a more spiritual dimension. I was all for listening to something more uplifting than a discussion of real estate prices in Israel. But her midrash gave me pause. In the story, the Hebrews who had fled slavery in Egypt crossed the desert and arrived in Canaan. Moses sent twelve spies to gather intelligence about the best way to enter the country. Ten of the spies returned with tales of grapes so huge that a single man couldn't carry them. That was the good news. The bad news was the cities were fortified and the warriors defending those walls were giants. The two remaining spies, Joshua and Caleb, tried to convince their friends the Canaanites were ordinary men like them. But the Jews, weakened by years of servitude, couldn't believe their own strength, so God ordered them back in the desert, where they wandered for a wearying but confidence-building forty years before Joshua led his men to the Promised Land and conquered Jericho.

If I hadn't visited Jericho a few days earlier, the story might have been inspiring. As it was, when I thought of Joshua and his army marching in and killing every last man, woman, and child in the city, I couldn't help but think of the nice cashier who had forgiven me for thinking that just because he was an Arab, he might cheat me, and who, to show he harbored no ill will, instructed me to go back and try the rice pudding.

The next morning, the rabbi in Spandex shorts complained about having to put on a dress and go to services, which made me feel better about my refusal to do the same. After she and Rivkeh left, I sat around reading an article about a government official who had been arrested for swindling his constituents. Oh no, I thought, he had a Jewish last name! Then I realized I needn't fear that Christian readers might use this gonif's indictment as proof of every vile Jewish stereotype they ever had.

Later, I leafed through the pile of women's magazines Rivkeh kept in her bathroom. The articles were in Hebrew, but as I studied the photos, I wondered why the models seemed so coarse-featured, so wiry-haired, so zaftig, so short, so dark—in other words, so much like Rivkeh, the rabbi, and me.

After that, I couldn't stop looking at those photos. Was this why the men in Israel were friendlier to me than the men back home? By the end of the day, I had managed to convince myself the models here were every bit as beautiful as their tall, thin, flat-chested, regular-featured, and fair-skinned counterparts in the American magazines I had grown up ogling.

In the evening, I finally had the chance to hang out with Rivkeh. She was a few years my junior, an inch or two shorter, quite a bit curvier, but otherwise, we could have been sisters. I sensed she was wary, as many Israelis are, of what an outsider might say about her country. But I found the courage to ask how she managed to cover such a volatile conflict—as far as I could tell from reading her articles, she was wonderfully adept at getting sources from both sides to open up and confide their stories.

Well, she said, I needed to understand that many Israelis were the descendants of Holocaust survivors. Many had lost fathers, brothers, husbands, sons, daughters, and wives in the succession of Israeli wars in which their families fought. Many also had friends who had died in a suicide bombing. For example, did I know the coffee shop down the street?

Sure, I said. I had taken to sitting there in the evenings, writing up my notes. Well, Rivkeh said, not long before, a suicide bomber had blown up that coffee shop, killing seven people and wounding fifty. Someone Rivkeh knew—a young woman who was getting married the next day—had died in that bombing, along with her father. What if someone had blown up my favorite coffee shop in Ann Arbor? What if my friend and her father died there? How forgiving would I be?

What made everything so complicated, Rivkeh said, was the Arabs were the victims of trauma, too. Many had lost their land. Their husbands, brothers, and sons had been prisoners in Israeli jails. As a reporter, she tried to see everyone's point of view. She drew the line at violence. But with most people, she thought: *I know who you are. If I were you, I would be feeling the same thing you're feeling.*

Maybe I was only tired, but Rivkeh's philosophy struck me as the secret to peace in the Middle East. Certainly, it was more useful than my own philosophy, which was that both sides were crazy, even as both sides were right. I took her display of empathy as an opening to tell her about the incident in which I had been dragged from my cab by a mob of right-wing Jews. What did she think about what had happened, I asked.

What did she think? What did I mean, what did she think! Such an incident was outrageous! Why hadn't I reported it to the police? If I had given the police the license plate of the car in front of me, they would have found the guy and arrested him.

"Really?" I said, heartsick to realize it never had occurred to me to report my attackers. Their unembarrassed hooliganism—in broad daylight—had convinced me everyone in Israel had been hijacked by the anti-democratic right to such an extent only a naïve American tourist would even care. How could I have assumed all of Israel had become so racist? What if a visitor to America witnessed a mob harassing someone who was Jewish, Black, Muslim, or gay and hadn't bothered to notify the police because she assumed America was so backward and xenophobic no one would care?

On my last day in Israel, I took the bus to Yad Vashem. I had always been uneasy about Holocaust museums, which seem to reify suffering and turn Judaism into a cult of hair and shoes whose main tenet is "Never again." But I wasn't visiting Yad Vashem to reinforce my commitment to the prevention of future Holocausts. What I wanted to do was look up the records of my grandmother's family, who, I recently learned, had been murdered by the Nazis and their Ukrainian henchmen in a town called Chertkow.

Steeling myself to go inside, I strolled along the Avenue of the Righteous, paying my respects to those gentiles who had risked their lives protecting Jews. I knew if Marian and I had been living in Poland during World War II, he would have done everything he could to save me. (Even his father, who blames the Jews for everything that has ever gone wrong in Poland, might have done the same, if only because he is at heart a decent man and because he hates the Germans even more than he hates the Jews.) In fact, if it hadn't been for Marian and his obsession with Polish-Jewish history, I would never have pressed my mother to tell me about my grandmother's family, and I wouldn't have known where to look to find out what happened to the Jews of Chertkow.

I sat on a stone and cried. If not for Marian, I would never have visited Israel, just as I would never have visited the old Jewish cemetery hidden inside the GM Cadillac plant in Hamtramck, Michigan. I wouldn't have attended the All-Navajo Rodeo in Lukachukai, Arizona. I wouldn't have been one of only two white people at Lola's Bar and Restaurant in Detroit the night Barack Obama was proclaimed the first African-American president of the United States. I found cultural tourism to be wearying and confusing. But I wasn't sorry I had let Marian drag me to so many places I otherwise wouldn't have gone. I was only sorry he and I hadn't managed to surmount whatever differences prevented us from getting married. If I couldn't find a way to share my life with my Polish Catholic boyfriend, how could I criticize the Israelis and Palestinians for not finding a way to surmount their differences and share their lives?

Drying my eyes, I made my way into the museum, which was crowded with Israeli soldiers on a field trip. In the archives, I sat at a computer whose memory banks served up a page of testimony filled out in 1953 by some relative of my grandmother's brother. Most of the data was in Hebrew and offered little but the facts. But when I sounded out my great-uncle Nachman Teitelbaum's name, I gasped. There really had been a Holocaust. There really had been Ukrainians who chased people into barns and lit those barns on fire. There really had been German soldiers who mowed down men, women, and children in the woods outside a town called Chertkow simply for being Jews.

What would have happened if my grandmother's brother and his family had escaped that burning barn and outrun the Nazis? People say the Jews got pushed out the windows of Europe and fell on the Palestinians. But isn't it also true the Arabs, like the British and Americans, showed very little mercy to those few Jews who managed to survive the terrors of Europe? Maybe it is time to stop justifying everything Israel does in the name of an atrocity that took place three quarters of a century ago and wasn't committed by the people who are—or are not—threatening Israel's safety now. On the other hand, it might not hurt to remind the world that the millennia-old hatred of the Jews so pervasive in Europe, Russia, and the Middle East created the need for a Jewish state, and now that Israel exists, it has the same right to protect its citizens as every other nation in the world.

Yad Vashem is on the outskirts of Jerusalem, and as my bus made its way to the center of the city, it picked up every kind of Jew and Muslim. Someday, there had to be peace. How could there not be? Hadn't the warring factions in Ireland and South Africa made peace? Hadn't the Iron Curtain fallen? And maybe, once the peace was achieved, the fact that the two communities were so intertwined would make it all the stronger. If two former enemies shared the same highways, rivers, and lakes, didn't they need to cooperate to preserve their resources? Didn't they need to join forces to study the archaeology of the sites so important to both religions and to ensure the safety of the tourists both nations required to survive?

The question was, what would happen after that? Israel was going to need to commit itself to the same sort of civil rights movement America had struggled through in the past—and is still struggling through today. In what way was the driver of the taxi a threat to anyone's security? In what way was my experience in his cab not analogous to that of a white woman being pulled from a taxi in Mississippi or Alabama by Klansmen intent on preventing her from riding in a car being driven by "one of their men"? In America, we barely have begun to achieve some measure of tolerance and equality. But I no longer see the need to spend my time with fundamentalists or fanatics. To do so on a regular basis would leave me with no tenderness or energy to do much of anything else.

On my last night in Israel, rather than catch a few hours of sleep and rouse myself for an early-morning flight, I stayed up talking to Rivkeh. Then I lugged my suitcase down to the street to wait for the sherut to the airport. The neighborhood, usually crowded with young Israelis, now lay deserted, except for the feral cats slithering here and there in search of a meal.

As I stood by the curb, a taxi screeched up and the driver jumped out. "You going to airport? Come, come with me." I tried to protest—the fare would be far more expensive than if I rode in a sherut—but the driver, a secular Jew, grabbed my bag and locked it in his trunk. "I give you good price," he said, although, when I pressed him, the fare he quoted was exorbitant.

I pounded on his trunk. "Give me my bag!" I didn't care if his grandparents barely had survived the Holocaust and he had lost everyone he ever loved in every war against the Arabs. "Open this trunk!" I shouted, so loud the cats mewling around my feet ran off. "Open this trunk right now!"

Sullenly, he opened the trunk. I grabbed my suitcase. He muttered what sounded like an insult, then sped off. The sherut came and took me to the airport. There, a blonde, ponytailed soldier with a rifle asked me questions meant to gauge how Jewish I was and therefore how great a risk I might pose of blowing up my flight. Angry I should be subjected to such an inquisition but not willing to be prohibited from getting on my plane, I stammered out something about joining a temple in Ann Arbor but quitting when my son became a Marxist. Dummy! I thought. Why did you mention that? Now they'll never let you get on that plane. And wait until they find that keffiyeh in your bag!

The soldier smiled and shook her ponytail. "Don't worry," she said. "I'm not here to pass judgment on how observant a Jew you are. I only hope you enjoyed your time in my country. There are many, many ways to be a Jew."

"Yes," I said, "there are." And what I didn't say: I was the kind of Jew who hoped and prayed—although to whom I didn't know—that Israelis like Rivkeh, and the proprietor of the B&B in Safed, and my friend Ayla in the Negev, and the protestors in Tel Aviv, and the thousands and thousands of other Israelis like them would find a way to save their country from anyone who believes the question of who owned which temple or mosque or cave or mosaic one hundred years ago, or five hundred years ago, or five thousand years ago is worth killing another human being or depriving him of his dignity. I had spent the first fifty years of my life trying to avoid, ignore, or do battle with bigots in America. And as much as I did love Israel—even now that, at the insistence of my Polish Catholic ex-boyfriend, I had gotten on a plane and visited—I wasn't about to retire to a country where I would need to spend another fifty years doing more of the same.

DIDN'T ANYONE TELL YOU

ONE SUMMER, WITH A serial rapist roaming Ann Arbor, I asked my undergraduates to read an essay called "In the Combat Zone" by Leslie Marmon Silko, in which she argues that if women felt comfortable using firearms, they wouldn't present such passive victims for men intent on harming them. One of my female students, fair and lithe as a stalk of goldenrod, informed me that she had nothing to fear from anyone: she had been a track star in high school, and if any man tried anything she didn't like, she could outrun him.

I shuddered when I heard this, having said the same words to my mother when I was that age. Back then, I was sure my parents' prohibition against my living or traveling alone stemmed from nothing more than their old-fashioned sense that a woman was a fragile creature whose virginity needed to be protected, coupled with a willful denial of how resourceful I was. Though only five-four, I was fleet of foot and strong, and I had been trained by my older brother to withstand a tackle.

But even my brother shared their fears. "There's no man I couldn't get away from," I bragged, at which he came up from behind, wrapped his arm around my throat, and lifted me from the ground. Kicking, flailing, I choked out an admission that I was wrong, then went on living as if I weren't.

The choices seemed stark—stay at home until I was safely coupled with a husband, or get out there and see and do all I wanted to see and do, denying the reality that I was far more at risk for getting hurt than my stronger, fleeter, less sexually vulnerable brother. I didn't need lessons on how to shoot a gun. What I needed were lessons on how to navigate—wisely, bravely—that terrifying first year out of college.

That first year, I am convinced, is a time most women decide it isn't worth their while to carry out any unnecessary solo missions in the combat zone. For my parents to have provided such lessons would have been to concede their approval of my plan to spend the summer working in Philadelphia and the two years after that studying in England and exploring Europe. (My mother was so upset at my announcement that I had won a Marshall Scholarship to study abroad that she shook her head sadly and said, ''I will break the news to your father.'')

After graduation, I packed my bags and, without my parents' blessing, took the bus to the City of Brotherly Love to begin my internship at the insurance company where my older sister was an up-and-coming executive. She had been the first to test our parents' wariness about a woman living on her own. As an undergraduate at Barnard, she had been mugged in the Manhattan subway, but our parents seemed to worry far more about me than they did about her. She was the responsible, clear-headed sibling, while even in junior high I had shown a penchant for taking risks. Having earned her MBA from Wharton, my sister worked her way up the ladder at one of the largest insurance companies in the world. Although she had been transferred to Atlanta, she finagled me a summer internship at the home office in Philadelphia and found me a place to stay at a boardinghouse run by an elderly woman who used to work for the company. The neighborhood was poor and rundown, but the landlady, Mrs. Plummer, was a feisty raconteur who told me stories about the misdeeds of her former bosses, who were *my* bosses now. Clearly, she was one of those women who should have run a department rather than take dictation from the less competent men who did.

The only disadvantage was that Mrs. Plummer owned a cat that frequently vomited on my bed. Also, the lock on my bedroom door didn't latch properly. But Mrs. Plummer assured me that I would be safe because the door that led in from the street was secured by two heavy deadbolts. The only other lodger was a grossly overweight and unhappy Finnish guy named Ron, who had been forced to drop out of Wharton for reasons as yet unclear to me. He claimed he managed a Radio Shack in the suburbs, but whenever I got home, he would be sitting in the living room, watching TV and drinking beer. He never said anything provocative, but I could tell he resented me for holding a better job than he did, as he resented my sister for having earned her MBA from the same business school that kicked him out. "You wouldn't have this job if not for your connections," he grumbled, as if my sister and I belonged to some privileged Old Girl network rather than having grown up in a desolate town in upstate New York, the daughters of a dentist who himself had grown up poor; as if my sister hadn't been one of the first women to earn a degree from Wharton; as if I didn't wear the same three hideously out-of-date suits—my sister's castoffs—in rotation every day and rent a room in the same crappy boardinghouse as he did.

Still, I was determined to enjoy the summer. Undaunted by the hundred-degree heat or the endless sanitation strike that had left mountains of garbage rotting along the sidewalks, I spent my spare time exploring the city. Of course, this was exactly the sort of behavior my parents feared. Back in the 1970s, there was still an unspoken assumption—which frequently was spoken—that the greatest danger facing any white female lay in poor, Black neighborhoods. The racism inherent in such paranoia struck me as ugly and untrue, so I planned my excursions based on other considerations.

One weekend, I decided to visit the art museum, and rather than take the bus to Center City and walk north, I started walking due east. On and on I went through the blazing, garbage-mounded streets, until I found myself passing buildings that were burned out or deserted. The neighborhood seemed devoid of habitation, but then, on one slightly less devastated block, I saw that each stoop was populated by a few shirtless Black guys lolling in the heat. No woman would have relished passing through such a gauntlet, especially in the T-shirt and shorts I had on, but I didn't want to hurt the young men's feelings, so I made my way between them, nodding and saying, "Hey." Too tired and hot to move, they nodded almost imperceptibly and murmured, "Hey" or "How you doing."

As the weeks wore on, though, I began to absorb the fear rising from the streets with the heat and the stench of garbage. That was the summer the Philadelphia police laid siege to a Black back-to-nature commune called MOVE, which had taken over a building in the same blighted neighborhood through which I had passed on my walk to the museum. Most Black Philadelphians felt little sympathy for MOVE's diatribes against zoos, cooked food, medicine, and technology. But the mayor's attempt to starve into submission a group that included pregnant women and toddlers raised the community's ire. Early in August, the cops stormed the compound. One officer was shot in the head, possibly by his own men. Most of the adults were arrested, and the violent beating of one MOVE member was recorded by a reporter's camera.

After that, the city grew so tense I suspected something bad would happen, although, as usually is the case, I

179

wouldn't have predicted the danger lay not among strangers, but among people I knew. One evening, I came home from work to find Ron in his usual spot. He offered me a beer. When I declined, he muttered, "Snob." I climbed the stairs, fixed dinner in Mrs. Plummer's kitchen, then showered in the bathroom Ron and I shared. Even when I switched on the fan in my bedroom window, the room remained stifling hot. Dejected, I took off my clothes and crawled beneath the sheet to sleep.

Only to be startled awake in the middle of the night by a two-hundred-and-fifty-pound naked white guy towering above my bed.

There must have been a light outside—I remember the sickly radioactive glow of all that flesh. My first thought was to jump up and run, but I was naked beneath the sheet. Mrs. Plummer's bedroom was on the third floor, and with the fan clattering in my window, she wouldn't hear me scream. Not that I *could* scream. I was silenced by the terror that freezes you in a nightmare. I remember thinking: So this is why people get killed. If you're really scared, you're too paralyzed to escape or fight.

Ron did nothing but stare down at me with such a scornful expression I wanted to cry out: *Why do you hate me? You don't even know me!* Then it occurred to me that he did know me, at least well enough to hate me. He hated me because I was a woman. Because I was more successful than he was. Because my sister had graduated from Wharton and gotten me an internship at the insurance company where she worked. Because I had refused to watch the ball game and share his beer.

"Ron," I said, "you don't want to do this."

But apparently he did. Maybe he didn't intend to rape me. Maybe he intended only to exact revenge. But he certainly managed to put me in my place. Cock in hand, he pissed up and down the bed. The urine spattered the thin sheet covering my bare skin. I was so shocked I couldn't move.

"Ron!" I shouted. "No!" He shook his head, as if startled from a dream, then turned and lumbered off.

I barricaded the door. I must have ventured out to take a shower, but how would I have found the courage? I know I balled the sheets and left them in an acrid heap beside the bed. I must have put on one of my sister's suits and taken the subway to work, because I was sitting at my desk when the cleaning crew came in to clean. I remember thinking I could never tell my parents because they would blame me for sleeping in a room with a door that wouldn't lock. Nor could I tell my landlady. What was I supposed to say, "You know your other boarder, Ron? Well, he came in naked last night and peed all over me." It all was too embarrassing. I would, I decided, blame the wet sheets on the cat.

At nine, my sister called from Atlanta. I had no intention of confessing what had happened—like my parents, she would blame me for sleeping in an unlocked room. But the catatonia in my voice betrayed me. "What is it?" she said. "What's wrong?" I was afraid she would insist I tell our parents—she did, in fact, chide me about the unlocked door—but she understood my reasons for not wanting to remind them why a young woman shouldn't be living on her own. Instead, she made me promise I would tell my landlady. I gave my word, then hung up and called Mrs. Plummer. Horrified, she said she would take care of the matter, then called me back to report she had issued an ultimatum: Either Ron signed himself into rehab, or she would turn him over to the police. Apparently, he had no memory of what he had done, but he allowed Mrs. Plummer to drive him to a facility.

By the time I got home, she had washed the linens and

remade the bed, but the cat had vomited on my pillow, and I decided I couldn't spend another night in that house. I quit my job and flew to Los Alamos to spend the rest of the summer with my boyfriend, Kevin. He and I had met the summer before, working at Oak Ridge National Laboratory in Tennessee. Back then, nuclear weapons and reactors didn't scare me, but in the intervening year, I had left physics to become a writer, and within days of arriving at Los Alamos, I realized I could never live with a man who worked at a facility where nuclear weapons were manufactured. Dejected, I asked Kevin to drive me to the bus station in Albuquerque, where I used the last of my savings to buy a ticket home.

As if the summer hadn't been upsetting enough, a few miles outside El Reno, Oklahoma, a series of loud popping noises rang out and a bullet hole appeared in the window above my head. As the sheriff told us later, life in Oklahoma got so boring the good old boys sometimes sat on the hill outside the Burger King with a six-pack of beer, taking pot shots at the Greyhounds. I wasn't targeted as a woman—there were bullet holes above the heads of the two male passengers behind me. But the men on the bus, most of them foreign tourists, romanticized the shooting as a big adventure. ("Cowboys!" they shouted. "Indians!") I, on the other hand, had to hurry to the fetid restroom to heave up the rancid taco I had wolfed down two stops before.

I made it to my parents' house without further mishap and spent the next few weeks recuperating. I wanted to tell my mother about all the terrible things that had happened to me, but our unspoken agreement was that she and my father wouldn't ask why I had quit my job, why I had traveled to Los Alamos, why I had returned by bus weeks earlier than I said I would be arriving, and I, in turn, wouldn't volunteer the information. Why bring any of it up? All they would say is:

Didn't we tell you this is what happens to young women who insist on living on their own?

In September, I traveled to Washington, D.C., and took a cab to the British Embassy to meet my fellow Marshall Scholars. Exhilarated to be traveling abroad for the first time, I crossed the Atlantic with the group, and we passed a glorious day touring the Houses of Parliament. The other Marshalls were studying at Oxford or Cambridge, but I had chosen one of the newer, less stuffy universities where the term started later, so I stayed in London to sightsee. Amazed to be treading the same streets that Shakespeare, Dickens, and Virginia Woolf had trod, I walked until my feet were blistered raw. At a first-aid station in the Tower of London, a nurse pronounced the wounds infected, and I needed to seek out a foot surgeon to have my feet tended and wrapped in gauze.

Undaunted, I hobbled to the theater to spend my last night at the premiere of a new musical called *Sweeney Todd*. I emerged from the theater trembling. It was pouring, I could barely walk, and the prospect of descending to the Underground having witnessed so many bloody executions didn't thrill me. I could hear my father's outrage if I told him that I had gotten mugged in a subway at eleven o'clock at night. For once, I would shell out a few more dollars—or rather, pounds—and take a cab. I stepped out in traffic and raised my arm. "Taxi!" I shouted. And there I stood, raising my arm and shouting in the rain for half an hour.

Finally, a car with an antenna on the roof pulled up. The kindly man in the passenger seat rolled down his window and said, "Luv, didn't anyone tell you? You can't get a taxi right off the street, especially on a rainy night. We're all on the radio, see?" He held up the receiver. "Where you going, luv? We can squeeze you in before our next call."

Grateful, I slid in the back and named my hotel. The driver maneuvered expertly through the London traffic, and soon we were speeding south across the Thames. "Wait," I said. "My hotel is north of here, not south."

"Shut up!" the man ordered. His companion drove faster. I thought of jumping out, but the car didn't slow until we pulled up beside a midnight-black park. The thought crossed my mind that if my kidnappers didn't slash my throat and turn me into a meat pie, I was going to be sexually assaulted for the second time in three weeks, but all they did was demand my wallet. I threw my cash over the seat and jumped out. I tried to run, but my bloodied feet wouldn't take me far. Luckily, my kidnappers sped off, and I was able to find a hotel and rouse a clerk, who let me in.

By all rights, I should never have gone anywhere alone again. But waiting in the lobby for the Bobbies to show up, I decided if I didn't want to forgo the pleasures of the world— traveling, living in a city, going to the theater—I would need to stop getting taken advantage of. If misfortune did befall me, I couldn't allow whatever happened to shake me up.

The police came and said that fake cabbies often preyed on solitary female tourists. Given I hadn't taken note of the license plate, they could do little except give me a lift to my hotel, where I unswaddled my ruined feet, downed a few Tylenol, and vowed to put the disasters of the past few months out of my mind.

In the years that followed, I traveled back and forth across Europe and America, sometimes alone, sometimes in the company of other women. I became a writer and covered stories that led me to infiltrate a religious cult in New Hampshire and to camp out at a Sun Dance on a remote reservation in South Dakota. When my partner and I broke up two weeks before the vacation we had been planning, I went anyway and drove around Israel and the West Bank on my own. From time to time, I found myself in precarious situations. But I stayed calm, and nothing ever went so wrong that I couldn't handle it.

And yet, I still suffer flashbacks about big, naked men looming over my bed, and I can't sleep in a room with an air-conditioner or a fan droning in the window. I take my phone to bed, and I warn each new lover there is a high probability I will, in the throes of a nightmare, clobber him in my sleep. When I told a therapist about the awful summer during which I had been peed on, shot at, and kidnapped, she raised the question of whether I might still be in the throes of post-traumatic stress. "Me?" I said, ticking off all the risky assignments I had covered as a reporter and the faraway destinations to which I had traveled solo, to which the therapist gently replied that this behavior might constitute its own version of PTSD.

Until recently, I assumed that whatever misfortunes I experienced that first summer out of college were the result of my own bad choices, even as I read essay after essay in which my female students described the assaults to which so many of them had been subjected—not only rapes, but weird, disturbing shit that never would have happened to a man. Eventually, I was forced to admit my parents were right—girls *are* more vulnerable to sexual assault than boys. A fake taxi driver isn't likely to target my six-foot-two son. If I had been a male intern at that insurance company, Ron might have resented my good fortune. He might have picked a fight. But I doubt he would have felt the need to humiliate me by breaking into my room and urinating on me. Besides, if a young man did awaken to find a huge, naked drunk guy peeing on him, he would likely punch the intruder in the face and shout: "You asshole, I told you not to drink so many beers!"

The answer isn't learning to shoot a gun. What if I had panicked and shot one of those Black guys lounging on his stoop in West Philadelphia? Given the choice, I am glad Ron ended up in rehab rather than dead. I was safer throwing my money at those fake cabbies than I would have been to pull a gun and risk having them wrest it from my hand, and far less traumatized than I would have been by blasting them in their heads and getting spattered by their brains and blood.

What I am advocating isn't target practice, but the kind of self-protective training I gave my son. When Noah was sixteen, he bicycled from Ann Arbor to Detroit, a forty-five-mile trip through some of the most blighted neighborhoods in the country. He locked his bike to a lamppost, explored the city, then returned to find his mode of transportation stolen. I grounded him for a month—mostly because he had lied about where he was going—but the first time I gave him the keys to my car, he drove right back to Detroit. Rather than ground him again, I accompanied him on his next excursion and showed him where he could park so my car wouldn't get stolen. I bought him a cell phone and urged him to call if he got into trouble. Then I took him on a two-week road trip around Mexico so I could teach him how to travel safely on the cheap.

Would I have done this for a daughter? I doubt it. I probably would have ended up passing along a version of the mothering passed on to me. Most of Noah's friends' parents were appalled at what I allowed him to do in high school. If he had been a girl, they would have turned me in to social services. As far as I can tell, my female students have been raised in a bizarrely confusing atmosphere in which they are obsessively sheltered and instilled with a vague but overwhelming sense of the terrors that might befall them if they don't check in with their parents every half hour on their cell phones, yet they are led to believe the world treats men and women equally. Their mothers refrain from sharing their horror stories because they still find those stories so embarrassing, or because they are afraid of giving their own parents cause to say "we told you so," even if those parents no longer are alive, or because they don't want to terrify their daughters out of boldly sallying forth and achieving all they might achieve. Often, the mothers no longer take risks themselves.

I am not saying any of this is easy. Raising a child is like acquiring a priceless vase, then being told you are supposed to leave it in the street unguarded. But the answer isn't to hover above your kids, terrifying them into leading timid, risk-free lives, nor to pretend the perils facing young women today aren't (still) more prevalent and insidious than those facing their young male counterparts.

We all know we should do whatever we can to make women's lives safer. In the meantime, we need to teach our daughters that the world does harbor dangers not even the fastest track star can outrun. If they end up the victim of an assault, we should make sure they get the counseling they need to get back out in the world without being crippled by fear. But what I really hope is we instill in them a pride no one instilled in me, a pride that they ventured out into the combat zone and accomplished what they wanted or needed to accomplish, without a gun.

HALLUCINATIONS

"DO YOU HEAR THEM singing?" my father asked.

I wished I could tell him yes.

"I can't make out the song, but it's something from before the war." Beneath his blanket, my father shrugged. "Must be some new gimmick—they send a group of fellas around to all the condos, singing from door to door."

Christmas had passed a few months earlier. My father lay dying in the hospital bed we had set up in my parents' den. This was Boca Raton, in southern Florida. It was ninety degrees outside. Not only were there no carolers going from door to door, all but one or two of the retired couples who lived in my parents' development were Jews. The hospice doctor said the cancer in my father's lungs was depriving his brain of oxygen. "He will hallucinate more and more. Then, toward the end, he will see people he knew and loved from long ago. That's how you'll know that he's nearly gone."

I turned up the dial on the oxygen machine, but my father's breathing came in ragged gasps. He would wheeze, then choke, at which my mother and I would try to argue him into letting us put a drop of morphine beneath his tongue. The nurses assured us the morphine would allow my father's diaphragm to relax and ease his breathing. But he refused to take the drug because the morphine might cloud his brain, the irony being that the lack of oxygen was leading him to hallucinate.

My father never had the slightest use for drugs, except for the Novocaine he injected to dull other people's pain. The only alcohol he ever drank was the finger of Manischewitz he poured in a juice glass to enjoy on a Friday night, smacking his lips and sighing at how sweet a man's life could be. Every year, his patients would show their appreciation by giving him fine liqueurs; the bottles stood gathering dust on the top shelf of our pantry, so every time I sneaked in to steal more than my daily allowance of Tootsie Rolls or licorice sticks (I was a dentist's daughter, after all), a tall, stiff porcelain soldier filled with something yellow and vile looked down in disapproval.

Once, my friend's older brother, Preston, went to my father to get his teeth cleaned. "Gee," my father said, "your teeth are kind of discolored. Do you smoke?" "Uh, not really," the young man said. "Except, you know, some pot." That anyone would so casually admit to smoking marijuana—which, to my dad, was a pharmaceutical of the same brain-destroying powers as LSD or heroin—blew my father's mind. He repeated the story for years without understanding why, of all the jokes he told, this one got the fewest laughs, especially from his kids.

My father was resolutely opposed to any substance that altered a person's ability to judge reality. His favorite advice was: "Use your head." If anyone got sentimental, he muttered: "Cut the bullshit." My mother and I are such creative dreamers we would happily spend the entire morning recounting our adventures of the night before, but my father could never recall a single dream. He wanted me to succeed as a writer, but he couldn't imagine a life in which a person sat around all day inventing stories. His greatest pride was in his ability to look into a patient's mouth and fix what needed fixing. A man couldn't afford to daydream while maneuvering a high-speed drill.

His only form of fantasy was the kind of deadpan "true story" that wasn't true. (You would be amazed how many people believed a patient showed up at his office one day with a billiard ball stuck behind his teeth and my father had no choice but to insert a cue stick you-know-where to poke it out.) After so many years listening to stand-up comics perform their shtick at his parents' Borscht Belt hotel, my dad had developed an encyclopedic repertoire of dirty jokes, which he combined with a disarmingly sweet delivery that provided an ironic contrast to the vulgar nature of what he said. (My father so resembled the comedian Red Buttons that people used to stop him on the street and ask for his autograph, which my father sometimes gave. Oddly, Red Buttons died just a few months after my dad, and we learned from his obit that he and my father had been born a few months apart, a coincidence my father would have loved, if only we could have told him.) You might assume this regular routine made him a caricature of the dentist who gets you in his chair, renders you immobile and mute, then regales you with tasteless jokes. But if you had asked my father who he was, he would have told you that he was a practical, straight-talking man who was good with his hands, treated everyone as his equal, and liked to make people laugh. Which assessment, I suspect, most people who knew him would agree was true.

Then, in his early sixties, his hands began to shake. It was only a familial tremor; it didn't threaten his health or impair his ability to do a good job once his hands were in someone's mouth. But the sight of those shaking hands made his patients so nervous he was forced to give up his practice. He and my mother retired to Florida, where he was able to enjoy a good twenty years kibitzing around the pool and playing in daily foursomes of tennis and bridge before he was diagnosed with bladder cancer. Slowly, he grew too weak to hit a tennis ball and too fuzzy-headed to play out a grand slam at bridge. He started to forget the punchlines to his jokes.

Then the middles began to go. He stopped accepting visits from his friends, not wanting them to return home without a laugh. Finally, he refused to speak to my siblings and me when we called on the phone.

I knew he was dying, but I wasn't prepared for the shock of flying down to Florida and discovering he had lost so much weight he couldn't keep up his pants. By then, the cancer had metastasized to his lungs, and the nurses set up an oxygen pump in the living room, with a very long tube connected to my father's nose. Hurrying to use the bathroom, he would undo his belt, which caused his pants to fall. He wore cotton socks, the floor was slippery, and since the oxygen tube kept tangling around his feet, it was only a matter of time before he tripped.

Not to mention he got up so often during the night to use the bathroom that my mother, who'd had two bypass operations and was debilitated by Parkinson's, was going downhill herself. Against my father's wishes, I set up a hospital bed in the den. Also against his wishes, I hired a nurse's aide to help us get through the nights. Until then—the youngest of three, a girl—I had been my father's pet. I listened to his stories about growing up at his family's hotel or serving in India during World War II. If I heard a good joke, I would call my dad and offer it as a gift; in return, he would tell me whatever new jokes were making the rounds in Boca.

But he was furious when I set up that hospital bed in the den. He accused me of kicking him out of his "marital bed" so I could sleep with my mother. He refused to believe he got up more than once or twice a night to use the bathroom. And he hated that we were wasting his money on a nurse's aide instead of keeping it to support my mother. He insisted the aide, a sweet Haitian woman named Michelle, was actually a man, and when she tried to help get him out of bed, he hit her. The wages we were paying Michelle preyed on my father's mind; he claimed he found a stack of hundred-dollar bills beside his bed, but when he tried to pick them up, the bills kept dissolving. "Why would anyone make money that dissolves?" he cried. "It doesn't make sense!"

That's when he heard the carolers. I explained about the lack of oxygen, but the hallucinations were driving him crazy. I always thought losing a parent meant you received a call in the night saying he was gone, after which you underwent a period of intense grief and missed him terribly. I lived in fear some misfortune would befall my son and I would be forced to watch him suffer. But it never occurred to me that I would watch my parents suffer.

In fact, my father suffered so badly that after a while it became impossible to believe he ever had told a joke. Only once, when the hospice doctor visited, did he rouse himself from his hallucinations and put on a final show. He did this, I suspect, because he feared if he didn't demonstrate the clarity of his mind, the doctor might force him to spend his final days at the hospice center. The doctor, who wasn't much younger than my dad, led him to the screened-in porch, helped him get comfortable on the lounge chair, then engaged him in a dueling-banjos contest in which the two men tried to top each other in telling dirty jokes in Yiddish while my mother and I marveled at my father's last performance, his voice clear and strong, not a single muffed word or mistimed line. It was as if a dying athlete had stepped back onto the court and wowed his fans with the powerful serve and forehand that had won him Wimbledon years before.

The performance convinced the doctor to allow my father to remain at home, but he continued to decline, lying in the den, listening to the carolers sing their songs, gasping for air, drifting in and out of sleep.

Until he resumed his dental practice. Eyes closed, arms lifted, he would move his fingers deftly, reaching for an instrument, inserting gauze in a patient's cheeks, murmuring instructions—*turn this way, open wider*—or if a procedure was going poorly, shaking his head and muttering. Some people gather so much momentum doing what they have always done they can't stop doing it even when they are dying. If you were to cut off that person's head, it would likely keep thinking the thoughts it used to think and coming up with what it used to say—which, in my father's case, meant telling dirty jokes and instructing his patients to floss more regularly. Most of the time this made him happy. Rather than seeing relatives from his past, he was seeing his former patients.

He grew agitated only when he couldn't make out the cavity he was trying to fill or see the crown he was installing. "Why aren't I wearing my glasses?" he would demand, and though his eyes were shut, I would slip his big plastic glasses on his nose, at which he would go back to work. When he would complain the light was bad—"More light! Give me more light!"—I would bend the lamp closer to his face, and he would mutter and nod his thanks, thinking, no doubt, I was one of his loyal assistants from the old days, Mrs. Decker or Mrs. Weyrauch, and he would cheerfully resume his work.

I was glad my father's brain was providing him with a dream that allowed him to spend his final days in peace. But dentistry? That was the best his brain could do? I never understood how anyone could be content to be a dentist. Granted, my father used his skills to relieve his patients' pain. ("A man walks into my office," he told me once, as if this were the prelude to a joke, "and all he can think about is the pain from his abscessed tooth. I lance the abscess and fix him up, and he walks out the door a new man.") But when it came time to choose my career, making sentences seemed more noble and artistic than fashioning a perfect crown, and I wanted a wider audience for my talents than the patients in a small-town practice, the irony being I hadn't achieved the happiness or success my father had achieved. No matter how many stories or books I published, the rejections made me fear I had chosen the wrong profession and would come to recognize on my deathbed that I had wasted my life in the service of a delusion.

Still, as I sat trying to pass the time while my father practiced dentistry in the air, watching over him in case he imagined himself engaged in a more dangerous hallucination (once, he thought he was being pushed from a moving car and reached out to grab the door, pulling the television down on his stick-thin legs), what else could I do but write? Worse, I was writing a comic novel—and the writing was going well. It was as if I were channeling the sense of humor from my father's head into my computer's hard drive.

My only excuse for this theft was that the novel was a tribute to my father. The main character had grown up in the Borscht Belt and was trying to make it as a comic; the working title of the book was *The Bible of Dirty Jokes*. As is true when any novel is going well, I was living in my characters' world rather than in the real one; someone watching me might have had the impression I was the one hallucinating.

My father held on longer than predicted, as if he had promised to work his way through the remaining patients in his appointment book before he retired again, for good. The only real crisis came when he decided he had been guilty of practicing dentistry without a license. "Abe," my mother said, "how could you ever think you've been drilling anyone's teeth without a drill?" But she couldn't dissuade him from believing the police would show up any minute and haul him to jail, where he would spend his final few days humiliated and disgraced.

Then he became convinced I had sold my novel. Not only that—*The Bible of Dirty Jokes* had garnered a huge advance. Two million dollars! Now I was set for life. When my mother tried to disabuse him of this new belief, I shushed her. Why rob my father of the joy this delusion brought? Besides, if I ever did sell my book (if not for two million dollars, then for a plausible advance that wouldn't dissolve in my hands the minute I tried to grasp it), my father would no longer be there to celebrate. Why shouldn't he go to his grave believing in a truth that eventually might come to pass?

Content in this reassuring new conviction, my father went back to work. And it occurred to me as I watched that it didn't really matter if you were deluded to pursue some calling. The trick was to engage in a line of work such that, when you were on your deathbed, your greatest peace would come from imagining you were doing what you had done before, all those days and weeks and years. My father's cry for more light was the funniest, most touching echo of Goethe's famous deathbed plea that any comic novelist could invent. And even though I have since learned that the etymology of "hallucinate" has nothing to do with *luce*, I can't help but think the tacky fifties lamp above his imaginary dental chair provided my father with just enough illumination to implant a perfect crown.

HOJO'S

THE SUMMER I TURNED sixteen, I secured a plum spot as a secretary at an insurance company. But that was a bookish, elitist sinecure, and I was desperate to join my friends who were waitressing at Howard Johnson's. Why would I have traded a job that allowed me to sit behind a desk taking accident reports on the phone for a backbreaking marathon that demanded I run around carrying a heavy tray and taking orders from customers who, unlike the lawyers at the insurance company, didn't know and didn't care that I was the top student at our local high school, a national debate champion, a girl who was headed for a better future than serving fried clams at HoJo's?

For one thing, I was determined to prove myself worthy of the respect of the girls I had considered my friends before they turned on me in seventh grade, bullying me, mocking me because I did too well on our exams and didn't get drunk on Boone's Farm or high on pot like everyone else, not that anyone invited me to the parties where the drinking and smoking happened. Everyone could see I was headed for an easier, more privileged life than they were, even if I envisioned my future as one in which I would be as friendless and unloved as I was that summer. I wanted to be hard and strong, even as I suspected I was soft and weak. Real life came in twenty-eight flavors, and I had sampled nothing but vanilla.

And so, the following summer, I applied to HoJo's. Did I lie and claim that I had experience? Even if I had told the truth, it wouldn't have mattered. The coming weekend marked the start of the tourist season in the Catskills, and the restaurant was seriously understaffed. The manager handed me a turquoise-and-white-checked polyester uniform, told me to buy white shoes, white stockings, and a hairnet, and ordered me to show up the following night to work.

When I informed the other girls I had been hired at HoJo's, they laughed and rolled their eyes. I wouldn't last my first shift, they predicted, let alone the next three months.

They had reason to doubt my fortitude. The summer we all turned twelve, I had decided I would spend a week at 4-H Camp with my friends Carol and Jane, even though I was terrified of insects and had never so much as camped out in a tent. I wanted to feel closer to nature, and closer to my two non-Jewish friends, who seemed far more at ease in the natural world than I was.

Unfortunately, the first task I was assigned was cleaning the latrines, which were not only filthy but grimed with the carcasses of flies and spider webs. Lunch consisted of a slab of ham and a carton of milk; I had been raised to eat only kosher food, and the sight of that rubbery pink meat revolted me, let alone the idea of washing it down with milk. That night in our lean-to, which seemed to be missing a wall, giant moths and daddy long-legs massed around the one bulb, which hung directly above my bunk. A bat flew in, and even the most seasoned campers screamed. I wriggled to the bottom of my sleeping bag, pulled in the pillow, and spent the night trying not to suffocate in the ninety-degree heat.

The next day, I begged the camp director to allow me to call my parents. When he said no, I threatened to climb to the top of my lean-to and jump off. He relented, but only if I agreed to stand in front of the other kids and admit I was too spoiled to make it through another day at the camp they loved. I accepted the dare, disgracing myself forever. By the time I got home, everyone in town seemed to know how pampered I was, how soft.

Of course, such qualities are often relative. I lived in a rural village of five thousand mostly poor and working-class inhabitants, where my family was considered rich because my father was a dentist and we lived in a modest 1950s ranch house. I had always loved racing the boys, playing football, and getting dirty. My brother teased me mercilessly and made sure I could take a punch.

It was more that everyone assumed a girl who did well at school could not succeed at "real life." And real life was what I yearned for. My friends' existences struck me as more adventurous than my own, their families warmer, more generous, more authentic. I thought working at Howard Johnson's would prove I was willing to suffer and sweat the way my friends did. I craved what I called "experience," although "experience" doing what besides serving fried clams and ice cream I couldn't yet articulate.

We had known each other since kindergarten, if not before. Melissa, Cindy, and Betty Ann (I've changed everyone's names) lived within shouting distance of each other; Lisa lived a few streets over. I lived on the opposite side of town, but my father and Cindy's father had been friends their entire lives, and Cindy and I spent every night in seventh grade talking on the phone, reviewing the minutiae of our slights and triumphs.

Cindy was as thin as a sparrow, with a narrow face and features framed by the layered haircut we all wore in the seventies. She had a giddy, girlish laugh and a kind, sweet smile. If I sound wistful toward someone who sometimes bullied me—once, she and the other girls invited me to a nonexistent party in Cindy's backyard, then hid behind the bushes so they could watch my disappointment when I found no other guests—it is because even when the other girls were at their meanest, Cindy would invite me over so we could sit on her roof, oil ourselves with baby oil, and use our giant reflectors to blast our faces while we gossiped and discussed our crushes. After we had fried ourselves in the sun, we crawled back inside and raided her mother's cupboards for peanut butter, Frosted Flakes, cocoa, oatmeal, and honey we could mix in a bowl and gorge on. When Cindy's baby sister, Jill, was brought home from the hospital, we sneaked in and tickled her tiny baby-feet until she squealed.

Lisa, whom everyone loved, was only four foot eleven, with an adorably round face and cheeks you couldn't help but pinch. She always seemed to be quivering with excitement; a photo in my yearbook shows her tilting backward in a chair, an assignment book pressed to her mouth as if to hold in a laugh that threatens to erupt with such force her legs will push back from the desk and send her cartwheeling beyond the page. She had a beautiful singing voice and could play the piano and compose; when our music teacher, Mr. Bynum, chided her for not practicing her piece for the state competition and asked what the Chrissake she had been doing all month, Lisa piped up that she had never liked the piece and had spent her time composing a jazzy ragtime number called "On the Rag Rag."

"Get it?" Lisa giggled. "That's what women called it in the twenties when they had their period."

Melissa was the most serious of the four, olive skinned, with short dark hair and piercing eyes she could train on a victim like a death-ray. She was the one who told the rest of us what to do, pronounced judgments on our clothes and hair, informed me that I would never learn to dance because I had no soul. Once, on a field trip, I fell asleep on the bus and woke with my head in the lap of whomever I was sitting next to. "You really want to be loved, don't you," Melissa uttered solemnly. If she had said this with a smile, I wouldn't have minded. But I knew she had happened upon a weapon she might turn against me.

And then there was Betty Ann. A stunning redhead, willowy, tall, with creamy skin, green eyes, and a watchful expression, Betty Ann was almost as abused as I was. I hate to complicate my narrative by admitting this, but sometimes, if I found myself an inch higher on the social ladder, I turned on Betty Ann and tried to nudge her down.

If Melissa hadn't been there, the rest of us might have gotten along. One night, Cindy, Betty Ann, and I slept over in Lisa's basement. Cindy rolled around on the floor, hugging her pillow and moaning the name of the boy she had a crush on while Betty Ann and I lolled on our mattresses, eyes closed, listening to Elton John croon "Come Down in Time." Suddenly, Lisa jumped up on her bed and started bouncing. Then she sprang off, landing on one of the mattresses on the floor, then bounded to the other, then back to the bed, wearing nothing but her Rolling Stones T-shirt. The rest of us did everything Lisa did, leaping and bouncing until our hair clung damply to our necks and our nightgowns molded to our bodies with sweat. Cindy crumpled to the bed, I fell on top of her, and Betty Ann landed on top of me. Lisa collapsed beside the four of us and we lay there, panting and blank and cleansed of our desire.

So yes, I wanted to work with the other girls. I wanted to achieve the closeness I had felt dancing in Lisa's basement. I didn't want my friends to think of me as privileged or effete. Cindy, Lisa, Melissa, and Betty Ann had worked at Howard

Johnson's the summer before, along with the older women who waitressed there year-round and the Black and Hispanic men who sweated in the kitchen, cooking and washing dishes. And so, late on a Thursday at the very end of May, I joined them.

At first, I followed a more experienced waitress around the dining room, observing her as she took her customers' orders, handed those orders to the cook, then prepared her diners' beverages, brought them their rolls and butter pats, fetched their appetizers, soups, and salads, fetched their entrees, then checked back to make sure everything was to the customers' liking, until it was time to ask what they wanted for dessert and prepare their sundaes, cones, and banana splits. Then there was all the side work—the cleaning, prepping, and restocking of condiments the waitresses were required to perform when they weren't crazy-busy taking orders.

I might have been all right if I had been given a table or two to practice on. But when I returned that Friday night, the manager said the waitress who trained me quit and I would need to take over her entire station.

"Just do the best you can," he said, which, given that I would be facing Memorial Day Weekend in the Catskills, meant he hoped I would get some amount of food on some percentage of my tables without injuring or killing anyone and I would survive that one shift before I ran out screaming.

I did survive, although I have no memory of how I did. I understood the *theory* of taking orders. What I lacked was the *experience* of how to balance four mains and four sides on a single tray, then remove each dish without causing the remainder to become unbalanced; how to consolidate my errands so I wouldn't keep retracing my steps; how to sweet-talk the cooks into filling an order out of turn because I had

201

forgotten to submit it when the family of six came in; how to draw beer from a tap so the head wouldn't become too foamy; how to stack my dirty dishes, cups, glasses, and utensils so everything would fit inside my bus box before I hefted it to the dish room; how not to collide with the other waitresses as we tangoed around each other in our fat white shoes.

The real killer came when a family ordered not only food but ice cream, which we waitresses were required to prepare ourselves. A complex specialty like a Fudgana or Tasty Tester took precious minutes to assemble; it also took skill. When a customer ordered an ice cream soda, you needed to serve it with a scoop of ice cream balanced across the top of the glass, which required that you first flatten the bottom of the scoop against the side of the freezer in such a way that it would hold its weight until you had ferried the whole concoction to your customer. If, when you set the soda on the table, the ice cream plopped inside the glass, the soda would overflow and the manager would shout: "I'm going to fire you!"

And yet, in the middle of that hellish night, I realized I was tougher than I had imagined. Who would have thought there was pleasure to be found in enduring the tasks impossible to keep up with, the pain in your lower back, the burns on your hands and wrists from brushing against scalding surfaces. And yes, there was satisfaction to be found in showing up the next day, and the day after that, to take on even more abuse and pain.

At the insurance company, everyone had treated me with respect. Here, I was one of "the girls," all of us equally disrespected. The manager didn't care if we lost our footing on a kitchen floor made slick by the coffee leaking from the urns. The break room was in the basement, down a tightly curved metal stair; when one of the waitresses slipped and cracked her head, the manager ordered her to return to her station anyway.

Not that we had time for breaks. By the middle of a shift, we would be so ravenous we would cram a customer's uneaten French fries in our mouths as we carried the bus box to the kitchen. (We wouldn't touch the fried clams—we saw what those looked like, the raw pink strings, before the cook dumped them in the fryer.) I remember how much I used to love a Howard Johnson's milkshake . . . until I was taught to take the powder from a giant bag, dump it in the machine, add a few gallons of lukewarm water, and beat out the lumps with a mammoth whisk. I remember one of the older waitresses whispering that even though the law forbade returning an uneaten dinner roll to the bin behind the counter, that was exactly what the manager required us to do. I remember rushing into the walk-in freezer to find twelve salads that weren't wilted and brown, then rushing out with the least offensive dozen, only to have the hairnet snatched from my head by a wire shelf, a violation so extreme I felt I was being scalped, which caused me to scream and toss the salads in the air, and then, to avoid being yelled at, quickly scoop up the lettuce leaves, mound them in their bowls, and hurry out. Most of all, I remember how exhausted I felt at the end of each shift, when there were still floors to be mopped, condiments to be refilled, tubs of ice cream to be replaced, counters to be swabbed and dried, and how the older waitresses helped me, even though their bodies must have ached far more than mine.

No one believed I would last longer than a week. But the fact that I was even trying granted me a greater share of camaraderie than I could have hoped for. Weren't we all forced to wear the same hideous checked uniforms, which made even a girl as beautiful as Betty Ann as sexy as a linoleum floor? (One afternoon, I found the courage to ask the manager whether business wouldn't be better if he allowed us to wear more attractive uniforms. Oh no, he said. Wives refused to allow their husbands to pull over at a restaurant where the waitresses might be too good-looking.) Didn't I offer to fill in for whoever couldn't work her shift? Didn't I have my own stories of abuse to share when the other girls shared theirs—like the time an important judge promised a "big reward" if I found seats for his party of twelve and "took good care of them," and after I had run myself ragged seeing to their every whim, made a dramatic show of shaking my hand and pressing a quarter in my palm?

Once, I was trying to pack a scoop of vanilla against the wall of the freezer so I could set it across the glass of strawberry soda I already had pumped when I saw my number flash above the window to the kitchen, announcing my order of fried clams was ready to be picked up. Should I set the ice cream across the glass, even though it was too soft and might fall in, or should I run and pick up my order before the clams grew so greasy and cold my customers might complain? I inhaled the sour odor of baked beans and stroganoff from the bus box I hadn't had time to empty. Out of the corner of my eye, I saw a family of five settle on the vinyl stools at the far end of the fountain, which was my responsibility to attend to. I held the metal scoop above the glass and squeezed the lever. The ice cream hovered, then sank, pink foam oozing across the counter.

Lisa brushed past and unloaded three California Burger Platters from her tray. Her uniform—three sizes too large—sagged around her ankles. Her hairnet drooped. Her glasses had slipped to the tip of her nose, which caused her to appear cross-eyed. "Get your buggers!" she singsonged to the three men who had ordered them. "I mean, get these *burrrrrgers* while they're hot!"

"Lisa!" I begged. "I'm going down."

She surveyed the overflowing soda and unemptied bus box. Then she put down her tray, hooked her arm in mine, and as Cindy hobbled past to refill four pitchers of coffee, grabbed her by her free arm and pulled her in. "And a one, and a two, and a three," Lisa shouted, leading us in a cheer: "We are HoJo's girls. We couldn't be any prouder. And if you can't hear us, we'll yell a little louder. WE ARE HOJO'S GIRLS! WE COULDN'T BE ANY PROUDER! AND IF YOU CAN'T HEAR US . . ."

The three of us shouted the cheer a few more times. Then Lisa announced we would now perform a little number she'd just made up. "It's called 'Travellin' HoJo Girl,'" she said, then started to sing in her high, clear voice: "I was born in a bowl of New England clam chowder, raised for ten years in a turkey pot pie. . . ." I was almost too shy to join in—my voice is terrible—but then I did. Even now, in my sixties, I remember how the fried clams glistened beneath the warming light, how the white lump of ice cream sat dissolving in its glass, and how, when Lisa, Cindy, and I finished singing "Travellin' HoJo Girl," every customer in the dining room applauded.

Waitressing brought out a side of me I hadn't known existed. Despite my shyness, I enjoyed kibitzing with the guests, and despite the uniform, I found myself flirting with the waiters and busboys who came in for dessert after their own shifts at the hotels were finished. After the restaurant closed for the night, my friends and I would carefully descend the spiral staircase to the break room, where we plucked our hairnets from our heads and tried to freshen up, excavating our tips from our pockets and counting the bills, which were sticky with chocolate syrup. I had never been one to drink alcohol, but I couldn't imagine going home and trying to sleep while still reciting that litany in my head—*a booster seat for table eleven, more butter for twelve, a clean soup spoon for three*—and so I would wander next door to the Triangle Lounge to wind down with a glass of wine (at seventeen, we lacked a year to drink legally, but no waitress would deny another girl her relaxant). Sitting there at the bar, I found what I had been longing for—the bone-deep satisfaction that comes from a long night of physical labor, the belonging that derives from a shared sense of being abused by your customers and your manager.

I might have defied everyone's expectations, including my own, if not for an accident that took place about a month after I started work. The restaurant had closed for the night, and all I needed to do was sponge down the equipment. I was running a soapy cloth along the back side of the shake machine when I sliced my hand on a metal vent. I tried blotting the cut with a stack of napkins. But blood kept dripping into the vats of ice cream.

"Honey," said one of the older waitresses, "you'd better go tell the manager you need to leave. Then drive yourself to the emergency room and get yourself stitched up."

Faint-headed, I realized she was right, and I wobbled to the office to ask if I could go. But the manager barely looked up to inspect my cut before he said I needed to finish cleaning.

Dutifully, I went back to work, but no matter how many napkins I pressed to the wound, it wouldn't stop bleeding.

"Sweetheart," the older waitress said, "just tell that bastard you quit and go."

I stuck my head in the office door and did what she'd suggested. Then I drove myself to the hospital, where an intern stitched up my hand. By the time I got home, it was four in the morning and my father was furious. Didn't I see? This was why he and my mother hadn't wanted me to give up my nice, safe job at the insurance company. This was the sort of danger they had been trying to protect me from all these years.

I might have returned to the restaurant and begged the manager to take me back—given how short-staffed he was, he would have grunted and said okay. But I never got the chance. While I was waiting for my hand to heal, the HoJo's caught fire—it wasn't completely gutted, but no one was going to be working there anytime soon. Instead, I begged the lawyers at the insurance company to give me back my old job for the remainder of the summer. A few days later, as I sat typing with my one uninjured hand, two police officers showed up at the door and, with everyone listening, demanded I tell them where I had been the night the HoJo's was set on fire.

Set on fire? I echoed.

Yes, they said. The fire had been intentionally set, and as a "disgruntled employee," I was by far the most likely suspect.

"Really?" I said, bizarrely proud that I was the chief suspect in a crime for which, if I actually had committed it, my friends would have regarded me as a hero.

Sadly, the arsonist turned out to be the manager. From what I heard, he had been skimming cash from the daily profits and set fire to the restaurant to cover the shortfall, not realizing the safe would be the only part of the restaurant to survive the flames.

At some point, the Howard Johnson's did reopen. Whoever bought the property turned it into an Italian bistro where, decades later, my family gathered for my father's funeral. (By then, the motel attached to the restaurant had grown so squalid that my nephew was reluctant to leave our car, let alone spend the night there.) The bistro's menu was far more upscale than the menu at HoJo's had been, but I couldn't help noting that the layout remained the same. Here was where the manager kept the bin to which we returned the uneaten dinner rolls. Here was the tap where I had learned to draw beer without creating too much foam. And there was the spot behind the fountain where Lisa grabbed Cindy and me before all of us started singing.

And that was where Cindy had been standing the afternoon a member of her family came to report the news that her father had died of some terrible cancer none of us knew was killing him. Looking back, I wish the crime I was guilty of committing had been burning down that restaurant. But my actual crime was worse. After her father's funeral, I followed Cindy home and, like some emotional vampire, spent the night sleeping on her bedroom floor. What could I have been thinking? It was as if my hunger for experience only could be sated by drawing close to her family's grief. Did Cindy understand what I was doing? Was that why, after we left for college, she and I barely remained in touch? By the time she died—in her early forties, from the same cancer that killed her father, leaving four motherless sons behind—I didn't bother to attend her funeral.

And Lisa? She had plenty of her own experiences. Freshman year at Cornell she suffered a schizoaffective break and has been in and out of hospitals and halfway houses ever since. At the start, I tried to call or visit her whenever I could. But entire decades have passed when I couldn't summon enough courage or love to even talk to her on the phone.

And Betty Ann? Judging by her online profile, she remains as strikingly beautiful as ever. (Once, when we were young, she answered a request to deliver room service to the motel behind the restaurant and found the customer to be Dustin Hoffman, who was filming a movie nearby and apparently made a pass at her.) She married a former priest and seems to have created a family and a life anyone would be proud of.

I don't want to mention Melissa, except to say that when I saw her at our last high school reunion, she made a remark about my father so cruel that I nearly punched her.

And me? Did I ever get to experience the "real life" I was yearning to experience? Well, I have suffered my share of setbacks. No matter who you are, you are going to sample most of the flavors life eventually dishes out—the ones you like and the ones you don't. But I also have been privileged to enjoy the excitement and drama everyone knew I was going to experience. Everyone, that was, but me.

So maybe it isn't strange that I feel nostalgic for a place where I served lousy fried clams and lumpy, lukewarm milkshakes to my customers, where I slipped on a greasy, wet floor while carrying a loaded bus box, where I sneaked cigarette breaks with my friends who weren't really my friends, even though I loved them, and for all I know, they loved me.

As I sat in that Italian restaurant with my family—missing my father, whom we had just left at the cemetery in a plot beside Cindy's father's—the young, attractively dressed waitress recited the specials of the day.

"I used to work here," I interrupted. "When this place was a Howard Johnson's."

"Really?" she said, with a flicker of curiosity. But then, under the gaze of her imperious boss, she hurried to the kitchen to put in our order.

ONE A DAY

1. SWEETS

MY FATHER WAS A dentist, so I was allowed only one sweet a day. The reasons for this restriction were not mysterious. The water in our town wasn't fluoridated. When my father tried to convince his fellow citizens they should add this chemical to the well, they accused him of fomenting a Commie Jew plot to poison them. (Why else would a dentist want his neighbors' teeth to be so healthy they wouldn't need his services?) Every morning, I was required to take a tiny pink pill to make up for our lack of fluoride. But I still developed a mouth full of cavities. Visiting my father's office had its rewards. I was allowed my pick of the magic tricks in his closet. I got to play with the leftover globs of mercury. But I hated the whine of the drill, the nauseating jolt when it hit a nerve.

So I understood why I wasn't allowed to consume too much candy. The rule applied to my parents, too. They didn't believe in bragging, but they were inordinately proud of their self-control. I never heard my parents disparage another family for their religion, race, or nationality. But they couldn't conceal their disdain for anyone who permitted their children to fall asleep with a juice bottle in their mouths or consume huge quantities of sugary soda, sticky candies, cookies, cake, or ice cream.

My parents grew up during the Great Depression. Having clawed their way out of poverty and, in my father's case, returned safely from World War II, they couldn't comprehend how drinkers, gamblers, adulterers, or profligate spenders could risk destroying the stability that allowed them to enjoy a clean, comfortable house and a healthy family. As a child, I couldn't understand why anyone would do that either.

I remember my parents throwing parties only twice. With an elaborate flourish, my father would pour an ounce of whiskey in a jigger. ("Jigger," he kept repeating, delighted by the ridiculousness of the word.) In would go the ice and the whiskey sour mix. He made a comic show of jumping up and down to shake the shaker, then pouring the frothy cocktail in the glass. He popped in a maraschino cherry, and I was allowed to take a sip. My parents couldn't imagine any child of theirs developing a taste for alcohol. But those whiskey sours were so delicious! After the party, I went around fingering the cherries from the bottom of everyone's glasses and swallowing them on the sly.

Other than his weekly tipple of Manischewitz and those few whiskey sours, my father never drank. Yet, Christmas after Christmas, his patients brought him bottles of expensive scotch, wine, champagne, and fine liqueurs. These stood on the top shelf of our pantry, guarded by a ceramic soldier who held a urinous fluid called Galliano. In the thirty-five years we lived in that house, I never saw my father tap into anything except the whiskey for those whiskey sours and a flask of sweet Danish liqueur called cherry heering. (Given my family's proclivity for pickled fish, I thought the drink was called cherry herring , which is why I never sneaked sips, the way I sneaked sips of the Manischewitz.)

Apparently, in her more hedonistic days, my mother had smoked a cigarette. She still put out a fancy lighter and an ashtray for guests. But I don't recall the lighter containing fluid or the ashtrays being dirtied by a single ash. My father owned a pipe. I remember him teaching me to clip the tip from a cigar. But he had spent too many hours staring into the dirty, diseased mouths of smokers to take up that habit.

When I was in high school, my parents were aware some of my contemporaries used marijuana. That nearly every kid I knew was smoking dope, that some were shooting heroin or taking trips on LSD, while I took maybe two puffs on a joint my entire time in high school, earned me no credit from my parents. They simply assumed no child of theirs would be so irresponsible as to get hooked on drugs.

Don't get me wrong. There are worse child-rearing strategies than modeling self-control. The problem was, everything my parents taught me was a lie. They didn't *want* to do the things they refrained from doing. They hated the sensation of being drunk. Inhaling cigarette smoke made them ill. They weren't the type to shoot up heroin. But they suffered as much as anyone in trying to restrain their intake of sugar, fat, and calories.

In the pantry, beneath those unopened bottles of liquor, my mother maintained a constant supply of Tootsie Rolls, Twizzlers, Hershey's bars, and caramels. Usually, there was a big bag of marshmallows, which I would jam in my mouth two or three at a time, choking on the gluey glob; if no one was in the kitchen, I would jab a marshmallow on a fork and set it on fire at the stove.

My mother loved candy apples. We bought them in Atlantic City, or she made them at home by pouring molten red Karo syrup over each tart Macintosh arrayed on a sheet of waxed paper, a stick jammed through the navel in each.

In the cookie drawer, she stocked bags of Oreos (which my brother consumed in towering stacks when he got home from school), Chips Ahoy (which my father loved), and crumbly vanilla cookies called Lady Joans (the cookies were delicious, but the name irked me because my sister's name was Joan and I was always being chided to act more like a lady, like her).

In the baking drawer, my mother kept mixes for Bundt cakes, brownies, and Boston cream pies (my favorite). Before I was born, she made birthday cakes in the shapes of animals. I would stare longingly at the recipe book that described how to use toothpicks, coconut flakes, jellybeans, licorice sticks, and M&Ms to fashion lambs, butterflies, bunnies, and cocker spaniels, wishing she hadn't gotten tired of baking such masterpieces before I came along. Dejected, I consoled myself with the stale silver beads, sprinkles, and red-hot candies left over from those earlier projects.

Even in her less ambitious days, my mother baked us rich, moist, sour-cream coffee cakes, Toll House cookies from the recipe on the bag, and butter cookies, the dough for which she would pack into a metal cookie-press, changing the disc so she could crank out an amazing array of shapes. Once, I dashed into the kitchen between batches, grabbed a fistful of butter-cookie dough, then ran upstairs and sat in my own private heaven, nibbling that baseball-size gob of buttery, sugary dough for the remainder of the afternoon. To this day, eating that fistful of dough remains the epitome of culinary bliss in my life.

Perhaps bliss of any kind.

After her first coronary bypass, my mother ruthlessly avoided every milligram of cholesterol. But none of this stopped her from enjoying a fat-free slice of angel food cake, a box of bright pink Peeps, or an entire pan of Rice Krispie crunchies.

In the upstairs freezer, she kept the Cool Whip she used to make Jell-O molds (the Cool Whip tasted like machine oil, but I sneaked spoonfuls when she wasn't looking), as well as cubes of Hawaiian Punch (my mother considered the juice to be fruit, so the punch-sicles were exempt from the one-treat-a-day rule).

In the basement freezer, I could always find ice cream sandwiches, Popsicles, Creamsicles, and Eskimo Pies. By the garage door, the seltzer man left us beautiful beveled bottles of cherry and cream soda, which we drank with dinner because the laws of *kashruth* prohibited us from drinking milk with meat.

In the attic, where my grandmother lived, she kept a ceramic dish of chocolate kisses. I felt guilty sneaking those kisses, but my grandmother loved me so much, she would have given me the entire bag if I had asked. She had the sweetest tooth of anyone in the house. When I was six, she taught me to drink coffee with cream and three or four spoonfuls of sugar. (These days I leave out the cream, but I still heap in all that sugar.)

In the summer, when the Good Humor truck came tinkling around the block, my parents would give me money to buy a chocolate éclair, a chocolate-covered cone, or that crunch-coated vanilla bar that hid a solid chocolate core. From a very young age, I was allowed to walk down the hill to the Dairy Queen, where, for a dime, you could get a vanilla cone, and for another five cents, ask that it be dipped in a bath of molten chocolate. On special occasions, my father drove us to Howard Johnson's for a dish of pistachio or butter pecan, a milkshake, or an ice cream soda. (I lost my taste for those treats only later, when I worked at HoJo's.)

Our town used to be famous for its Jewish resorts, and we had a bakery so good that vacationers would load up on pastries to take back to Manhattan. Whenever we went downtown, my friends and I would stop at Katz's for a chocolate éclair, an almond horn, or a chocolate-covered cream-filled pastry called a Liberty Bell (the name of our town was Liberty).

In the summer, I would visit the concession stand at my grandparents' hotel for a frozen chocolate-covered marshmallow bar and a bottle of Orange Crush. The hotel employed a baker whose job was to turn out trays of those colorful European cookies that taste of almonds and jam, as well as seven-layer cakes, Napoleons, cream puffs, rugelach, and who can remember what else.

On Halloween, hundreds of families would truck their children to our street, figuring the Jews who lived there would hand out the most expensive candy. So even though my father's career revolved around the scientifically proven fact that candy rotted teeth, we were responsible for pumping sugar into a very high percentage of the kids in our town. Afraid of running out, my mother would buy even more candy than she needed, not to mention that my siblings and I would go around the block trick-or-treating; we were finishing off all that candy well into the new year.

From September through June, my mother packed my lunch with a Devil Dog or a Yodel. The high point of any day was nibbling off the hard chocolate shell that coated the Yodel, unrolling the cakey roll, licking off the icing, then eating the roll itself.

At three p.m., my friends and I would stop at the gas station across from our elementary school to grab a snack on our way to Hebrew school. For reasons I no longer comprehend, I picked those vile novelties that contained colored sugar-water in waxy straws, fake cigarettes, and candy dots you bit off a backing of white paper, getting as much paper in your mouth as candy.

I also bought Bonomo's Turkish Taffy, which would have caused my father to blow his top because so many of his patients chipped their teeth biting into those plasticized bars. The trick was to smack the taffy against a sidewalk or a desk, shattering it into fragments. Hadn't the grownups listened to the commercial?

> *Give it a smack! Bonomo!*
> *Give it a crack! Bonomo!*
> *Lift off the flap! Strip off the wrap!*
> *We're gonna taste Turkish taffy—hey, it's delish!*
> *We're gonna taste Turkish taffy—answers every wish . . .*

I doubt my parents snacked much during the day. But in the evenings, they had as difficult a time sticking to their rule as I did. Why else would my mother have kept us supplied with all those treats? I couldn't have been the only one making those boxes and bags of sugary snacks disappear.

My parents both had terrible teeth. My father had grown up at his parents' hotel, where he had unlimited access to the same cookies and cakes that later tempted me. By the time he became a dentist, the damage to his teeth was already done.

My mother inherited her sweet tooth from her mother. Her father died when she was in her teens; she sank into a deep depression and her weight shot up precipitously. She thought no one would ever marry her. (Luckily, my father liked his women zaftig.) The only reason my mother slimmed down was that she loved being married to my father. Also, she suffered from an undiagnosed gall bladder ailment that made her sick if she ate anything fatty. Heart disease ran in her family: her father and eldest brother both dropped dead of heart attacks; her two middle brothers and elder sister barely survived their own coronary woes.

After my mother underwent the first of her two quadruple bypasses, she summoned her self-control and avoided every molecule of cholesterol. She lived in terror of regaining the weight that had ruined her youth or dying of the heart disease that had felled her family.

Unlike other members of their generation, my parents knew how unhealthy sugar and fat could be. Yet, having survived their own impoverished childhoods and a war in which sugar and fat were rationed, how could they fail to find the plentitude of the 1950s and '60s to be irresistible? They prohibited us kids from consuming what tempted them. What shamed them. What frightened them. What threatened their self-control. But in those days, parents didn't admit their weaknesses to their kids. They simply laid down the law.

Sadly, telling someone she mustn't have something, then surrounding her with that forbidden substance, is an effective way to drive her nuts. As soon as I hit seventh grade and began to put on a few pounds, I was subject to remorseless scrutiny and humiliation. Because I felt so watched, I became conscious of every morsel I put in my mouth. I took to weighing myself two or three times a day. I bought one of those booklets that lists the calories in every food, then devoted ninety percent of my brainpower to figuring out how many pounds I might gain or lose by consuming what I was consuming.

When none of that worked, I invented what I thought was a unique method of maintaining a normal weight. If there is anything I remain ashamed of, it's all those years I spent bingeing and throwing up. Of course, I now understand the reasons I developed an eating disorder—the mixed messages about food I received from my parents; the unrelenting bombardment by images of sexy, thin women; the ostracism by my classmates, who made me feel lonely and odd because I loved reading books and studying science; the scorn heaped on any girl who enjoyed hitting a ball, running a race, jumping a hurdle, or even jogging. Most pernicious of all, no one talked to me about what might constitute a satisfying life, other than getting married and having a child who wasn't allowed to consume too much candy or cake or fall asleep with a juice bottle in her mouth.

Not until graduate school did I cure myself of my bulimia. I didn't do this by exerting some magical form of self-control. I simply developed more satisfying ways of spending my time than eating. Instead of taking in sugars and fats, I gorged on novels, essays, stories, ideas, and poems. I saw a therapist. I made new and better friends. I purged myself of anxiety and rage by writing. I played tennis. I practiced the piano. No one put limits on what I ate. No one watched. No one tried to shame me. I stopped eating so much because everything else in my life became so much more pleasurable and fulfilling.

That, and I started to have great sex.

2. SEX

I am sure all sorts of biological, social, and environmental factors contribute to eating disorders. But I am equally sure people who have found a satisfying way to earn a living and who enjoy regular sex with people they love are more likely to resist addictive behaviors than people who hate their jobs and spend their evenings and weekends alone.

In my mid-twenties, I met a kind, brilliant, handsome man. We fell in love. We had sex. In fact, we had far better sex than I'd ever had with anyone. On our honeymoon, we had sex in a Finnish sauna. In a cramped bunk in a ship moored in a Stockholm harbor. In a cheap boardinghouse in Copenhagen after a night searching for an X-rated movie, because we had heard that Danish porn was the sexiest in the world. We went skinny-dipping in a stunningly blue pond amid the glaciers high in the Norwegian fjords, then hiked to the hut where we would be spending the night and had sex before the other hikers got there.

After our honeymoon, we had sex in our marital bed in Cambridge. We had sex in a ski chalet north of Montreal, where we got snowed in for three days. In southern Spain, after imbibing too much sangria and sneaking into the local bullfighting ring to see a flamenco competition, we had sex and conceived our son.

After that, my husband's career as a research scientist took over his life, our marriage fell apart, and we pretty much stopped having sex. But I loved kissing and hugging my son and rolling around with him on the floor so much that I hardly minded. Besides, I was too busy teaching, writing, cleaning the house, doing the laundry, shopping, and cooking to find time to eat. I lost so much weight my mother kept telling me I was too thin and urging me to eat.

Even after I left my husband, I managed to have great sex. Not sex with a lot of men, but a lot of great sex with the few men I loved. I think the reason I am not screwed up about sex the way I am screwed up about eating is that my parents didn't send conflicting messages about sex the way they did about food. Having grown up hanging around with the comedians at his parents' hotel, my father constantly told dirty jokes, even with his daughter present. Where I grew up, sex wasn't shameful or sinful; it was funny. Sex was sexy. Sex was human. Sex was one of the reasons that life, with all its *tsuris*, was still worth living.

My mother often told my sister and me about her own sister advising her before her wedding night to "just close her eyes and get through it." But my mother didn't think that sounded right, so she went to the library and found a book that offered better advice as to how a woman could enjoy sexual relations with her husband. As a result, I never felt I was being told to abstain from a pleasure everyone else was indulging in on the sly. I didn't feel watched. I didn't feel shamed. I wasn't constantly being told not to want—or even think about wanting—something I wasn't supposed to have.

3. SOLITAIRE

Not long ago, I got dumped by someone I truly loved. I moved from the Midwest to Manhattan and suffered a series of terrifyingly bad online dates. I retired from teaching. I still had my writing to keep me occupied. I made new friends with whom to play tennis or go out to eat. But I found myself with far too much time on my hands. I began to grow afraid of getting old. Of never again having sex. So I shouldn't have been surprised my obsession with food crept back.

Here I was in a city whose restaurants serve the best food to be found anywhere in the world. American food. Chinese food. French food. Italian food. Thai food. Malaysian, Ethiopian, Middle Eastern, Korean, and Japanese food. To get from the subway to my apartment, I have to pass a pizza place that serves, if not the best pizza in Manhattan, then a pretty good runner-up. If I dodge the pizza place, I need to hurry past a joint called Koko Wings, whose specialty is double-fried soy-garlic chicken strips that call to me like the Sirens singing to Odysseus.

Instead of shopping for ingredients and cooking dinner, I simply point to my selections amid the rows of delicious prepared foods at the West Side Market. Or Fairway. Or Citarella. Or Eataly. Or I stop at one of the taco trucks that dot my neighborhood. I struggle not to order a fruit tart from the Silver Moon Bakery. Or a chocolate bapka from Zabar's. Or a slice of strudel from the Hungarian Pastry Shop. Or a thick wedge of caramel pecan cheesecake from Café Lalo. Or a cupcake, cronut, muffin, or chocolate truffle from any of the boutique vendors on every block.

At sixty, I am too healthy and sane to binge and purge. And so, to keep from eating, I watch episode after episode of my favorite TV series. At first, I needed to make up for having been too busy with my career to watch *Breaking Bad*, *The West Wing*, or *Arrested Development*. Given that I was now living in Manhattan, I needed to re-watch every episode of *Seinfeld*, *Sex in the City*, *Saturday Night Live*, and *30 Rock*. Then I moved on to *Orange Is the New Black*, *VEEP*, *Transparent*, *Inside Amy Schumer*, *Unbreakable Kimmy Schmidt*, *The Great British Baking Show*, *Project Runway*, and purely for sociological reasons, *The Bachelorette*.

I even started watching porn. I am not *addicted* to porn. But that is only because most porn is so misogynist. That, and my computer crashes no matter which site I try. Still, I have come to understand why so many men—and for all I know, women—spend so many hours watching porn. It's right there on the computer you are trying to use for work.

I find it impossible to stay off my laptop. Whenever I get stuck writing—which is every few minutes—I check my email. Then my Facebook account. Then my Twitter feed. I watch movies on Netflix. I watch *Modern Family* and *Black-ish* on Hulu by using a password I stole from my cousin's husband. I use that same password to watch tennis on ESPN and Chris Hayes and Rachel Maddow on MSNBC.

I am so addicted to computer solitaire, I can't start writing in the morning unless I have won a hand. Or another hand. Or another. I play solitaire on my iPhone while I am watching Netflix or Hulu on my laptop. I force myself to go for a walk in the park, only to find myself sitting on a bench to check my email, then my Facebook account, then my Twitter feed. Then, as long as I have my phone out, I play another round of solitaire.

Not long ago, I gave in to the urge to click on one of the ads for a game called Panda Pop that kept appearing on my phone between hands of solitaire. I vowed I would play only the free sample. Then I downloaded the app. Now I am far more addicted to Panda Pop than I ever was to solitaire. How can I let those poor baby pandas suffer at the hands of the evil baboon? How can I watch the panda mother cry if I don't save all her babies?

Solitaire is a meditative game. I can calm myself, even think, while I play it. Panda Pop is far more frustrating and rewarding. If I fail to save all the babies, I feel terrible; if I pop a cascade of bubbles and the babies come parachuting down and the panda mamma claps and smiles, I am flooded with an adrenaline high. Even when I am not playing, I see bubbles ricocheting around the margins of the book I am reading or the screen of the computer on which I am typing. It's all I can do to finish this paragraph before giving in to the urge to pop some more bubbles and save another batch of baby pandas.

4. POT

Most of the behaviors to which I am addicted aren't dangerous. Sometimes, they provide much-needed relaxation. But living in a constant state of vigilance, fighting everything I am tempted to indulge in, makes me feel so crappy and full of shame I obsess about the behavior I just engaged in, which makes me want to engage in it yet again. I keep thinking: Is this really how I want to spend my remaining years on this planet? Is this what the human race evolved to do?

The truth is, nearly all of us now live in a world that is as crazymaking as the house I grew up in. Even as we find ourselves surrounded by more and more stuff that has been engineered to be irresistible, we are constantly being lectured to refrain from giving in and consuming it. Often, we are being told this by doctors who are obese, or government officials, celebrities, or members of the clergy who are addicted to drugs or porn. Our children are being ordered to put down their phones and turn off their iPads by parents who can't tear themselves away from their own phones and iPads.

Unlike the candy in my mother's pantry, which at least required a fair amount of effort and ingenuity to acquire, the flashing, buzzing games, the television shows, the social media accounts, the porn sites, and the YouTube videos that tempt us today exist in limitless quantities within devices we can hold in our hands and whose buttons we can push twenty-four hours a day, with no one looking. Never before have human beings been inundated by such craftily persuasive advertisements, brought to us via media that are impossible to avoid and as addictive as the products they are selling us. Entire magazines and television shows devote themselves to seducing us into desiring the finest gourmet foods and the richest, trendiest desserts. If I found it so hard not to put on weight in a house where my mother served boiled chicken and frozen green beans for dinner, in a town where the only ethnic offerings were chop suey and pastrami sandwiches, in an America in which dark chocolate hadn't been invented, how are our children going to resist all the carefully formulated snacks and delicacies that have become so plentiful, even as we adults go on and on about how vital it is to avoid sugar, fat, gluten, salt, and artificial additives?

We caution our children not to binge on alcohol, even as we extol the virtues of the finest wines or crafted beers. Smoking pot has become so acceptable even a woman of sixty like me keeps an entire bag of weed in her fridge. (If the SWAT team breaks in, they will never think to look in the Tupperware container in the crisper drawer.) Then there are all the mood stabilizers, anxiety relievers, attention focusers, sleep inducers, opioids, and other habit-forming pain medications that are being pushed on us by our physicians, therapists, and television sets.

We have all read that children who can delay eating one marshmallow now because they have been promised two marshmallows later are more likely to succeed than the losers who lack the discipline and restraint to wait. But does anyone have the faintest idea how to instill willpower in a child who lacks it? And has it ever occurred to anyone that the child who eats one marshmallow now rather than two marshmallows later is going to end up healthier?

5. NUTELLA

As an infant, my son was so overweight strangers stopped me on the street to berate me for overfeeding him. On his pediatrician's orders, he went straight from breast milk to skim. Even so, he remained obese. He didn't walk until he was eighteen months; he was so heavy I could barely carry him. When I sent my mother a professional photograph of her grandson, she ripped it up and urged me to do the same with the other copies.

For his first three years, I made sure Noah didn't eat anything sugary or fatty. He thought Halloween entailed dressing up in a costume and handing out bags of raisins to the other kids. Then I realized I had become as obsessed with controlling my son's diet as my parents had been obsessed with controlling mine.

After that, I tried never to make a big deal about what he ate. I didn't stock a lot of sweets in the house, but on special occasions, I baked cookies or a cake, or we would take a walk to the Dairy Queen to celebrate. When his friends began spending hours playing *World of Warcraft*, I bought my son a few video games for his own computer. But I also tried to make sure he got outside and found other pastimes that absorbed him. He loved watching *Rocko's Modern Life* and *The Simpsons*. We laughed at these shows together. But we also had plenty of talks about what he might do with his life that would bring him more satisfaction than watching TV.

Now, in his twenties, my son stands six feet two inches tall and weighs little more than he weighed in grade school. He jogs. He rides his bike. He boxes. He is studying for his doctorate in history, a subject he loves, and devotes most of his free time to organizing for social justice. I don't want to violate his privacy, but let's just say I raised him to think of sex as a vital part of a healthy romantic relationship. He exhibits little interest in sugary snacks, alcohol, drugs, or social media. Until recently, he lived in a co-op where I never saw anyone chow down on anything more decadent than a whole-wheat muffin.

In fact, when I visited him at his new apartment—a single room in a converted funeral home in a drab, working-class neighborhood in Chicago—I thought I might have raised a kid who has *too much* self-control. When I offered to treat him to dinner at the restaurant of his choice, he drove us to a modest Uzbeki restaurant. When the waiter offered us dessert, my son declined.

Sadly, I still craved a bedtime snack.

Well, Noah said, he did have something sweet squirreled away in his pantry. He took me into the kitchen he shares with his housemates, stepped inside the closet, and emerged with a half-eaten jar of Nutella and a barely opened package of graham crackers.

"You like Nutella?" I said.

"I love it," he admitted.

We settled at the grimy Formica table, spread the former on the latter, scraped the jar clean, and—guiltily, happily—demolished the pack of crackers.

MAYBE IT'S ME

THE ONE-WOMAN SHOW I'LL NEVER PERFORM IN PUBLIC

I TURNED SIXTY, I moved to New York. People said: *Why would you move to New York? The streets there are smeared with dog shit. With people shit. It's so hot in the subway, your blood bubbles in your veins. The train you want is never coming. For the price of a bed-bug-infested shoebox in Manhattan, you could afford an entire house in the nicest neighborhood in Ann Arbor, Michigan.*

Which is exactly what I traded for my lousy shoebox in Manhattan.

I told everyone: *I love the theater! I love ballet! Opera! Great restaurants! World-class museums!*

The truth is: I wanted to find true love before I died. You think just because a woman is in her sixties, she loses her interest in sex and romance? You think desire is like a battery? It runs down? A good-looking man walks by and you don't feel that flutter in your vagina? When you are young and no one has ever done a really good job of making you feel so beautiful that even your tiniest toe is worthy of being sucked on, then sure, you are dying for a man to take you in his arms and kiss you. If you have only ever seen people eating chocolate on TV, you wonder what chocolate tastes like. But after forty years enjoying everything from Reese's Peanut Butter Cups to the finest, darkest Scharffen Berger truffles, are you going to say: *Nah, I don't care if I ever taste chocolate again?*

Not so much as an M&M?

When you are a kid, you assume women in their sixties should be content to sit around playing mahjongg or canasta or whatever games old ladies play. *Just shut up and go play canasta! Put on your track suit and your old-lady shoes and go for a walk around the mall with your other old-lady friends!* If a woman in her sixties is looking for a man, that might be cute. But if she complains no one wants to date her? *Hey! You ought to be glad you're not tied to a wheelchair, drooling on your pajamas.*

When you are young, you don't understand that old people feel exactly the same as you. *It's still me in here! Someone zipped me inside this old-lady suit, and I can't get out!* Maybe you are a little wiser. But all that means is, you are less willing to settle for the bullshit you settled for as a kid.

I do not need a man to complete me. The last time I looked, I wasn't missing any parts. Most of the time, I am happier to be alone. It's just, if you only get touched when some drunk on the subway presses up against you, you come down with an emotional flu. You know how everybody says, *Healthcare isn't a privilege, it's a right!* Well, it ought to be a right to have someone who can hug you once a month. Someone you can compare notes with after you see a movie. Someone you can go shopping with so you don't need to lug home all those bottles and cans and jars. Someone who will make the salad while you make the pasta. And really, shouldn't everyone be guaranteed a special someone who is obliged to drive them home after a colonoscopy?

I don't need a man to fertilize my eggs. I am not a science-fair project. I already have a son. My biological clock isn't ticking. You know the hourglass in *The Wizard of Oz?* That's the timepiece we are talking about here. I get to spend however many years I have left on this planet locked in the witch's tower, with only Toto to keep me company, and when the sand runs out, the witch flies back with her monkey men and uses her giant axe to lop off my head.

Here is what it is like to be in your sixties. You lie in bed wondering if anyone will ever see your breasts again. Touch them. Kiss them. Appreciate how smooth they still are, how soft. It's like buying a bag of oranges, and you aren't sure you can eat them fast enough before they wither and attract the fruit flies.

So I moved to New York. Because if you live in a college town in the Midwest, you are going to run through the eligible men very quickly. At least the ones who aren't your students. Or your therapists. Or you best friends' ex-husbands—who aren't worse than other men, except you already know they never empty the dishwasher and they occasionally sleep with prostitutes.

Also, I thought men in New York might not find me as intimidating as men in the rest of the country find me. I am only five foot three. I weigh one hundred and twenty-five pounds. But when I was young, I made the tragic mistake of earning a degree in physics, and apparently that makes a woman as undatable as the Incredible Hulk. Men are afraid they will be sucking on a nipple and the woman will whisper: *The sum of the square of the legs of a right triangle equals the square of the hypotenuse.*

Also, I have published a lot of books, and men worry I will write about how small their penises are, or how they aren't any good at giving head. Which I would never do. Unless they treated me in such a way as to justify such a comment.

The men in New York say they are looking for a woman who is "funny and smart." Except what they really want is a woman who is smart enough to appreciate how smart *they* are. A woman who will laugh at *their* jokes, even if the jokes are racist, sexist, or not the least bit funny.

I understand why men my age want to have sex with a younger woman. I wouldn't mind having sex with a younger man. But women in their sixties have been studying how to give blowjobs all their lives. You go to a doctor, do you want Doogie Howser to walk in the room, or Marcus Welby? Okay, with doctors, the younger they are, the more up-to-date their methods. But blowjobs? It isn't as if anyone has been dreaming up technological innovations every year.

This one guy was in his seventies. After two dates, he tells me he really likes me but he isn't feeling "fireworks." "Fireworks?" I say. "Seriously? Those fireworks of yours have been lying in a moldy basement for seven decades. You think the gunpowder might have gotten a little damp? You think maybe you shouldn't expect such a spectacular display? Maybe you should be content with sparklers?"

Sorry. I don't mean this to be a rant about how older men are all Harvey Weinstein and every woman over sixty is a combination of Helen Mirren, Ruth Bader Ginsburg, Betty White, Halle Berry, Meryl Streep, Tina Turner, Sigourney Weaver, Cher, and Maxine Waters. Although such a comparison should give you pause. This is about being a woman who was born in the 1950s and witnessed an earthshaking change in the way women live their lives and who now wonders if her expectations weren't a little high. If she might have made a few mistakes. If she might need to overlook a few flaws in a man's behavior if she doesn't want to spend her last twenty-five years alone.

For instance: I can't help wondering if I was wrong to leave my marriage. My husband was one of the kindest, most brilliant men you could ever meet. Handsome. Tall. When he was in graduate school, he found the gene for a childhood cancer. Then he devoted his life to figuring out why some people are born without eyes. But it turns out, if you want to figure out why people are born without eyes, you need to spend every waking minute—and most of the minutes you ought to be in bed—working in your lab.

Before we got married, my husband promised my career would be as important as his. And it was. It was. Except, he expected me to do all the housework. All the childcare. Pay the bills. Do the taxes. Be there when the Roto-Rooter guy came to unstop the drain so our basement wouldn't be flooded with feces. All this while I was teaching full time and trying to research and write a book so I wouldn't be humiliated when I came up for tenure. So I got a little out of sorts. A little frustrated. A little tired. I moved out. I moved back in. We tried couples counseling. But he said he had worked too hard to earn all his degrees and set up his laboratory and he couldn't cut back on his hours without ruining his career, so I finally left him.

Should I have stayed in my marriage? If I *had* stayed, I never would have found out how much worse my other options turned out to be. This is a paradox so important, it ought to have a fancy German-sounding name, like that paradox about the cat that's alive and dead at the same time, until you open the box and kill it. Except, in this paradox, the woman in the bad marriage is the one who is alive and dead at the same time, until her best friend says, *You really ought to leave your husband*. At which, the woman is only dead.

I am sure you have heard the theory that we exist in an infinite number of universes, and in every one of those universes, some version of ourselves is living with every possible choice we could have made? Well, whoever figures out how to peek into all those parallel universes and *Star Trek* themselves into the one universe in which they made all the best decisions . . . that person is going to be more famous than

Sir Isaac Newton, Albert Einstein, Sigmund Freud, and that Schrödinger guy rolled into one. My bet? She is going to be a woman who can't stop trying to figure out if she should have stayed in her marriage or left it.

In *this* universe, I left my marriage. And ever since, I have been trying to find a man who is sexy, smart, and good-hearted enough to fall in love with. But here is what I needed sixty years to learn: It isn't enough that I fall in love with the man; he needs to fall in love with *me*. And I don't mean some version of myself I have trimmed down and diminished until it is quiet, demure, and delicate enough to fit inside a snow globe. I mean the me that earned a degree in physics and loves thinking about space and time. The me that wrote a bunch of books and earned tenure as a full professor. The me that can be a little bit loud and raunchy. The me that loves slamming a volley at my opponent in tennis. Of course, I would nurture and support my lover. I would listen to him talk about his work. His hobbies. His opinions. I would laugh at his jokes—if the jokes were funny. But here is a radical proposition: I would expect him to do the same for me.

I almost found what I was looking for. I dated a Polish Catholic man who came to enjoy making love to a woman with whom he could share his passion for reading books and traveling. Sadly, in the end, we couldn't overcome our many differences.

Then I fell in love with a man who was breathtakingly smart and whose writing I admired. Just reading this man's sentences made me come. We had the kind of sex most women only dream about. He knew so much about music, literature, and art, I could have listened to him talk for hours. I thought I finally had found someone who understood me. Who saw me for who I am.

But he kept breaking off the relationship. He loved the

sex, but he thought I wasn't cute enough. I wasn't sweet enough. I wasn't *nice* enough. Let me tell you, I am plenty nice. But I am nice in a New York sort of way. I would be the first person to carry your stroller up or down the steps to the subway. I would rush into a burning building to save your child.

But I beat the guy at Scrabble. By more than two hundred points. I didn't mean to. He was drunk. I drew exceptionally good letters. I made a seven-letter word. And I ruined an opening where he could have used a triple-word square. He told me nice people don't intentionally ruin another player's chance to use a triple-word square. I said: "Is that why you broke up with me? Because I beat you at Scrabble?" He assured it wasn't. But I think it was.

Maybe it is a fantasy to think I can achieve physical and mental intimacy with the same person. Men have been trained to satisfy their intellectual needs with other men. What they are looking for in a woman is someone to provide them with comfort and support. A boost to their ego. Someone to watch Netflix with and get naked with them in bed. I could fulfill my need for intelligent conversation with my female friends. But I want what George Eliot found with George Henry Lewes: I want communion of the body *and* the mind.

Am I too picky? Am I crazy to think a man who grew up in the 1950s could be a feminist?

Because men my age never had any real reason to change. Imagine if all the male chimpanzees on some island grew up believing they were entitled to eat the ripest, most delectable kumquats and bananas while the female chimps got only the seeds and peels. Then, one day, the female chimps realized if only they could find the courage to crawl through this narrow, dark tunnel, climb this really steep cliff, and swim across this really deep lake, they would find the juiciest, most delicious fruit, and they could eat every bite without needing to put up with their male companions. The female chimps exercised day and night. They got very strong. They overcame their fear of heights. They taught themselves how to swim. And then, one by one, carrying their babies on their backs, those female chimps crawled through that tunnel, climbed that cliff, and swam across that lake.

And the male chimps? What incentive did they have to stop scratching their balls and change? None. Except they no longer had enough female chimps to mate with. Oh, a few females were still hanging around, willing to make do with the seeds and peels. But if a male chimp wanted one of those stronger, braver females, he needed to find the courage to crawl through that same tunnel, climb that cliff, and swim across that lake.

Sadly, there weren't enough of these new, improved male chimps to go around. If a female chimp got desperate for male-chimp companionship, she needed to swim back to the island and put up with a chimp who still believed he was entitled to eat the kumquats and bananas while she made do with the seeds and peels.

I'm sorry. I shouldn't be comparing human males to chimpanzees. The truth is, I was raised to believe human males are the supreme arbiters of a female's worth. The reason I worked so hard to achieve everything I achieved is I wanted to impress the men. I thought if I proved myself to be smarter, stronger, and funnier than all those dumb, weak, unfunny women about whom the men spoke so disparagingly, I would be the woman they fell in love with.

Imagine if you had spent your first twenty or thirty years training to be a figure skater. Day after day, you practiced your jumps and spins because you thought that would impress the judges. And then, just as you qualified for the Olympics, someone cued you in that the guys holding up the cards would be judging you based not on what you did, but on how pretty you looked while you were doing it. You could perform a perfect quintuple Axel, and the judges wouldn't even notice unless you were wearing a sexy, shiny leotard with your hair done up in a ponytail and—no matter how much effort was required for all those jumps and spins—a smile plastered on your perfectly made-up face.

Bad enough that for thousands of years, women allowed men to rule the world. Couldn't the men have done a competent job? They fooled us into believing they were gods, and they turned out to be Donald Trump. Okay, not all of them are Donald Trump. But even Jack Kennedy and Bill Clinton turned out to be rapists.

Sorry! I promised this wasn't going to be a diatribe about how all men are rapists and all women are paragons of perfection. First, that isn't true. Second, who would pay to listen to a woman talk about how angry she is, how bitter? An editor once told me he wasn't interested in publishing stories about the dating practices of bitter middle-aged women. *Really?* I thought. *If Saul Bellow, John Cheever, John Updike, and Philip Roth had been women, you wouldn't have published them? Because every word those writers wrote revolved around the dating practices of bitter middle-aged men.*

If a woman complains she can't find a man, everyone assumes she must be hideous. Which is why I decided to convey my experience in the form of a comedy routine. I figured if I were up here on the stage, you could see that I am a very appealing person. I told myself if I were at my cutest and most self-deprecating, maybe my audience wouldn't write me off as a scary feminist. Also, I felt obliged to entertain the possibility that my frustration might be my own fault. There are some very sweet men online. In their profiles, these men tell me they are "spiritual." Although, if a person needs to convince you how spiritual he is, he probably isn't. Can you imagine the Dalai Lama trying to convince you he is spiritual? Mostly, this means the men are into yoga and meditation. Sadly, I fail to see that an ability to touch one's toes or monitor one's own breathing guarantees a person is willing to vote for a female president. These men say they are "easygoing" and "down-to-earth." They are "gentlemen" who are looking for the "perfect little lady" they can "spoil."

The trouble is, when I see the words "gentleman" or "lady," I think you are going to show up at my apartment in a top hat and tails, and you will expect me to wear white gloves and pearls, and you will hold the door and pay for dinner, but you will expect me to refrain from saying anything I truly think, and when you take me home, I will lie there politely and let you do whatever you want while I utter polite little oohs and ahs, but I need to be careful not to say anything the least bit dirty, let alone scream when I am coming.

What I am looking for is a man who is a little edgy. A little dark. Someone who earns his living in a more interesting way than filing people's taxes. This means I often end up dating clowns. As in, guys who put on makeup and big feet and yuk it up for Ringling Brothers and Barnum & Bailey Circus. I am not kidding. I have dated clowns not once but twice. One clown had a law degree and was teaching a college course on the history and theory of clowning. I enjoyed telling people I was dating a clown. But I found something off-putting about the way this man assumed each expression, as if he were trying to convey whatever emotion seemed most appropriate. I got the sense he was hiding behind a mask. I told my friend: "There is something so *performative* about this man." And my friend said: "Eileen, what do you expect? You are dating a clown."

Then there were all the artists. If you move to New York, you think nothing could be cooler than dating an artist. Artists get you into all the museums for free. And the museums own the artists' work! Of course, none of the artists I dated actually had paintings hanging on the walls of those museums. But knowing a guy's paintings were sitting in a closet at MOMA or the Met was all I needed to take off my clothes.

If you spend enough time with an artist, you start to see the world a whole new way. The problem is, artists make a living breaking rules. We would be in a museum, and this photographer I was dating, he would touch the exhibits! Who does that? Once, he touched this delicate glass sculpture hanging from the ceiling—by a thread! I kept expecting alarms to go off. We would be arrested! We would be shot! I am a person who is afraid to touch the trash cans in a museum. I am afraid to touch the toilet!

This other artist—he was raised by wolves. Almost literally. He grew up poor in the Bronx, he got beaten up all the time, his parents couldn't be bothered to protect him, and he saved himself by hiding at the zoo, learning from all the animals. By the time I met him, he was in his seventies. But I had this book of his early work, and it showed photos he had taken of himself—the guy was six-foot-four, dark and hairy, and the photos showed him naked, crouching on all fours, imitating a tiger on the hunt, an ape swinging through the trees.

These were the sexiest photos you could imagine. The guy was famous, or he had been, and I couldn't believe how lucky I was to be dating him, so I left the book open to the page that showed him swinging through the trees. These cousins of mine, they've been married a million years, they saw the photos. "You're dating this person?" my cousin said. And I'm, like: *Yeah, aren't I cooler than you?*

He turned out to be a wild man. Did I mention he was six-foot-four? Well, he wouldn't take off his hat, not even at the movies. We would go out to a Chinese restaurant, and he would keep asking the waiter to refill all those jars of condiments. The pickles. The chilis. The hoisin sauce. The mustard. The fish sauce. Over and over, ten or eleven times: Please, would you fill this up? He would come over to my apartment, and the minute he walked in, off would come the shirt, the jeans, the underwear. I don't have curtains, and he would walk around like that, his cock and balls hanging down—and I do mean hanging down. The guy broke up with me, and my cousins said: "Eileen, you were dating a man who swung naked from the trees, and you thought this was the basis of a great relationship?"

Then there was this whole category of men who, through no fault of their own, seemed too broken to be in a relationship. I met this lovely man who had lost his wife to cancer. He grieved a few years, then he fell in love with another woman, and he lost her to cancer, too. Five months after that second woman's funeral, he put his profile on Match and dated me. I knew he had lost his wife, but he didn't tell me about the second woman until I had fallen in love. "The heart is a very sensitive organ," I said. "Don't you think yours needs time to heal?" Oh, no, he said. He was ready to move on. He didn't want to lose me.

Now, this man was a serious rock climber, and even though I am terrified of falling off a cliff and getting smashed on all those hard, pointy, you know, *rocks* you would hit as you tumbled down, I went with him to a climbing gym and let him teach me about harnesses, ropes, and pulleys. In a gym, if you fall, you bounce on the rubber mats, so I overcame my fear and made it all the way to the top of one wall, and down, and up another wall. Which does give a person a certain satisfaction in her accomplishment. Not to mention, when I was on the ground looking up at my lover, who was skittering from ledge to ledge and crawling across the ceiling of a cave, that was quite a turn-on. So I promised I would try climbing a real mountain. The kind that doesn't come with a rubber mat.

Before we could do that, though, he went away on a business trip, and when he came home, he found his late wife's cat dead on the bathroom floor, and he fell apart. He was as smashed up as if he had plummeted from the top of Mount Everest. "I'm not sure why," he said, "but I suddenly don't want feel like seeing you."

So I said: "Maybe that cat was your last living link to your beloved wife? And you're finally grieving for her? And that other woman you loved and lost?"

And he said: "I don't really want to think about any of that right now. But I hope you can still be my best friend and come over and watch *Project Runway*."

And I said: "No. Not unless you go into therapy."

And he said: "Why would you think I need to go into therapy?"

And that was the end of that. Except I had blown out both my rotator cuffs climbing those walls, and I was in agony for months, although I only felt the pain when I tried to lift anything heavy, like my toothbrush.

I might be screwed up, but at least I have the courage to face my failings and get myself therapized. Men think they can tough things out. If they drink enough, if they get high enough, if they climb enough mountains, they can forget how much pain they are in from having been raised by their own fucked-up fathers. They think finding the right woman—someone who "isn't into drama" and "doesn't have any baggage," which means she has no needs of her own and likes to hang around with guys, drinking beer and watching football—can fill the emptiness they are experiencing.

These guys think they are Iron Man when they are more like Soap Bubble Man, and you walk around all day trying to protect them from getting popped. I know women who stick with drug addicts, alcoholics. Their husbands run up thousands of dollars of debt, they have affairs. And the women stay! They drive their boyfriends to rehab! Are these women so afraid to be alone they would put up with anything? Or do they love their husbands so much they overlook every fault? Are they more forgiving than I am? Do they have kinder, more generous hearts?

I met this very sweet man, another artist. He seemed to love me for who I was. But I wasn't allowed to touch his penis. I could give you details, but let's just say the sex was so bad, it made me want to tape a giant yellow X across my bedroom door. He asked if I would see a sex therapist with him, and I thought, *Well, at least he recognizes he has a problem. At least he wants to fix it.* And he was such a great person, I agreed to go.

I made it through four months, and he assumed we were getting married. When I said I wasn't ready to sign on the dotted line, he fell apart. What was he, on trial? Was I going to be judging everything he said and did, deciding whether to break up with him? How could he stand the anxiety?

He got so defensive, he started finding fault with *me*. And I wasn't allowed to answer back. When we talked, I needed to follow a set of rules he had printed on his computer. According to these rules, I needed to listen while he explained what was bothering him, and I needed to repeat what I heard, and I could not—ever—dispute his version of events.

So, he makes a date for us to discuss what he says is a terribly urgent problem. All right, if I am doing something that upsets the man I care about, we ought to talk. We agree to meet at a diner. He takes out the three sheets of rules and sets them on the table between us. Then he explains that whenever we go for a walk, I walk too fast. Obviously, I am embarrassed to be seen with him, and I am trying to run away.

Really? I think. *This is the urgent matter we needed to discuss?* I can't help but feel relieved. I am, in fact, a very fast walker. And this man is a very slow walker. So I repeat back to him: "I hear what you are telling me. I walk too fast. You think I am trying to get away from you." I admit I do walk too fast. I promise I will walk more slowly. "But really," I say, "I am not at all embarrassed to be seen with you. You are a very good-looking man. I walk too fast with everyone, including my son, who is my favorite person on the planet. My son is six-two, and even he can't keep up, but I am not trying to get away—from him or you."

No, no, he says. If he tells me I am trying to get away from him, I must be trying to get away from him. "Another thing," he says. "When we are walking, you don't match your gait to my gait." Apparently, I don't match my rhythm to his rhythm, so when we are walking arm in arm, which is a very important activity for this man, he doesn't find the experience to be enjoyable.

Now, this is an accusation I don't take lightly. First, I *do* match my gait to his. This is something I have done with every man I have ever dated. No matter what weird rhythm they shuffle or lope or gallop to, I alter my rhythm to match my date's. But why should the woman be required to match her rhythm to the man's? Why shouldn't my lover be matching his gait to mine? I know I am supposed to say: *I hear you that I am not matching my gait to your gait.* But I can't bring myself to say it. Because I disagree with the basic premise.

Which, according to the rules, I am not allowed to do. If he thinks something is true, it must be true!

I am so frustrated, I blurt out: "I am sorry, I just can't do this."

And the guy looks stricken. "Wait! Does this mean you are breaking up with me?"

And I think: *No. That wasn't what I meant at all.* But I look at the three pages of computer-generated rules lying on the table between us, and I think how difficult it will be to go for a walk with this man because of how self-conscious I will be as to whether I am walking slowly enough and whether I am matching my gait to his gait, and I say, "Yeah, I'm sorry, we're breaking up," and I throw a twenty on the table to pay for my sandwich and hurry out.

As crazy as it sounds, that was the best relationship I've had since moving to New York. Part of the problem is online dating. In the old days, an acquaintance fixed you up. Or you fell in love with your boss or your colleague across the hall. Now, if you hit on someone at work, you don't end up going on a date; you end up going to jail. Not that messing around with your colleagues was ever a good idea. *I mean, what could go wrong? We're adults! No matter what happens, we'll stay professional.* But in the best cases, you would get to know someone, they would get to know you, and the sexual attraction followed. I've tried hanging around at bookstores, tennis tournaments, concerts, museums, lectures on relativity. I took a comedy class at the Y. But most women my age don't get noticed unless they look like Kim Basinger or Christie Brinkley.

And seriously, how can you expect to accurately evaluate a man from his online profile? In real life, the minute you meet someone, your animal brain starts processing a million cues. Does he clip his nose hairs? How many buttons does he leave open on his shirt? Are his shoes the kind with all those little holes and tassels? The minute a man opens his mouth, you can tell everything by the way he talks. Online? You're supposed to suss out a man's character from a photo of him hanging off a zipline and a list of his favorite food groups.

The very first man I messaged looked so soulful, so, well, *spiritual*, I made the mistake of giving him my phone number. A rookie error. Within a few hours, he was bombarding me with texts accusing me of betraying him with other men. When I wouldn't answer the texts, he started calling and leaving me threatening messages, so I had to block him.

My therapist, who had encouraged me to try online dating, took one look at this guy's photo and said, "Eileen, can't you see by his eyes he is mentally ill?" And sure enough! What I had taken to be the expression of a man who could see things I couldn't see because he existed on a higher plane was the look of someone who was delusional.

Then again, even experienced daters can't always tell if someone is out of his mind by studying his online profile. I saw a write-up for a weedy little man who was a professor of linguistics. I have always been fascinated by how human beings went from grunting and pointing to asking politely for a piece of meat. How did the word "apple" or "chair" or "sad" end up representing an apple, or a chair, or how fucking suicidal a person can feel after she has spent too many days alone in her apartment? This seemed to be what this professor studied. Maybe I would fall in love with his mind and we would go trotting around the globe, exploring archaeological digs and deciphering the first scratches any human being gouged on a piece of stone.

So I show up at this coffee shop—which, not that I believe in omens, is named for Edgar Allen Poe—and right away the professor pulls out all these charts and diagrams, pages and pages of Hebrew lettering, Latin, Greek, Aramaic, languages I have never heard of. Apparently, he has figured out why every word in every language needs to be composed of exactly the letters it ended up being made of. I googled him before we met, and this man actually once had been a professor of linguistics at a prestigious university. But our date was like that scene from *A Beautiful Mind* in which John Nash draws all these equations on the walls and windows.

I didn't want to hurt the poor man's feelings. But after an hour studying the doodles and diagrams on his notepads, I excused myself politely, stood, and put on my coat. At that, his expression changed. He looked like Gollum! "You had better stay," he hissed. "A woman your age, with a degree in physics . . . I am the only man who would ever date you!"

A few experiences like that and you swear you will never go back online. But at three a.m., after you have spent another Saturday night watching some Netflix series about gorgeous, sexy people falling in love and boning one another, you find yourself logging back in and sending messages to guys whose profiles wave more red flags than the May Day parade in Kremlin Square.

The least of it is the lying. I expected women would make themselves younger, but I was shocked how many men shave ten years from their age. Do they think when they show up at the restaurant and are bent ninety degrees, their waistbands are up under their armpits, and they tell you about this scary movie they saw in high school and you know *Psycho* came out when Eisenhower was in the White House, you aren't going to figure out they are in their seventies?

Then there are the men who add six inches to their height. I can't blame them. Most women prefer to date taller men. But if you tell me you are six feet tall, and when you show up you are five foot two, you know what I am going to think you are? A liar.

The worst lie is men claiming they are feminists when they clearly believe they deserve all the bananas and papayas. Most of the men I date never ask me a single question. For the longest time, I couldn't understand this strategy. Didn't they care what I thought? Or what I did for a living? Or what I liked to read? Or whom I was voting for in the election? Then it hit me. All they cared about was whether I was willing to listen to *them* talk about what they did for a living and whom *they* were voting for in the election. If I looked like someone they might want to fuck, that was all that mattered.

One man spent three dates complaining how hard it is to be a straight white male now that women and people of color have taken over the publishing industry. Apparently, he went to a bookstore and asked for help finding a volume of poems by a straight white male, and the owner gave him a disparaging look, and my date found this to be offensive.

"Would he have minded if I had asked for a book by an African-American female poet?" my date demanded.

And I told him: "Almost every book of poetry published since the printing press was invented was written by a straight white male. I doubt you would have had trouble finding one on your own."

And this other guy? The first thing he told me was his ex-wife left him because he yelled at her all the time. "She was crazy!" he said. "I've never raised my voice to a woman in my life!" But I instantly understood what his ex-wife meant. He might not have raised his voice, but he criticized her. How do I know? We had barely met, and he was already criticizing me! "If you want me to think you're interested," he said, "you need to sit up straighter. And you need to lean closer, across the table." This man criticized the coffee we were drinking. He criticized the cups! I could only stand listening to him for half an hour, then I told him I had to go. He said he would walk me to my apartment.

"Uh, no," I said. "That's okay." But by this time, we were out on the street and he was walking me to my apartment.

"What do you think I am, an axe murderer?"

I said, "How do I know you aren't?"

"Ha ha," he said, and kept walking me to my apartment.

Okay, he didn't show up with an axe. But that night, he sends me an email that is the equivalent of five single-spaced pages in which he details everything he thinks is wrong with me. He has googled me, and he is very impressed that I have published so many books and earned a degree in physics. The problem is, I shouldn't have kept this information to myself. Obviously, I am neurotic. He would like to date me, but only if I swear I will start seeing a psychiatrist. And lucky me! I live on the Upper West Side, where there are hundreds of great shrinks to choose from. In fact, he has attached a list of psychiatrists he recommends, and I can take my pick!

I don't answer this email, so he sends me another, even longer, pointing out even more of my neuroses. I don't answer that letter, but I get another. And another. And another. And *I* am the one who needs the services of a mental health professional!

The biggest know-it-all, though, was Swing Dance Guy. I have taken swing dance lessons for many years. I may not be the girl you see getting swung upside down over some Lindy Hopper's head, but if a man knows how to lead, I know how to follow. This person insists on accompanying me to an outdoor swing dance festival at Lincoln Center.

I say: "Are you sure you know how to swing dance?"

"Of course!" he says. "I am one terrific swing dancer."

He tells me to meet him at the fountain at Lincoln Center. The one where Cher met Nicholas Cage in *Moon-*

struck? I am a sucker for romance, so against my better judgment, I tell him yes.

In his photo, this man is wearing a suit and tie. He claims to be a successful inventor. Which maybe he is, because the person who shows up at the fountain looks exactly like the professor from *Back to the Future*. His hair is standing straight up as if his skull is giving off radioactive waves. But he isn't wearing a suit. He is wearing a filthy, ripped T-shirt, baggy shorts, and knee-high black socks with sandals. By now, I can spot someone who is nuts by looking at his eyes, and this man's eyes are rolling around in their sockets. He looks like someone who *thinks* he invented a time-traveling car, except some other guy stole the patent, and he is going to spend the entire night telling you about the lawsuit.

Oh, and even though he doesn't have the slightest idea how to swing dance, he thinks he can grab me by my arms and hurl me around the floor—these being the same arms that already have sustained considerable damage from climbing walls to please the dude who dumped me—until I am in so much agony I say: "Stop yanking me around! This isn't swing dancing! You're just making up the steps as you go along!"

To which my date indignantly replies: "It's your fault! You aren't following my lead!"

"Your lead?" I say. "How can I follow your lead if you are randomly throwing me around the dance floor? What am I supposed to do, read your mind?"

And my date says: "Yes! If you were a good dancer, you could read my mind!"

I have never been so embarrassed. The man got down on his knees and performed a move that was a cross between Bernie Sanders break dancing and Al Jolson singing "Mammy." I told him I wasn't dancing with him anymore. "Who cares?" he said. "Lots of women would be very appre-

ciative of my asking them to dance." To prove this point, he
went up to a young Asian-American woman—she couldn't
have been eighteen—and because it is considered rude not
to dance with anyone who asks, she accepted his invitation.
I stood there watching this poor woman get pushed and
pulled around the dance floor as if she were a mop and he
was using her to swab the plaza at Lincoln Center. When
the music stopped, he came back to me and said: "See? That
beautiful Oriental girl enjoyed dancing with me! She and I
were the best couple on the floor! You know how I could
tell? Everyone stopped to watch!"

At least Swing Dance Guy didn't pretend to be woke.
That artist I dated, the one who liked swinging through the
trees? He got beaten up a lot as a kid, so he thought that
gave him permission to say whatever he wanted about Black
people. First, he said they complain too much about how
oppressed are, even though they aren't any more oppressed
than anyone else.

"Are you kidding?" I said. "I don't see cops stopping
white people for busted headlights and shooting them in the
back."

"Oh, give me a break," he said. "When does that ever
happen? Besides, they make too big a fuss about slavery."

The guy was Jewish, so I said: "Yeah, and Jews really do go
on about the Holocaust!" I told him I had just seen a Black
guy get taken off my bus in handcuffs because he was caught
without a receipt for the fare. If those same marshals caught
me, I said, I might need to pay a fine, but they wouldn't drag
me off in handcuffs. The artist told me I was lying. He said
I hadn't seen what I had seen. The cops would never take
anyone off a bus in handcuffs.

He also thought that because he had raised his daughter, he was a feminist. But to his mind, the entire purpose

of a girlfriend was making sure he never needed to spend a minute on his own. He was putting on a show in another city, and the gallery kept jerking him around, so he decided to fly down and straighten things out, and he asked me to fly down with him. I would have gone, but I was contractually obliged to give a lecture in Washington, D.C., on that Monday, and I already had a ticket to fly to Chicago on that Friday to visit my son, so I would have needed to rearrange all my flights, which not only would have been a pain in the neck, it would have cost a fortune I couldn't afford. I told the guy I would travel with him next time. But he wouldn't forgive me. If I were truly a devoted girlfriend, he said, I would cancel my own event, spend money I didn't have, and fly with him wherever he was going so he wouldn't need to spend a night alone in his motel room.

Still, that wasn't the reason I got dumped. I got dumped because I asked him to go down on me. I went down on *him* every single time we had sex, and he clearly derived great pleasure from this activity. But he never went down on me. Finally, with my birthday coming, I politely requested you-know-what as my present. To his credit, I had a very enjoyable birthday. But another few months went by and—nothing. Not for Christmas. Not for New Year's. I dropped a hint. But he admitted he wasn't confident in that department.

"Not confident?" I said. "You actually are very talented. You are an artist in more ways than one!"

"Thank you," he said, but he wasn't sure he enjoyed doing what I asked. Really? How could he not know if he enjoyed giving oral sex? Well, he said, that was the first time he had ever done it.

I was flabbergasted. He was seventy-two years old, he had lived in Manhattan most of his life, he was a famous and successful artist, and this was the first time he had ever gone down on a woman? Fair enough. I didn't want to shame him. If going down on me was not something he enjoyed doing, I wasn't about to force him. But *he* broke up with *me*! Why? Because we were "having issues in bed"!

Then there was the feminist who claimed he had helped Ronan Farrow bring down all the misogynistic monsters in broadcast news. I admit I dated this man because he was a celebrity. Not a *celebrity* celebrity. I mean, this was a man who was famous for being smart. He was one of the experts you see explaining the state of the world to Chris Hayes and Rachel Maddow. Plus, he specified in his profile he was looking for a woman who was "confident and scrappy" enough to keep up with him. I messaged him on OKCupid, and there he was, except, instead of talking to Chris or Rachel, he was talking to me.

True, without the makeup, he was just this short, pasty, balding, Jewish guy. He was missing a tooth—but it wasn't a front tooth. He kept plucking at his nostrils—but he wasn't *picking*, he was only plucking. Could I imagine kissing this man? The answer wasn't no. If you see someone on *Rachel Maddow*, that automatically makes them kissable.

And his politics were so progressive! He was devoted to ending the harassment of his female colleagues. He and Ronan Farrow were close friends, he said, and he had done a lot of work behind the scenes, helping Ronan research and write his book.

So I would have been judge-y to hold against him that he had been married and divorced four times. Or that none of those wives was Jewish. Or that he had never loved the mother of his children but married her because he figured she was "good breeding stock." He laughed when he said this. And when he noticed *I* wasn't laughing, he said, "Oh, come on. You can't fault me for being honest."

Despite the missing tooth and the plucking at the nose

and the four failed marriages, I was thinking: *At least he seems to be enjoying our conversation. True, he hadn't asked me a single question. But if I start talking about a topic, at least he listens.* We spent three and a half hours eating brunch and taking a romantic walk through Riverside Park, which ended with a kiss that might have led to our making out if we hadn't been standing in the middle of Broadway at four in the afternoon. He even texted to say how much he enjoyed our date.

Then I didn't hear a word for two days. I figured he was busy getting ready for his next appearance on *Rachel Maddow*, so I texted back a flirty "I'm still thinking about that kiss," only to receive a message that even though I had "nice breasts," he didn't feel enough "heat" for a real relationship. I suppose if he hadn't been such a feminist, he would have said "tits" instead of "breasts." To think a man can't see the contradiction between calling himself a feminist and not asking a single question about the woman sitting across from him for three and a half hours and judging her solely on the size and shape of her breasts and whatever else did or did not make her hot enough to fuck.

But the worst case of a man who billed himself as a feminist was Sapiosensual. In dating lingo, this means he is turned on by a woman's intelligence. What he was looking for, he wrote, was a woman who was "comfortable in her own skin," a turn of speech that makes me laugh because I picture a woman going to the beach and getting sand not only inside her bathing suit, in all those nooks and crevices, but beneath her actual skin.

Which is pretty much how I felt as a little girl. I couldn't sit still. My family was extremely critical. My parents and siblings were always nagging me about the way I looked, the way I dressed. All I wanted was to run around, climb trees, ride my bike, and play baseball with the boys, but these weren't acceptable ways for a girl to act. When I hit adolescence, my family criticized every ounce of weight I gained. So I developed not only an eating disorder, but a twitch. I couldn't sit still. Any halfway competent child psychologist would have understood *why* I twitched. But in the town where I grew up, there were no child psychologists. The family doctor told my parents I had something called St. Vitus' dance, the last case of which was diagnosed in the Middle Ages and cured by tying the little girl to a stake and setting her on fire.

I spent years in therapy. I studied the effects of the patriarchy on female behavior. I conquered my eating disorder. I came to be very comfortable inside my own skin, so I thought that maybe, after all that hard work, Sapiosensual might be my reward. Here was a man who appreciated the very qualities other men found threatening. He was looking for a woman who could engage him in "spirited conversation" about politics, literature, and art. A woman who was "powerful" and "independent." Best of all, he told me I was "gorgeous from head to foot."

Granted, he was a little stout. A little red in the face. He had an overly large head, and his teeth were too white and prominent. Imagine a shark in a tuxedo? But he gave off a hyper-electric confidence I found attractive. Most of the businessmen I knew read nothing but *The Wall Street Journal*. But Sapiosensual posted his favorite novelists—J. M. Coetzee, Nadine Gordimer, Alan Paton. Turns out he had been born in South Africa and helped to bring down apartheid. Now, as the head of his local Democratic party, he was trying to persuade more women and people of color to run for office.

There was the tiniest of red flags. I mean, this was a flag so small you might give it to an ant to carry in a parade. Apparently, I hadn't replied to the first message he'd sent me, and when I apologized, he chided me for being "naughty." *Naughty?* What was I, a toddler? But hey, maybe "naughty" was one of those British expressions that seems, well, naughty, when it isn't, like when the Brits say they will "knock you up" and all they mean is they will rap at your bedroom door. Christmas was on its way—maybe he had picked up "naughty" from that song about Santa keeping lists.

He asked me to meet him at a restaurant around the corner from my apartment, which seemed creepy, unless it was a coincidence—I hadn't told him where I lived. We had a lovely candlelit dinner, at which he seemed to prefer asking me questions to talking about himself. He walked me home. We shared a sexy, romantic kiss.

And then . . . nothing. Why? When he finally wrote back, he said he was "a highly passionate man" and in me he could "sense a certain reticence." He was hurt that I hadn't invited him up to my apartment. Really? I barely know you, you are much bigger and stronger than I am, and I am supposed to invite you up to my apartment, where you can do anything you want and get off without going to jail because whatever happened was consensual because I invited you up to my apartment, which everyone knows is a license to rape and kill me?

But he was willing to give me a second chance. I probably had an engagement for New Year's Eve, but if I could see my way clear to spend the holiday with him—I should add that he lived a two-hour train ride from Manhattan—he would be supremely honored.

You might think I am an idiot for saying yes. But it is very painful to be alone on New Year's Eve, especially in the city that made New Year's Eve such a big fucking deal in the first place. Besides, I was hurt that he thought I wasn't passionate. Me, not passionate? I would show him who wasn't passionate! The morning before New Year's Eve, snow started falling, so I emailed Sapiosensual a poem by Mary Ruefle about how, when the poet sees snow, she needs to stop whatever she is doing and have sex with a man who "also sees the snow and heeds it," a man for whom "the snow sign" is an ultimatum "beyond joy as well as sorrow."

I send the email, and five seconds later, my cell phone rings, and this man is beside himself with happiness. "Are you a witch?" he says. "How could you have known I had exactly such a contract with the woman who was once dearest my heart?" Apparently, whenever it snowed, this woman, no matter what she might be up to—and she sat on the board of several major corporations—was "contractually obliged" to show up at his door wearing nothing beneath her fur coat and engage in whatever he demanded. "Ah," he said, "such little games. Don't you think that they add the most delicious excitement to one's otherwise humdrum existence?" He had been waiting to confide his predilection until I visited him New Year's Eve. But as long as I had sent him that ever-so-exciting email, he might as well reveal his secret: he was a *SEX-sue-ally DOM-in-ant man*.

Sexually dominant? As in, he was into S&M? To be honest, I don't remember the details. You know how you get when you receive a shock? Here I thought I finally had found a man who valued me for my intelligence, my independence, my ability to make good conversation, and what did he want? He wanted to humiliate and debase me. Sure! What fun is it to order a woman who already is a dishrag to crawl across your floor? What you want is a highly intelligent and independent woman to tie to your bed and whip.

What upset me most was how turned on I was by the prospect of showing up at this rich man's door in nothing but my coat and doing whatever he ordered me to do. I almost went! Even after I knew what I might be in for! I was raised to be a masochist. What woman isn't? Every movie and TV show and advertisement we ever see, every novel we ever read, trains us to get hot and wet just thinking about letting some guy tie us up and whip us.

I know, I know. You can't hold anyone's sexual preference against them. Plenty of feminists are into S&M. I understand why two women or two men might get off on a little role-playing. A little acting out of sadomasochistic fantasies. But the power dynamic is not the same if you are a straight woman submitting to domination by a straight white man. Would it be all right if some politician who claimed to be helping Black people fight their oppressors secretly got off on persuading those same Black people to pretend to be his slaves? What if he dressed up as an SS officer and made Jewish women get down on all fours and lick his boots?

So, no, I did not get taken prisoner and held in some rich maniac's dungeon on Long Island. But that was the last time I went out with a man I met online.

To be fair, dating is hell for everyone. I told this story to one of my tennis partners, and he said, "Well, it's not much fun dating women who are submissive. The worse you treat them, the more attached they get." A lot of women say they are looking for a man who enjoys "fine dining," which is code for not wanting to date a man whose bank account doesn't qualify for a five-bedroom condo on the Upper East Side and two or three vacation homes in countries I am too much of a peasant to fill in the names of.

People say: *You should look for a widower. Widowers know what love is. They know how to make a marriage work.* Are you kidding? Widowers loved their wives! Those women might have had a few flaws while they were alive, but dead? Every single one is Joan of Arc. With a man who is divorced, the woman you need to beat was such a harridan he gave half of everything he owned to get away from her, or she broke his heart, or she ran off with the guy's best friend.

Except, if you end up in the relationship, you usually sympathize with the wife.

The up-side of all these horrible dates is, I realized: It isn't me! All those nights when the other girls went out on dates, and I prayed: *Please, God, let me get asked out on dates!* Well, God waited until I was in my sixties, then he sent me on a million dates, and most of the men I dated were insecure egomaniacs. So it finally occurred to me: *These are the same men who didn't want to date me when I was in my teens and twenties!*

Back then, the boys only wanted to date the cheerleaders. Now that the women who look like cheerleaders are too young to want to date them, these men have no idea what to go by. When I was young, I judged men by appearances, too. The guys wanted to date the cheerleaders, and I wanted to date the boys on the basketball team. At this age, without a handsome face and muscled arms and that tight, flat stretch of stomach between the bottom of a man's shirt and the tops of his jeans, with that sexy line of hair leading you-know-where, you have to focus on what the person says and how he treats you. It's not about his looks. It's not about his CV. It's not about what your friends or former boyfriends might think if they ran into you at the beach.

Of course, you still need to get turned on. If I think I am going to have sex with a man, I find a photo of what he looked like in his twenties. Some of these old guys were so breathtakingly handsome, so soulful, so strong, with their mustaches and beards and bouncy Afros or Jewfros, emerging dripping wet from a lake at Woodstock, their calves twisting this way or that as they reached out to grab a Frisbee, I would have considered myself blessed if they had smiled in my direction. So when I see someone trying to find the strength to do his pushups of love above me, I imagine I am seeing the younger version from the photo, which makes me feel I am cheating on him, until I realize he is probably picturing a cheerleader or a movie star when he looks down at me.

And that is why, despite everything, I can't give up. I know how comforting it can be to lie with your head nestled beneath a man's rough chin, stroking his broad and hairy chest, and I don't want to spend however much time remains to me without making love to a man who considers himself lucky that I am willing to make love to him. A great poet once said that a writer ought to write not from grievance, but from grief. So here is my grief: We are given only one life to live. And I am grieving because I don't want to blow my one life without knowing what it is to be loved by someone who loves my mind as much as he loves my body.

HOW SWEET THE SOUND

WE SAT IN A CIRCLE at the 92nd Street Y, recounting the traumas that had silenced us.

"My music teacher told me to move my lips but not make a sound," the first woman said. The rest of us nodded in recognition. Half of the fourteen members of that class—optimistically called "Everybody Can Sing"—had been shamed at karaoke night. (I refused to ever, ever go out with my graduate students after our weekly creative writing workshops.) Alicia, who spoke with a mellifluous Spanish accent, told us the last song she had sung was a childish version of "La Cucaracha."

The idea that in six ninety-minute sessions, all fourteen of us would stand in front of the room and sing a song that didn't make the others cover their ears in pain didn't seem believable. Hadn't we been born with ugly, distorted voices, the way some people are born with unfortunate features, a lack of rhythm on the dance floor, or a mind that blanks when required to solve a quadratic equation?

If genetics plays any role in musical ability, I was cursed from the instant my father's tone-deaf sperm pierced my mother's tin-eared egg. My parents' and siblings' voices were so tuneless, we never even sang "Happy Birthday" to one another. When my brother tried out for chorus, the music teacher told him, "You have a range of one note, and you sing even that one note off-key." At breakfast, my mother would wistfully recount a dream in which she opened her mouth and an operatic solo came pouring forth; in real life, if she so much as hummed along with a performer on TV, we groaned and shushed her.

I had been cautioned by my third-grade music teacher that when the rest of the class raised their voices to warn of the low bridge ahead in "Erie Canal" or pine for that rolling river called "Shenandoah," I should only pretend to sing. Even then, I was too dense to get the message. I thought Mrs. Many wanted me to allow the other children a chance to be heard, the way our regular teacher ignored my ever-raised hand in math class.

The truth didn't dawn on me until the next summer, when the staff at Camp Jubilee held auditions for our yearly production of a Gilbert and Sullivan operetta. I proudly marched to the center of the dining hall and belted out my rendition of—well, I don't remember what song I belted out, only the horrified looks on my counselors' faces. Rather than be awarded the female lead, I was relegated to the undifferentiated mass of aunts, uncles, and cousins who formed the chorus of *HMS Pinafore*, and even amid that vast and tuneless throng, I was asked to please sing quieter.

Still, the human urge to sing requires a tsunami of discouragement to drown it. I grew up in an Orthodox Jewish community in which women were not allowed to read from the Torah and so could not be bat mitzvahed. Outraged, I petitioned the rabbi to overturn this stern decree; when he instituted an alternative Friday night service, I was selected to be the first girl to lead one. Mostly, I would be conducting the congregants in songs they already knew, but on a few hymns, I would be soloing. I knew I didn't exactly sound like Sophie Tucker. But at that age, I still believed God would inspire me and tune my voice.

"I'm not coming," my mother said. Not coming? My own

mother was threatening to boycott my fake bat mitzvah? "I can't stand the thought of you embarrassing yourself by singing in front of everyone." Of course, she wasn't actually afraid I would embarrass myself; like most mothers, she was afraid I would embarrass *her*—in this case, by doing something she yearned to do but was too scared to try.

I am not sure how I found the nerve to mount the *bimah* and welcome the Sabbath bride. But in years to come, whenever I thought of standing in front of any group and singing, I saw my mother huddled at the back of the sanctuary, her face buried in her hands, as if I were standing naked on that stage and shrieking.

Even then, I wouldn't give up on my dream. I grew up in the Catskills, where the hotels featured singers like Tony Bennett, Leslie Uggams, Sammy Davis Jr., and Barbra Streisand. Our PTA put on musicals that would have been impressive even in Manhattan; each autumn, I looked on in frustration as everyone else in my town tried out and got a part.

Still, if I couldn't sing, I might learn to play an instrument. For years, I took lessons on the piano. But my teachers cared only that I play each note correctly. Not until years later, when I shared a house with a concert pianist, did I understand that music is meant to express the emotions of the performer, her desire, joy, or pain, or simply the beauty of the composition.

On top of all that, I suffered from some weird musical disability. I wasn't tone-deaf—I could hear how great a chasm yawned between the note I wanted to sing and the note my strangled throat gargled out. The trouble was that trying to memorize more than a few bars of music was like sticking a wet Post-it to a pane of glass. I could practice the same piece every day for a year and not be able to reproduce more than a measure or two by rote. If a musical savant is someone with a relatively low IQ who can memorize entire symphonies, I was a musical idiot who, despite a relatively high IQ, could hear a symphony a million times and barely be able to hum the opening melody.

Still, like a runt whose love for shooting hoops leads them to try out for the basketball team, I signed up for a class in music theory. The teacher was a dashikied jazz musician named Mr. Bynum, the coolest person any of us knew and the only African-American teacher in our high school. Of all people, he should have known better than to judge me by my appearance. But he seemed determined to prove that just because a student did well in her academic classes didn't mean she could play the piano, compose, or sing. Then again, that was the way most of our teachers acted: Anyone who did well in math was presumed to be lacking in musical or artistic talent, just as the musical, artistic, or athletically gifted students were presumed to be lacking in academic prowess. When I handed in the sonata Mr. Bynum had asked us to compose, he wrote that it was "mathematically correct but not the least bit musical."

As if that weren't bad enough, I was required to sight-sing to pass the course. I expressed fear that my friends would laugh. Oh, no, Mr. Bynum said. He would never let anyone laugh at another student. Reluctantly, I started singing. But I didn't make it past the second bar before I heard my friends giggling behind me. I looked to Mr. Bynum for support. But his cheeks were swelling like balloons as he attempted to stifle his own hilarity. Finally, he fell off the piano and went whizzing around the room. To his credit, he was so appalled by his behavior he granted me a passing grade. But that was the last time I sang in front of another human being. (I did sing "Kumbaya" to my infant son, but he put his hand to my mouth and shook his head no.)

* * *

This isn't to say I didn't deserve a humbling. I needed to learn that creating something beautiful, whether with a box of paints, a piano, or your vocal cords, is as difficult as scoring an A in calculus. But I couldn't bear to think I might leave this planet without ever knowing what it felt like to open my mouth and sing.

And so, at sixty-three, a few months before the coronavirus pandemic rendered singing in a group to be potentially fatal and confined us all to the loneliness of our apartments, I found myself sitting in a dingy classroom at the Y, my knee hammering up and down as rapidly as the needle on an earthquake detector. I have performed a comedy routine to a packed Manhattan nightclub. I think nothing of lecturing to an auditorium full of students or giving an interview on national TV or radio. But the idea of singing a single note in front of these fourteen strangers made me so nervous I couldn't stop shaking.

What saved me was listening to the din my classmates and I made as we followed our teacher in a dismal rendition of "You Are My Sunshine." I felt the way Rudolph must have felt washing up on the Island of Misfit Toys and meeting the train with square wheels, the Charlie in the Box, and the kite who was afraid of heights. One of our classmates might have been Beyoncé compared to the rest of us, but even she would have been accepted only grudgingly by her church choir, and never, ever—even if every other member had been stricken with the flu—been asked to sing a solo. Another woman didn't seem to know what singing *was*. A third sang so quietly she must have seen her third-grade music teacher standing behind her with a yardstick, threatening to thwap her on the head if she let out a sound.

Our teacher, Elissa, seemed roughly my age, with the

wavy, unstyled hair and sweet demeanor of every Jewish youth director who has leaned over her guitar and led her charges in Israeli folk songs. When I googled her later, I saw she had majored in math and economics at Princeton before going on to a distinguished career as a singer. She played the harp. She had sung at Carnegie Hall and Lincoln Center. After studying vocal acoustics and anatomy, she had come up with a method of helping people like me get over our fear of singing.

"We are all born able to sing," Elissa explained to our class. "Little kids sing all the time—singing is just part of life. And then people start saying, 'That doesn't sound good,' or 'That sounds good.' Everyone gets divided into the cans and the can'ts, instead of teachers saying, 'This is something everyone can learn to do.'" She didn't care if we had a pretty voice. Did Bob Dylan or Janice Joplin have pretty voices? All she cared about was that we told an interesting story with our song.

To provide us with a goal to shoot for, Elissa asked us to go around the room and tell her what song we fantasized about being able to sing. An elderly, aristocratic woman bewailed her "broken" voice and proclaimed her desire to once again be able to perform "La Vie en Rose." (She must have been appalled by our lack of talent, because after that first night she didn't come back.) Karen, a jovial bank clerk who was counting the minutes to her retirement, yearned to sing "The Impossible Dream." Frankie, our token male, wanted to be able to sing karaoke with his friends even when he was sober.

And me? What song did I fantasize I could sing? "'Amazing Grace,'" I said, although I had no idea why I had chosen it. The song seemed a strange choice for an Orthodox Jew who had been brought up in the Borscht Belt, but I figured my unconscious must have its motives.

As the class drew to a close, Elissa had us stride around the room lustily singing an easy round called "Viva la Musica" while shaking our classmates' hands. I suspected she was trying to get us so accustomed to fa-la-la-ling and singing as a group that we would forget to be afraid. I doubted her technique would work. It was like knowing you were about to be hypnotized—you would be too guarded to fall prey to the magician's tricks.

Despite myself, I was swept up in the communal glee. I might have been performing in the chorus of Italian peasants in an opera at the Met, that's how blissfully free I felt. If only my counselors hadn't grimaced when I auditioned for *HMS Pinafore*, I might have experienced this euphoria while striding about the stage as one of those aunts and cousins.

Sadly, the second class didn't go as smoothly. Elissa had asked us each to bring in a song so simple we could teach it to our fellow students. I spent a week practicing "Blowing in the Wind," which, if I went slowly enough—so slowly the wind couldn't have propelled a toy sailboat across a bathtub—I nearly could sing in tune. But the other members of my trio overruled me, and we ended up huddled in a corner, trying to rehearse one of the Temptations' greatest hits, "The Way You Do the Things You Do."

As I struggled to keep up the tempo while matching my partners' pitches—one member of our trio was the class Beyoncé—my vocal cords went as rigid and flat as dried-out rubber bands. When we performed for the rest of the class, the sounds I made diverged so wildly from my partners' voices, I might have been making up my own tune as I went along. Each of us had been assigned a single line as a solo, and when we reached the final line—*The way you do the things you do*—my voice dropped to a register so low I might have been the Temptations' original bass, Melvin Franklin. Even our teacher looked stunned. No one laughed. But I had to fight the urge to run out of the room and not come back.

But I did come back. The next week, and the next. And slowly, exercise by exercise, I began to gain a little confidence. "Just talk to the notes while you're singing," Elissa told me. I was offended. Did she mean I should give up and talk-sing, the way Rex Harrison did in *My Fair Lady*? Then I realized she meant I was trying so hard to SING that I was straining my vocal cords, the way my students try so hard to WRITE that they create overly purple prose and don't sound natural. Didn't my idol Leonard Cohen talk while he was singing? Maybe if you put your entire soul into every note, anything that came out was beautiful.

Elissa's biggest revelation was that singing is mostly mental: If you imagine the note you want, then your vocal folds will assume the right configuration for you to form it. This struck me as a sophisticated version of "Professor" Harold Hill's scam, in which he teaches the children of River City that if they simply think the right notes, they will be able to play the *Minuet in G* on their instruments. And yet, hadn't I learned to swing a tennis racquet with more accuracy and force only when I stopped trying to wallop the ball and allowed my body to imitate the image of a perfect swing?

I started practicing what Elissa preached. How could I have thought a singer didn't need to practice? That was like the children I tutored in math, who assumed you were either born with the ability to solve equations or you weren't. I would ask my computer to play an interval, then I imagined the notes and let my vocal folds do all the work. And even though I didn't end up like Harold Hill's students, marching through River City while performing a rousing version of "Seventy-six Trombones," I was astonished by my ability to imagine intervals in my head and match them.

In class, Elissa led us through some rudimentary Gregorian chants, which I've always believed to be the most haunting and uplifting music. We barely knew what we were doing. Yet I felt a part of something larger, something holy, as if I suddenly had become a monk.

Best of all, she taught us to sing the blues and asked us to compose two stanzas. Here was an assignment right up my alley. Hadn't I been blue my entire life? Hadn't I been painfully alone since moving to Manhattan five years earlier?

"*Got a bed*," I sang in my trembling but mellow alto. "*Got the emptiest bed in town. Got a bed, got the emptiest bed in town. Ain't had no one in that bed so long, I'm going down.*"

My classmates twisted in their chairs, as if they hadn't expected anyone to take the assignment seriously. And yet, they seemed oddly moved.

"*Got a heart*," I went on wailing. "*Got the loneliest heart in town. Got a heart. Got the loneliest heart in town. Ain't no one fill that heart soon, well, you know I'm going down.*"

Believe me, I have heard B.B. King, Buddy Guy, and Ella Fitzgerald perform in person, and I am under no illusion that the stanzas I composed that night would entitle me to share the stage with them any more than I could survive a single point on a court with Serena Williams. But I defy Mr. Bynum—who has long since died—to tell me that my composition was mathematically correct but not the least bit musical.

Thus emboldened, I prepared for our final exam, which required each of us to sing a solo. Elissa made us promise we would understand the story behind our song. I knew all about the foul-mouthed slave trader John Newton, who, during a violent storm, found himself calling to the Lord to have mercy on him and his shipmates; once saved, he became a minister and lobbied for the abolition of the very slave trade in which he had played a role. And yet, what did the lyrics mean to me? I had never traded in my fellow humans. I no longer believed in God. My undergraduate degree had been in physics. In what way could I possibly believe I had been saved by grace? Saved from what? Grace from whom?

Still, as I practiced in the privacy of my apartment, singing "Amazing Grace" with as much deliberation as if I had been accompanying my own casket at my funeral, I was astonished by the newfound richness of my voice and my ability to hit most, if not all, the notes. I found myself looking forward to the next-to-last class, when Elissa would listen to us perform and give us pointers so we would know what to work on for the final exam. Surely, she would be amazed at how well I sang. Maybe she would even praise me for having the best voice in class!

Sadly, I hadn't yet achieved enough grace to refrain from judging my fellow students. The stunning Chinese woman from Queens sang a song in English whose lyrics seemed to baffle her. Karen, the bank clerk, emoted her way through "Hey, Look Me Over" with such hammy gestures I couldn't bear watching. One woman prefaced her solo by explaining that one of her greatest disappointments was she had tried out to play Hodel in *Fiddler on the Roof* but didn't get the part; when she sang "Far from the Home I Love," I could sympathize—with the director. As for Frankie, he picked such a difficult song it was if someone who had learned to ski only that morning was setting off down one of those death-defying Olympic ramps.

None of this fazed Elissa. "Try singing in a lower key," she might suggest. Or: "Hold your fist a few inches from your mouth and pretend it's a microphone." Or: "Let's see what happens if you lower your head and relax your shoulders." Then she would ask the student to sing a few bars again. "See!" she would say, beaming. "Don't you think you are singing better?"

By the time my turn came, I remained confident everyone would be amazed by how well I sang. I strode to the front of the room, took a deep breath, and prepared to express my gratitude that, once blind, I now could see.

At which my knees started to shake so badly I barely could stand. Rather than rejoice in being saved, I squeaked like a mouse who has been cornered by a farmer's wife and is searching for a crack to hide in.

Chastened, I returned home and followed Elissa's advice that I continue practicing while waving my arms and marching around my apartment, which, she claimed, would relax my muscles and prevent my shaking. But none of that marching helped. I knew the minute I stepped in front of an audience, my legs would melt to a consistency that wouldn't support me. What was I so afraid of, embarrassing my mother? My mother had been dead for years. Getting laughed at? The other members of the class probably were more scared I would laugh at them.

Then I realized: I was still convinced I was a person who could never sing. Like most of us, I accepted the identity I had been given. As children, we are led to believe we are either gifted in mathematics, singing, art, dance, athletics, or we are dunces, we are clumsy, we are not creative. We are made nervous by teachers who tell us to move our mouths but make no sound, who stand above us tapping their feet and shaking their heads as we try to solve equations, who cover our essays with red-marked criticisms but rarely convey the purpose, let alone the beauty, of what they are asking us to do.

The reason I love those corny movies in which a coach

inspires a gang of Bad News Bears to overcome their lack of natural talent and win is that I so deeply believe in the fundamental importance of that story. And you would believe in such miraculous transformations, too, if you had heard my classmates and I warble and squawk those first few evenings, and then you had attended our final class, in which each of us stood in front of the room and sang our hearts out.

Did we succeed because we practiced? Because we learned what Elissa taught us? Or because we had overcome our fear of failing? Karen took Elissa's advice, dropped the hammy gestures, and sang as if she meant what she was singing: *Hey, look me over, I'm much more than a bank clerk! See what I can do now that I'm retiring!* The Chinese woman sang a song not in English, but in Chinese, and because she understood what the lyrics meant, so did we.

As for the woman who had always wanted to be cast in *Fiddler*, she offered such a fervent rendition of "Far from the Home I Love" that I easily could imagine her starring in, if not a Broadway version of that famous musical, at least a summer stock production. And Frankie! Never mind karaoke with his friends; if he had been leaning on a piano in a smoky cabaret, crooning the simple, honest ballad he sang, every man and woman in the room would have fallen hopelessly in love.

As for me, the moment I started to sing, my knees dissolved. I was afraid my trembling would overcome me. But I made it to the second stanza. *'Twas grace that taught my heart to fear, and grace my fears relieved.* As the meaning of the lyrics reached me, I found myself clutching my fist to my chest, then stretching out my arm and letting my fear fly free. Like Elsa in *Frozen*, I let everything go, and even if I was no Idina Menzel, I was shocked by how resonant and in tune I sounded.

What happened to me then was what happens to every singer in every biopic from *Coal Miner's Daughter* to *A Star Is Born*. As I gained faith in myself, my tone deepened and my voice grew stronger. I did what my mother only dreamed of doing: I opened my mouth and sang. A few notes sounded flat. But as I reached the final stanza, I knew I was telling the story the entire class had lived through, how we all had survived so many dangers, toils, and snares, how we already had come so far, how we needed to go much farther, but how grace, if only we trusted in our ability to transcend our fears, would lead us home.

ACKNOWLEDGMENTS

The following essays have appeared—some in slightly different form—in literary journals and anthologies:

"Pigeons" in *Prairie Schooner* and *Best American Essays 2013*; "Thin Air" in *Michigan Quarterly Review*, with an honorable mention in *Best American Essays 2011*; "The Jewish Shah" in *Fourth Genre*; "Ranch House" in *New England Review*, with an honorable mention in *Best American Essays 2013*; "A Friendly Book of Facts for Boys and Girls" in *Brainchild*; "The House of the World" in *Michigan Quarterly Review*; "I Tried to Raise a Jew and He Turned Out a Communist" online at *Kveller.com*; "Righteous Gentile" in *Harvard Review* and *Best American Travel Writing 2018*; "The Young Friends Pleasure and Benefit Society" online at *Tikkun Daily*; "All of Us, We All Are Arameans" as a *Ploughshares Solo* and reprinted in *Ploughshares Solos Omnibus Volume One*; "Didn't Anyone Tell You" in *Ploughshares*; "Hallucinations" in *New England Review*; "One a Day" in *Ploughshares*; "How Sweet the Sound" online at Medium.com.

I am deeply indebted to the editors whose tireless efforts keep these publications alive and thriving, often on minuscule budgets. I cannot thank them enough for helping me to make my work as strong as possible and providing me with an audience of dedicated readers.

I also owe immense gratitude to the friends, colleagues, and family members whose patience, encouragement, and wise suggestions have been crucial to me as I have struggled to figure out what I wanted to say and how to say it. Especial thanks go to Therese Stanton, who knows what I think and feel better than I do; to Marian Krzyzowski, who introduced me to so many new worlds and gave me permission to document our adventures; to Noah, who allows me to express the deepest truths about my life, even if that sometimes means exposing more about his life than any son should need to put up with; to Arthur Samuelson, who provided me with the title for this book; to Jenni Ferrari-Adler, my agent, who is so generous with her devoted support and sagacious counsel; and to Joe Olshan, Lori Milken, Jennifer Ankner-Edelstein, Colin Dockrill, and everyone else at Delphinium Books, whose loving devotion to literature makes my life as a writer possible.

ABOUT THE AUTHOR

Eileen Pollack graduated with a BS in physics from Yale and earned an MFA in creative writing from the University of Iowa. She is the author of the novels *The Professor of Immortality, The Bible of Dirty Jokes, A Perfect Life, Breaking and Entering*, and *Paradise, New York;* the short-story collections *In the Mouth* and *The Rabbi in the Attic*; and the nonfiction books *The Only Woman in the Room: Why Science Is Still a Boys' Club* and *Woman Walking Ahead: In Search of Catherine Weldon and Sitting Bull.* She has received fellowships from the National Endowment for the Arts, the Michener Foundation, the Rona Jaffe Foundation, and the Massachusetts Arts Council. Her novella "The Bris" was chosen to appear in *Best American Short Stories 2007*, edited by Stephen King; two other stories have been awarded Pushcart Prizes; and her essay "Pigeons" was selected for *Best American Essays 2013* by Cheryl Strayed, who also selected "Righteous Gentile" for *Best American Travel Writing 2018*. Formerly the director of the Hellen Zell MFA Program in Creative Writing at the University of Michigan, she now lives in Boston.